MY BOOK:— Robyn Fabe May '95

Spanish Observers and the American Revolution
1775 – 1783

SPANISH OBSERVERS
AND THE AMERICAN
REVOLUTION

1775 – 1783

Light Townsend Cummins

LOUISIANA STATE UNIVERSITY PRESS
Baton Rouge and London

Designer: Patricia Douglas Crowder
Typeface: Linotron 202 Galliard
Typesetter: G&S Typesetters, Inc.
Printer and binder: Thomson-Shore, Inc.

Publication of this book has been assisted by a grant from the Program of Cooperation of the
Ministry of Culture of Spain and the Universities of the United States; the book won the
"Spain and America in the Quincentennial of the Discovery" first prize for 1985, which was
sponsored by that program.

LIBRARY OF CONGRESS CATALOGING-IN-PUBLICATION DATA

Cummins, Light Townsend.
    Spanish observers and the American Revolution, 1775–1783 / Light
Townsend Cummins.
        p.   cm.
    Includes bibliographical references and index.
    ISBN 0-8071-1690-4
    1. United States—History—Revolution, 1775–1783—Foreign public
opinion, Spanish.   2. Public opinion—Spain—History—18th century.
3. United States—Relations—Spain.   4. Spain—Relations—United
States.   5. Spain—Foreign relations—18th century.   I. Title.
E249.3.C86   1992
973.3—dc20   91-13795
                                                        CIP

for V.H.C.

Contents

Preface

Spain's role in the American Revolution grew out of international forces set in motion during the period of intercolonial warfare that lasted from 1689 to 1763. Spain, along with its traditional ally France, was intermittently at war with Great Britain for almost a century, during which it fought the British in four major international conflicts: the War of the League of Augsburg (known in British America as King William's War), which lasted from 1689 to 1697; the War of the Spanish Succession (known in British America as Queen Anne's War), which was fought from 1701 to 1713; the War of the Austrian Succession (known in British America as King George's War), which began in 1744 and ended in 1748; and the Seven Years' War (known in British America as the French and Indian War), which saw fighting from 1755 to 1762.

In the Seven Years' War, which was the great contest for colonial empire in the Americas, Great Britain definitively defeated France and Spain. The Spanish had entered the war late, after neutrality during its early stages. In the closing year of the conflict, King Charles III of Spain declared war against Great Britain, just in time for his nation to experience humiliating military losses. The Spanish lost Havana and Manila to invading British forces within a few months. By early 1763, both France and Spain were at the peace table, forced to accept terms of defeat dictated by the British. The Peace of Paris, signed in 1763, was a resounding humiliation for France and Spain. By its provisions, France gave Canada to the British while Spain ceded Florida to them. In addition, the French king gave Louisiana to

Spain. The British did not want France to retain the Mississippi River province but did not want it for themselves either. For Britain, the expense to Spain of maintaining a colony in Louisiana held the advantage of debilitating the already weakened Spanish military presence in the Americas. The Spanish king and his ministers stewed in international embarrrassment over the Peace of Paris and waited for the chance to work revenge against Great Britain. The colonial crisis of the 1760s and 1770s in British North America provided them with the opportunity they wanted. Secret Spanish support for the rebels could be aimed at setting off a series of events that would weaken the British Empire. At the same time, Spain had to guard against provoking retaliation by the British in the form of attacks upon Spanish possessions. Given the indications for maintaining a balance between involvement and caution, Spanish participation in the events of the revolutionary era differed between two distinct periods: that of official Spanish neutrality, from 1775 to 1779, and that of open warfare against Great Britain, from 1779 to 1783.

During the period of official neutrality, Spain followed events in British North America by dispatching espionage agents and observers to locations scattered throughout North America and the Caribbean. The persons it sent provided a steady stream of information about the struggle and served as initial points of both diplomatic and commercial contact between the governments of Spain and of the infant United States. Two of the observers, Juan de Miralles and Francisco Rendon, resided in Philadelphia, where they eventually served as Spain's unofficial spokesmen. Others operated in Louisiana, Florida, along the Gulf Coast, and in the Caribbean. All of them provided copious news for King Charles III and his ministers.[1] The observers permit the historian an opportunity to study the development and implementation of Spain's policy regarding the American Revolution, since their activities touched almost every aspect of the relations between Spain and the new American republic during the course of the war.

1. Gonzalo Anes Alvarez, *El antiguo regimen: Los Borbones* (Madrid, 1975), 304–12. For general surveys of Spain during the era of the Revolution, see Richard Herr, *The Eighteenth Century Revolution in Spain* (Princeton, 1958), and Jean Sarrailh, *La España ilustrada de la segunda mitad del siglo XVIII* (Madrid, 1957). For a general introduction, consult *The Bourbon Reformers and Spanish Civilization: Builders or Destroyers?* ed. Troy S. Floyd (Boston, 1966), and the first essay in David Brading's *Miners and Merchants in Bourbon Mexico, 1763–1810* (Cambridge, Eng., 1971). Also important are Richard Herr's *Spain* (Englewood Cliffs, N.J., 1971), 50–51; Vicente Rodríguez Casado's *La política y los políticos en el reinado des Carlos III* (Madrid, 1962); and Antonio Ballesteros y Beretta's *Historia de España y su influencia en la historia universal* (2nd ed., 1929; 9 vols.; rpr. Barcelona, 1964), V, 159–222.

The observers have received surprisingly little attention from historians. In 1928, Kathryn Abbey Hanna wrote a short essay that appeared in the *Mississippi Valley Historical Review*. Entitled "Efforts of Spain to Maintain Sources of Information in the British Colonies Before 1779," it offered a very general analysis of several Spanish agents who observed the American Revolution. Over a generation after Hanna's study, an article by Helen M. McCadden entitled "Juan de Miralles and the American Revolution" appeared in *The Americas*. Using Miralles as her touchstone, McCadden highlighted the activities of the two Spanish observers who resided in Philadelphia. More recently, two brief essays of my own have considered the careers of several other observers. Because of the limitations imposed by the very form of the historical article, however, these four essays fail to provide a comprehensive account of the part Spanish observers played in the American Revolution.[2] The study that follows will provide for the first time the full story of Spanish observers in the American Revolution.

I deliberately refer to them as observers. They and their superiors, however, used the Spanish word *encargado*, or "one who is entrusted with a special task." It is misleading to translate this term literally as *chargé*, since most of the observers did not have diplomatic status. They instead operated as private citizens. Yet, to call them spies or espionage agents is equally inaccurate, though some of the observers did from time to time collect secret information. Others did not engage in spying but instead confined themselves to reporting on the revolt by gathering news from public sources, much as a journalist would do today. Leading Americans—including George Washington and members of the Continental Congress—certainly knew about a few of the Spanish observers, but they did not realize that Spain had a complex network of them. The Americans themselves used the word *observer* for those who came to Philadelphia, the term first having been employed by Henry Laurens during 1779 in reference to Miralles. This designation seems to capture better than any other the essence of what the agents were doing.

I ought to offer as well an explanation of other semantic conventions I have adopted. Persons of Hispanic heritage often employ compound sur-

---

2. Kathryn Abbey [Hanna], "Efforts of Spain to Maintain Sources of Information in the British Colonies Before 1779," *Mississippi Valley Historical Review*, XV (1928), 56–68; Helen M. McCadden, "Juan de Miralles and the American Revolution," *The Americas*, XXIX (1973), 359–75; Light Townsend Cummins, "Luciano de Herrera and Spanish Espionage in British Saint Augustine," *El Escribano*, XVI (1979), 43–57; Cummins, "Spanish Espionage in the South During the American Revolution," *Southern Studies*, XIX (1980), 39–49.

names, to delineate both patrilineal and matrilineal origin. I have abbreviated these in an effort to avoid peppering the narrative with cumbersome names. The Key to Spanish Surnames (pp. 207–208 below) coordinates my abbreviated nomenclature with complete names and titles. I have also adopted a somewhat unconventional usage of several terms. *America* here refers only to the British colonies that declared their independence in 1776, notwithstanding that all areas of the Western Hemisphere are of course part of America. I employ the words *England* and *Britain*—and *English* and *British*—interchangeably despite the admitted imprecision of doing so. I use the term *Spaniard* to denote any person who owed allegiance to King Charles III of Spain. Most observers lived in the Spanish-American colonies. Some of them had the perspectives of, and personally saw themselves as, Creoles rather than peninsular Spaniards. In some cases they are already known to history as Creoles because of their later, anti-Spanish endeavors. The distinction between peninsular and Creole had small bearing on the Spanish observation of the Revolution. All involved served as instruments of the Spanish imperium no matter what their personal background as residents of Hispanic America or Iberia.

Acknowledgments

A two-year grant from the Commission for Educational Cooperation Between the United States of America and Spain gave me the uninterrupted time in Spanish archives that I needed to review material dealing with Spanish participation in the American Revolution. I am indebted to Ramón Bela Armada, of the Commission, for his support and assistance. A stipend from the Andrew Mellon Fund for Southern Scholars, administered by the Rodger Thayer Stone Center for Latin American Studies, at Tulane University, permitted research trips to a number of repositories in Louisiana. A grant from the National Endowment for the Humanities supported a summer's work at the University of Florida. Several faculty grants-in-aid from Austin College partially underwrote research in Great Britain, Philadelphia, and Washington, D.C. A semester's sabbatical leave freed me from teaching duties at Austin College and let me work the manuscript into final form.

The directors and staffs of various archives and institutions in Spain extended me numerous courtesies. Above all, Rosario Parra Calla, Director of the Archivo General de Indias, and her staff met my every research need. For that I am most appreciative. Among the historians associated with the Escuela de Estudios Hispanoamericanos, in Seville, who aided me in many ways, I am indebted to Antonio Acosta Rodríguez, José A. Calderon Quijano, Juan Marchena Fernandez, Antonio Muro Orejón, Ramón Serrera Contreras, Pablo Tornero Tinajero, Bibiano Torres Ramirez, and Enriqueta Vila Vilar. I also acknowledge assistance provided in Spain by the staffs of the Archivo Histórico Nacional, the Archivo General de Simancas, the Biblioteca Nacional de España, the Real Academia de Historia, the Biblioteca del Instituto Cultura Hispánica, and the Biblioteca de la Escuela de Estudios Hispanoamericanos.

In the United States, I received timely assistance from the staffs of the Howard-Tilton Memorial Library, of Tulane University; the Louisiana Historical Center, of the Louisiana State Museum; the P. K. Yonge Library, of the University of Florida; the Historical Society of Pennsylvania; the Library of Congress; and the National Archives. I owe special thanks to John West, Nell Evans, and Helen Latham for their hard work as reference and interlibrary loan specialists at the Abell Library Center, of Austin College. I wish to thank the historians who took time from their own pursuits to give me advice: Gilbert C. Din, Edward Haas, Paul Hoffman, G. Douglas Inglis, Eugene Lyon, Linda Salvucci, Martha Searcy, J. Barton Starr, Stephen A. Webre, and the late Joseph D. Castle. The late J. Leitch Wright, Jr., kindly read the entire manuscript and made many insightful comments, most of which I have taken to heart. Bernice Melvin and Cynthia Manley graciously undertook the task of transcribing and translating various Gérard and Vergennes letters, thereby saving me from potential errors. I would also like to thank the staff at Louisiana State University Press, especially Margaret Fisher Dalrymple, for her encouragement, and Barry L. Blose, for his expert editing of the manuscript.

While in preparation for press, this manuscript received first prize in the international competition "Spain and America in the Quincentennial of the Discovery." The prize, sponsored by the government of Spain, marks the fifth centennial of Christopher Columbus' discovery of the Western Hemisphere, by honoring scholarly works that analyze the role Spain has played in the history of the New World. It is a pleasure to acknowledge the persons associated with the award for their courtesy and support: the Honorable Don Carlos Abella, Minister for Cultural Affairs, the Embassy of Spain, Washington, D.C.; the Honorable Don José F. de Castillejo, Consul General of Spain; Professor Antonio Ramos-Gascón, General Coordinator of the Program for Cultural Cooperation Between Spain's Ministry of Culture and United States Universities; and Don Juan Lladró Dolz, President of Lladró Ceramics, Valencia, Spain.

Finally, I must acknowledge the contribution of three persons to this study. The late Hugh F. Rankin awakened my interest in the American Revolution and in the history of the southern United States. I first learned from his books, and later, having had the opportunity to study with him, I came to appreciate the high standards of scholarship that his life and his work embodied. Richard E. Greenleaf, as a professor and then as a friend, has been of assistance every step of the way. My greatest debt is to my wife, fellow historian, and departmental colleague, Victoria Hennessey Cummins. Although occupied with her own writing on sixteenth-century Mexico, she has always been ready to offer needed advice and support while she successfully balanced the demands of her own research, publication, teaching, departmental administration as chair, and motherhood. This study is respectfully dedicated to her.

PART ONE

Spanish Neutrality

During the years after the Peace of Paris in 1763, Spain closely observed occurrences in British North America. Spanish ministers at court were especially concerned to guard against a surprise British attack upon Spain's New World colonies. The captain general of Cuba at Havana and his subordinate, the governor of Louisiana at New Orleans, superintended Spain's surveillance activities in the region. The captain general relied upon the commercial fishing fleet based in Cuba to observe British maritime movements. He corresponded with a Roman Catholic priest living in British East Florida, Father Pedro Camps, who relayed information about events there. The captain general encouraged merchants of the Asiento de Negros, Spain's slave-trading monopoly, to report what they learned while visiting British ports. Luciano de Herrera, a Spaniard living in Saint Augustine, became an agent spy for the captain general, furnishing regular reports from that city. The governor of Louisiana, Luis de Unzaga in particular, also played an important role in maintaining Spanish observation of British America in the years after the Seven Years' War. The governor monitored the British settlement of West Florida, especially the Mississippi River districts around Baton Rouge and Natchez. He talked with Englishmen traveling through New Orleans on the Mississippi. He dispatched agents to Pensacola and Mobile to collect news about the British colonies. In 1772, the governor sent Juan de Surriret to New York in order to learn about problems stemming from colonial dissatisfaction with the New Colonial Policy.

Hence, by 1775, Spain had long been following the growing political disorders in British North America. The policy makers at court, relying on information developed by the captain general of Cuba's espionage network, decided upon a course of formal neutrality. In addition, the Spanish king and his ministers set their own goals for any war between Great Britain and its colonies which the crisis might bring. They hoped for a return from British control of Gibraltar, a possession they had lost at the Peace of Utrecht in 1713. They wanted to regain the Floridas and clear the British from the lower Mississippi Valley and the coasts of the Gulf of Mexico. They sought to clear the eastern coast of Central America of the British logwood-cutting establishments that were there. They wished to end the special trading privileges in Spanish America granted to British merchants by treaties signed in connection with earlier intercolonial wars. After 1776, they came to desire the American revolutionaries to win their independence, thereby diminishing the size of the British Empire, though Spain, as the largest colonial power in the Americas, clearly never supported the general concept of rebellion against the authority of monarchy. The Spanish policy of secret help to the rebels came not from solidarity with the American cause but out of a powerful hatred for Great Britain.

Despite the decision of official neutrality, the court at Madrid directed the captain general of Cuba to observe the course of the prospective revolution from his base at Havana. During much of the late 1760s and early 1770s, the captain general's observers had routinely provided news about events in the English-speaking colonies to the north. Starting in 1775, Spain refocused the attention of the observers on the coming American Revolution. They reported everything they might learn about the revolt, and the Spanish court depended upon them as important sources.

The Spanish observers from 1775 until late 1778 operated with guises and subterfuges meant to keep them inconspicuous. They plied the trading lanes of the Caribbean and made contact with rebels along the Atlantic Coast from Florida to Pennsylvania. They sent to Spain an abundance of news about the revolt, much of it favorable to the rebel cause. Their reports eventually motivated Spain toward a tilted neutrality, in which Spain provided the Americans with supplies and other forms of assistance. The Spanish observers, especially those based near the rebellious colonies, became the conduits through which Spain channeled its material help. They were thus Spain's primary source of regular contact with the rebellious colonists prior to 1779, when it openly entered the conflict. Information from the observer corps, although favorable to the American cause, also convinced Spain that the infant United States would replace Great Britain as the major territorial rival in North America. Nevertheless, so great was Spain's desire to discomfit England that it was not deterred by that prospect. Spanish leaders walked a fine line of foreign policy between 1775 and 1779: on the one hand, they gave secret assistance to the rebels; on the other, they remained overtly neutral to avoid offending Great Britain. It was the observer corps that enabled the Spanish court to maintain the delicate diplomatic balance its position required. The existence of the observers made it possible for Spanish policy makers to wait until conditions appeared propitious for Spain to take a more active role in the conflict.

I
The Search for Information
1763–1775

Stationed at Havana, the captain general of Cuba had broad military and governmental powers. He served as ranking Spanish commander for the northern Caribbean. He exercised civil government at Havana while his subordinates administered the remainder of Cuba, its neighboring islands, and—after 1766—all of Louisiana, including much of the Mississippi Valley. Like the viceroys of New Spain and Peru, the captain general enjoyed greater autonomy than most officials in the Spanish Indies. Unlike many regional commanders, he communicated directly with the king and royal ministers, bypassing viceregal bureaucracies at Mexico City. All of this made his office an ideal clearinghouse for information regarding the nearby British colonies.

The Spanish rank of captain general was one of Spain's oldest institutions of governance, having grown out of the military needs of the medieval re-conquest of Iberia from the Moors. A *capitanía*, a company composed of five hundred men, formed the basic tactical unit of the Castilian army during the Middle Ages. During late medieval times, the commander of all *capitanías* within a region came to be called the region's *capitan general*, or its general captain of the companies. Once the conquest of the New World began, the Hapsburg monarchs of Spain made the captains general the primary agents for the military administration of their colonies. In the Spanish Indies, however, the office eventually came to be more than merely a military rank. By the seventeenth century, captains general governed Spanish America outside the established vice-regencies. In addition to exercising military command, they had responsibility for civil administration, and ensured the execution of royal directives, in the territories under their command. By the end of the Hapsburg period, captaincies general—along with judicial councils known as audiencias—governed in Santo Domingo, Chile, Guatemala, and Cuba. The Bourbon monarchs of Spain retained the institution and made extensive use of the captaincy general during the administrative reorganization begun on the Iberian Peninsula in the early 1700s. On the peninsula, King Philip V created new captains general for Aragon, Valencia, Mallorca, and Catalonia. In the Americas, he retained the captain general as the official who governed in political jurisdictions outside the geographic boundaries of the viceroyalties. Philip retained the four existing captaincies general, and he created a new one in Venezuela in 1742. By the time of the American Revolution, captains general held military and civil command in five important areas of the Spanish colonies: Guatemala, Venezuela, Chile, Puerto Rico, and Cuba. The captaincy general of Cuba, based at Havana, ranked as one of the oldest of the five of that time, having been created in the 1580s.[1]

The collection of information about British America became an important assignment for the captain general in the decade after the Seven Years' War. Havana's surrender to an invading British force during that conflict had given Spain pause and had brought it acute embarrassment. Although Great Britain had returned Havana at the peace table, King Charles III and his ministers realized that they had to strengthen Cuba's military defenses. Never again could Havana, the strategic gateway to the Spanish Sea, as Charles and his subjects pridefully viewed the Gulf of Mexico, be permitted to fall to an invading enemy.[2] After 1763, Havana became perhaps the most important military command in Spanish America as Spain undertook its military revitalization. Accordingly, a series of talented military officers filled the post of captain general during the 1760s and 1770s, including the Conde de Ricla, Antonio María Bucareli, the Marqués de la Torre, and Diego Joseph Navarro. Through force of character and the support of Spain, these four commanders brought new military strength and vitality to Cuba and its dependencies.

The military rehabilitation began when the Conde de Ricla took com-

1. José Sucre Reyes, *La capitanía general de Venezuela* (Barcelona, 1969), 132–50.
2. Light Townsend Cummins, "Spanish Administration in the Southeastern Borderlands, 1763–1800," in *Latin American Frontiers: Proceedings of the P.C.C.L.A.S., 1977*, ed. Matt S. Meier (Berkeley, Calif., 1981), 1–8. See also Hugh Thomas, *Cuba; or, The Pursuit of Freedom* (London, 1971), 61–65; and Allan J. Kuethe, *Cuba, 1753–1815: Crown, Military, and Society* (Knoxville, Tenn., 1986), 24–49.

mand at Havana after the Peace of Paris in 1763. He had instructions to restore the island's fortifications to a state of full readiness. Ricla brought with him for his purpose an able group of subordinate officers who assisted in the revamping of the island's defenses. Among them, Alejandro O'Reilly and Antonio Raffelin helped rebuild its garrisons.[3] They would spend much of their remaining careers in the Spanish Indies, where they were to distinguish themselves in a wide range of pursuits, including the collection and evaluation of information about the American Revolution. Ricla also expanded Cuba's militia system and the naval squadron; the king reassigned the Regiment of Córdoba to Havana and created a new company of dragoons for the city. Anticipating the need for swifter communication with Spain, the administrator of the Spanish mails began regular packet service between Havana and the peninsula in 1764.[4]

The military reinforcement continued under Bucareli, Ricla's successor beginning in 1766.[5] An able and innovative administrator, Captain General Bucareli initiated regular observation of the British possessions that bordered on his command. He created a network of contacts, agents, and operatives whose primary job was to collect news about those colonies. He recruited ship captains from the commercial fishing fleet at Havana and merchants of the Asiento de Negros as sources. The British in East and West Florida tolerated the presence of the Cuban fishing fleet. Each year some three or four hundred Cuban fishermen in several dozen vessels plied the Florida coasts, occasionally setting up temporary camps along the shore or on islands in British territory. The fishermen sometimes traded with local Indians. James Grant, the governor of East Florida, apparently tolerated the fishermen and their *ranchos* because he did not wish Cuban reprisals against British subjects engaged in illegal trade with the Spanish islands.[6] The cap-

---

3. Ramiro Guerra, *Manual de historia de Cuba desde su descubrimiento hasta 1868* (1938; rpr. Havana, 1971), 177–93; Joaquín Llaverías, ed., "Documentos acerca del estado de defensa de La Habana con un plano ó cuadro relativo al particular, 1766 a 1776," *Boletín del Archivo Nacionál de Cuba*, XLII (1946), 121–31.

4. Angel Torredemé Balado, *Iniciación a la historia del correo en Cuba* (Havana, 1945), 123–24.

5. Bernard E. Bobb, *The Viceregency of Antonio María Bucareli in New Spain, 1771–1779* (Austin, 1962), 19–20.

6. James W. Covington, "The Cuban Fishing *Ranchos:* A Spanish Enclave Within British Florida," in *Anglo-Spanish Confrontation on the Gulf Coast During the American Revolution*, ed. William Coker and Robert R. Rea (Pensacola, Fla., 1982), 17–24; Charles L. Mowat, *East Florida as a British Province, 1763–1784* (Berkeley, Calif., 1943), 20.

8

tain general also ordered the captains of the Spanish naval squadron based at Havana to report routinely on the movement of British vessels in the region. Bucareli's chief objective in this was defensive. He wanted to keep Cuba safe from surprise attack by the British.

In 1767, the lieutenant governor at Puerto Principe sent Bucareli word that a Spanish merchant vessel had called there with news of more troops being assigned to the British garrison at Jamaica.[7] The captain general quickly dispatched a Havana merchant to Kingston to serve as an observer under the cover of engaging in trade. Bucareli probably had no difficulty in recruiting his man, since he allowed him to keep the profits from the venture. With ears and eyes open, the observer did his job well. He learned that a ship belonging to Spain's Asiento monopoly had recently loaded a cargo at Kingston—something Spanish law permitted on a limited basis. At the time, the town was buzzing about the London ministries' supply of additional army troops to Jamaica. Bucareli's observer surmised that the Spanish captain, who had been bound for Puerto Principe, was the lieutenant governor's informant. The observer also ascertained that the new military units appeared to be part of normal reassignments and did not involve large numbers of soldiers. In the opinion of the observer, they posed no new threat to neighboring Spanish colonies. Bucareli corroborated this report from other sources. He questioned the captain of a Cuban fishing boat who had seen English ships under sail along the east coast of Florida and also queried some of the Asiento merchants then at port in Havana. None of them had noticed anything more than normal naval and merchant shipping. After plotting the locations of the various observations, the captain general concluded that a large flotilla of British troop carriers could not have passed undetected through the area. He decided that events at Kingston were unexceptional and that the first report from Puerto Principe had been exaggerated. The new troops at Kingston, no doubt small in number, failed to constitute an augmented British menace to Cuba.[8]

Bucareli also monitored events in British East Florida, a colony that belonged to Spain prior to the Seven Years' War. The Peace of Paris had in 1763 transferred most of the Spanish Gulf Coast east of the Mississippi to British control, and the English king had created two new colonies, West

7. Antonio María Bucareli to Julián de Arriaga, January 6, 1768, reserved, no. 523, AGI, Santo Domingo 1214.
8. Bucareli to Arriaga, February 5, 1768, no. 548, *ibid.*

Florida and East Florida, with Pensacola and Saint Augustine as their respective capitals. Both cities quickly became important British military centers, but Saint Augustine, the site of one of the largest military fortresses in North America, particularly worried the Spanish in Cuba.

Securing a regular source of information about events there initially posed a difficulty for Captain General Bucareli, because most of the Spanish residents of East Florida had moved to Cuba when the British took control of the province. But he gained a welcome and unanticipated source of information during 1770. A group of Roman Catholics had moved to British East Florida and settled along the Mosquito River, some twelve leagues north of Cape Canaveral, as part of a proprietary scheme organized by Andrew Turnbull, an English planter who hoped to reap his fortune in the Florida wilderness. Turnbull had received a large land grant from the British government and settled the area south of Saint Augustine with Minorcan and Greek peasants he had recruited to farm his extensive properties. He established the town of New Smyrna on his tract as an agrarian community organized along almost feudal lines. But his colonists from the Mediterranean soon found living and working conditions harsh, and disenchantment festered among them.

In particular, the Minorcan Roman Catholics complained about the difficulty of holding regular mass at the settlement. Although Turnbull permitted religious freedom and allowed a priest to minister to the settlers, New Smyrna's distance from an established bishopric created problems. The colonists' priest, Father Pedro Camps, found it difficult to secure religious supplies such as consecrated water, oils, wafers, and wax. He also lacked access to the sacraments normally performed by a bishop. His small congregation belonged to the episcopal see of the bishop residing in London, who was so far removed from contact with East Florida that the priest despaired of ever securing the support he needed. He therefore decided to approach clandestinely, on his own authority, the Roman Catholic bishop in Cuba.

Father Camps wrote the bishop in late 1769, requesting holy oils and other religious supplies from Cuban ecclesiastical stores for his small congregation. He thereby unwittingly opened an important channel of information for the captain general. The bishop, Santiago Joseph Echevarría, had no prior knowledge of the settlement at New Smyrna, nor apparently did anyone else in Cuba. When Father Camps's letter was brought by a Cuban fisherman who had been hailed from the Florida beach by a Minorcan, Bishop Echevarría immediately told Bucareli of the settlement and the captain general realized that it could be used as a post for observing the British at Saint Augustine. He ordered fishing boats from Havana to maintain regular secret contact with New Smyrna and to furnish accounts of whatever might be learned from its Minorcan residents about British activities.[9] The settlement eventually played a significant role in the captain general's information-gathering network.

The lower Mississippi Valley, too, became an area of concern to the Spanish during the captaincy general of Bucareli. The Peace of Paris of 1763 transferred Louisiana from France's control to Spain's. But the area east of the Mississippi and north of New Orleans became British.[10] As the British settled in West Florida, commercial contacts in open violation of Spanish law soon developed throughout the region. Turning his head, Bucareli permitted a limited volume of this illegal trade in order to keep abreast of events in British territory. And the British seemed only too happy to accommodate him, since they anxiously desired the trade.[11] In September, 1767, the West Florida provincial sloop called at Havana in order to advertise the availability in Pensacola of goods for the Cuban market. Spanish merchants in Havana responded quickly. A private Cuban merchant vessel soon called at Pensacola and purchased merchandise valued at thirty thousand *pesos fuertes*.[12] The following months saw the arrival of five or six Spanish ships in West Florida, where they exchanged cargoes of bullion and logwood for British goods.[13]

Although the trading voyages provided some opportunity for the captain general to glean information, by questioning the Spanish crewmen involved, the trade remained contrary to Spain's closed commercial policy and could not be allowed to continue brazenly. With the establishment of Span-

9. Don Pedro Camps to Santiago Joseph, Obispo de la Havana, October 20, 1769, Obispo to Bucareli, January 10, 1770, Bucareli to Arriaga, January 11, 1770, no. 1322, all *ibid.* 1223; Jane Quinn, *Minorcans in Florida: Their History and Heritage* (Saint Augustine, Fla., 1975), 39–60; E. P. Panagopoulos, *New Smyrna: An Eighteenth Century Greek Odyssey* (Gainesville, Fla., 1966), 54–66.
10. Cecil Johnson, *British West Florida, 1763–1783* (New Haven, 1943), 24–25, 47; Garland Taylor, "Colonial Settlement and Early Revolutionary Activity in West Florida Up to 1779," *Mississippi Valley Historical Review,* XXII (1935), 352.
11. Johnson, *British West Florida,* 14, 44.
12. John B. Born, Jr., "Governor Johnstone and Trade in British West Florida, 1764–1767," *Bulletin of Wichita State University,* LXXV (1968), 8.
13. Johnson, *British West Florida,* 63–64.

ish colonial government at New Orleans, Bucareli turned to the governor there, his military subordinate, as a source of information. The first Spanish governor of Louisiana, Don Antonio de Ulloa, arrived at New Orleans during May, 1766. Ulloa, however, soon faced insurmountable problems, and his administration was doomed to failure.[14] Hampered by a lack of troops and funds from effectively taking possession of the former French province, he issued his orders through the French commander, who remained on the scene.[15] His difficulties owed less to his administrative abilities, which were adequate, than to circumstances in the colony: money remained scarce and fluctuated wildly in value; cash subsidies from the Spanish treasury could not cover the costs of government and, besides, generally arrived late; anti-Spanish feeling ran high among the populace; and the inhabitants feared the imposition of new Spanish commercial regulations that would close them off from their traditional trading partners.[16]

In spite of being reduced to inaction by the adversities he encountered, Governor Ulloa did enjoy a limited success in gathering news about the neighboring British for the captain general. His first achievement of this sort came in 1768, when the British cabinet, in London, decided to reduce military expenses in the trans-Allegheny area of North America. In carrying out the cabinet's directive, General Thomas Gage, the British military commander for the continent, consolidated troops in the southern district by closing English forts on the Mississippi and removing their garrisons to Saint Augustine. In West Florida, only Mobile and Pensacola retained garrisons, although the British naval presence on the Mississippi continued. Ulloa was able to furnish the captain general with the salient details of the reassignments within two months of General Gage's orders. The Louisiana governor had learned of the developments from English subjects passing through New Orleans. In one case, he talked at length with a British army

14. John Preston Moore, *Revolt in Louisiana: The Spanish Occupation, 1766–1770* (Baton Rouge, 1976), 103–23.

15. John W. Caughey, *Bernardo de Gálvez in Louisiana, 1776–1783* (Berkeley, Calif., 1934), 43. See also Arthur Preston Whitaker, "Antonio de Ulloa," *Hispanic American Historical Review,* XV (1935), 155–95; John Preston Moore, "Antonio de Ulloa: A Profile of the First Spanish Governor of Louisiana," *Louisiana History,* VIII (1967), 189–218; Vicente Rodríguez Casado, *Primeros años de dominación española en la Luisiana* (Madrid, 1942); Marqués de Casa Mena [José Montero de Pedro], *Españoles en Nueva Orleans y Luisiana* (Madrid, 1979), 21–25.

16. Jack D. L. Holmes, "Some Economic Problems of Spanish Governors of Louisiana," *Hispanic American Historical Review,* XLII (1962), 521–24; Antonio Acosta Rodríguez, "Problemas económicos y rebelión popular en Luisiana en 1768," in *Actos del congreso de historia de los Estados Unidos* (La Rábida, 1976), 131–46.

officer who had been sent to New Orleans to sell surplus supplies. Ulloa also came into possession of a letter from General Frederick Haldimand, the British military commander in West Florida, which discussed the troop reassignments and mentioned plans for maintaining an English commissioner at Natchez.[17]

Although Ulloa showed promise as an observer, the problems of his administration eventually rendered his government ineffective. Dissatisfaction among the residents of Louisiana grew to dangerous levels. The hostility mounted during the summer and fall of 1768, when Ulloa promulgated trade regulations that, in the eyes of the inhabitants, disrupted the commerce of the colony. Under the new trade restrictions, commerce could be conducted only with Spanish ships. Moreover, the requirements he instituted concerning registered cargo lists, sealed and certified consignments, bonded captains, and designated ports of call severely circumscribed the colony's commercial activity.[18] Indignation on the part of the residents reached crisis proportions on the night of October 27, when a mob spiked the guns at the gates of New Orleans. A throng numbering over four hundred gathered the following day to demand a restoration of French rule. Faced with the deterioration of civil order in the city, Ulloa took refuge on a Spanish frigate in the river. That was enough for the superior council, the municipal governing body of New Orleans, which was constituted of local residents, to order him from the colony permanently. Ulloa sailed for Havana, never to return. Spain's first attempt to govern Louisiana had failed.[19]

King Charles and his ministers in Spain were dismayed by the insurrection at New Orleans and vowed that their next attempt to establish Spanish control in the colony would be successful. During the summer of 1769, they sent an occupation force of over two thousand troops under the command of the stern and forceful General Alejandro O'Reilly to plant the flag of Spain firmly on the banks of the Mississippi.[20] O'Reilly succeeded un-

---

17. Johnson, *British West Florida*, 14; Caughey, *Bernardo de Gálvez*, 24; Antonio de Ulloa to Marqués de Grimaldi, August 23, October 6, 1768, both in *Spain in the Mississippi Valley, 1765–1794*, ed. Lawrence Kinnaird (3 vols.; Washington, D.C., 1949), II, 69–72.

18. Holmes, "Some Economic Problems," 523. The trade decree for 1768 has been translated and reprinted in *Spain in the Mississippi Valley*, ed. Kinnaird, II, 45–70. For a full discussion of Louisiana's trade problems, most of which the local populace blamed on Ulloa, see John G. Clark, *New Orleans, 1718–1812: An Economic History* (Baton Rouge, 1970), 158–80.

19. Moore, *Revolt in Louisiana*, 163.

20. Bibiano Torres Ramirez, *Alejandro O'Reilly en las Indias* (Seville, 1969), 97–183; David K. Bjork, "Alexander O'Reilly and the Spanish Occupation of Louisiana, 1769–1770," in *New Spain and the Anglo-American West*, ed. George P. Hammond (2 vols.; Lancaster, Pa., 1932), I,

equivocally in his effort, although in the process he did not ingratiate himself with the local population. His harsh treatment of the uprising's leaders earned him the nickname of Butcher O'Reilly among New Orleanians. Nevertheless, the general established a stable Spanish colonial government in the province. He reorganized the governmental structure of the colony along Spanish lines, created a cabildo for New Orleans, instituted the Spanish legal system, extended Louisiana's trade to Cuba and certain Iberian ports, established a militia, organized military defenses, set guidelines for relations with the Indians of the area, and promulgated regulations for awarding land grants. He also attempted to stop the British commerce in contraband goods which dominated the local economy.[21] O'Reilly, an able general and tactical field commander, did not go to Louisiana with the idea of serving as governor. Instead, he took a governor with him in the person of Luis de Unzaga y Amezaga, who in theory held the office even while O'Reilly was establishing Spanish rule in the province. Unzaga waited, however, to assume more than nominal command until O'Reilly departed in March, 1770.[22] After that, he played an important role in gathering information about the British for the captain general.

The growing British population along the Mississippi above New Orleans was a special worry for Governor Unzaga as he took command of the province. A widely read book by Captain Philip Pittman entitled *The Present State of European Settlements on the Mississippi* was advertising the charms and benefits of the Mississippi Valley to Englishmen. In August, 1770, a group of some seventy white settlers and eighteen blacks arrived at Natchez by floating down the Ohio and Mississippi from Fort Pitt, and British administration soon followed. The next year, the Indian agent for the southern district, John Stuart, appointed Lieutenant John Thomas to deal with tribes in British-held areas along the Mississippi. Thomas arrived on the river, having outfitted his agency with supplies purchased from New Orleans mer-

---

165–82; Casa Mena, *Españoles en Nueva Orleans*, 25–31; Eric Beerman, "Un bosquejo biográfico y genealógico del General Alejandro O'Reilly," *Hidalguia*, XXIV (1981), 225–44; Carl A. Brasseaux, *Denis-Nicolas Foucault and the New Orleans Rebellion of 1768* (Ruston, La., 1987), 75–90.

21. Alejandro O'Reilly to Grimaldi, October 17, 1769. AGI, Cuba 560. For a concise review of the efforts by O'Reilly, see Caughey, *Bernardo de Gálvez*, 29–42. See also Charles Gayarré, *The Spanish Domination* (1866; rpr. Gretna, La., 1974), 1–41, Vol. III of Gayarré, *A History of Louisiana*, 4 vols.

22. Caughey, *Bernardo de Gálvez*, 43–57; Chevalier Guy Soniat Du Fossat, *Synopsis of the History of Louisiana from the Founding of the Colony to the End of the Year 1791*, trans. Charles T. Soniat (New Orleans, 1903), 22; Casa Mena, *Españoles in Nueva Orleans*, 31–34

chants. Governor Unzaga made every effort to keep Captain General Bucareli informed about the events. He noted that Governor Peter Chester actively encouraged the settlement of British areas on the Mississippi north of New Orleans, and he presented his superiors in Havana with a full description of the settlements.[23]

The Louisiana governor secured the services of a valuable observer when, in late 1770, James O'Kelley visited the Spanish fort at Manchac, upriver from New Orleans. An Irish Catholic by birth who wished to become a Spanish subject for reasons of religion, O'Kelley had apparently settled in West Florida, become disaffected with British rule, and decided to seek the favor of the Spanish. He offered Unzaga stolen copies of letters that had been written to the Indian agent Stuart by British settlers north of New Orleans and that clearly indicated Lieutenant Thomas to be influencing the Indian tribes to switch their loyalty from the Spanish to the British. One letter in particular showed that Thomas had made a reconnaissance of New Orleans and had observed that its fortifications needed bolstering. Thomas estimated that the town could be taken with as few as one hundred well-trained British troops provided the Indians in the area allied themselves with Great Britain. To this end, Thomas promised his superiors that all tribes in the region would be under his control within a short time.[24] Infuriated by that letter, Unzaga made a full report to the captain general and the ministries in Spain. The minister of the Indies advised Unzaga to employ the best methods available to continue observing the British and to keep the captain general fully aware of all developments.[25]

The Louisiana governor kept close watch on the situation, with O'Kelley continuing to furnish reports on events across the bayou at British Manchac. In late May, 1771, the governor entertained at dinner the master of an English barge that had arrived at New Orleans from the Illinois country. Unzaga learned from him that English colonists continued to settle at

23. James A. James, *Oliver Pollock: The Life and Times of an Unknown Patriot* (1937; rpr. Freeport, N.Y., 1970), 40–41; Johnson, *British West Florida*, 136–37; John Stuart to Luis de Unzaga, August 25, 1771, Unzaga to Stuart, May 4, 1772, [John Thomas] to Stuart, December 12, 1771, all AGI, Cuba 189-B.

24. James O'Kelley to Captain Descoundreaux, January 23, January 27, 1772, [John Thomas] to Stuart, December 12, 1771, all AGI, Cuba 189-B. All the information developed by Unzaga proved to be substantially correct. For the British side of this affair, see John Thomas' correspondence in the Public Record Office, London, Colonial Office 5, LXXII, 424–51.

25. Marqués de la Torre to Unzaga, March 11, 1772, draft, no. 13, AGI, Cuba 1146.

Natchez and that five hundred persons from North Carolina planned to locate there in the succeeding months.[26] Unzaga also talked with British traders passing on the river, Spaniards going to and coming from the Illinois country, and French inhabitants in the province. He instructed his outlying post commanders to send him at once any news about occurrences in British territory. By piecing together information from his sources, he decided that the Englishmen coming to the Mississippi Valley intended to settle near the post at Natchez or at Baton Rouge. The governor personally observed an English brigantine filled with settlers as it passed upriver through New Orleans. The possibility of British settlements at either Baton Rouge or Natchez was disturbing to Unzaga, since it would bring the English frontier perilously close to that of New Spain. He foresaw that in times of peace with Great Britain the British population centers would be an additional lure for illegal commerce and that in wartime they could create military problems. The best counterbalance to the settlements, he supposed, might be to establish a loyal Spanish population north of New Orleans and prepare to meet force with force.[27]

Governor Unzaga made a full report on the settlements to the captain general and the minister of the Indies, and the information he had assembled caused Charles and his advisers considerable anxiety. Their deliberations, however, highlighted some basic misunderstandings by the Spanish about the nature of English colonial institutions. Some ministers at the Spanish court argued that the settlements proved a conscious effort on England's part to erect military fortifications that could be used as bases from which to attack Spanish territory in case of war. King Charles, familiar with the Spanish presidio system in frontier areas—which united military and settlement activities—mistook the new settlements for military garrisons and agreed. But other ministers saw no logical reason why Great Britain would want to add to the number of its military establishments on the Mississippi.[28]

The minister of the Indies, Julián de Arriaga, decided to enlist the assistance of General O'Reilly, then in Spain, in interpreting the information from Louisiana. When O'Reilly had examined all the reports provided by Governor Unzaga and the captain general, he explained that, according to

---

26. Pasqual de Cisneros to Arriaga, September 20, 1771, no. 49, AGI, Santo Domingo 1211.
27. Unzaga to Torre, February 27, 1772, *ibid.*
28. Torre to Arriaga [February, 1772], draft, February 22, 1772, both *ibid.*; Torre to Unzaga, March 20, 1772, no. 15, AGI, Cuba 1146.

British law and custom, the government of West Florida had made land grants to private interests that hoped to settle the area or to promote settlement there. Personal profit was the motive, with people seeking their livelihood and fortune from rising land values and agricultural production. English settlement in the areas north of New Orleans, O'Reilly assured the court, went forward independently of British military expansion. Therefore it was doubtful, he thought, that what was happening in West Florida was a direct threat to Spain. Still, O'Reilly told the king, "It is certain that it is not convenient for the royal interests to have them so close as neighbors."[29]

In the general's opinion, Spain's course could only be to continue to observe the settlements. In accepting that judgment, the king ordered the captain general of Cuba and the governor of Louisiana to keep the British in West Florida under close, continuous scrutiny. Unzaga was to take whatever action he felt necessary to obtain information about developments in the area. The court also authorized Bucareli and Unzaga to send an observer into British territory along the Atlantic coast in order to report on general developments and events in the seaboard colonies.[30]

A diplomatic crisis at this time made observation of the British even more urgent. Spain and Great Britain had long disputed possession of the Malvinas—or Falkland—Islands, off the coast of South America, then occupied by the British. Spain considered the islands its own although it had neglected them after their discovery in 1592. In the 1760s, both England and France established naval stations in the island group. King Charles immediately protested to both courts, with the result that King Louis of France surrendered his claim to Spain and vacated the islands. But the British navy refused to leave. After several minor confrontations, a military force sent by the Spanish governor in Buenos Aires landed in June, 1770, near the English base and forcibly evicted the British. With that, diplomats at the three interested European courts frantically set to negotiating a settlement, to keep the crisis from degenerating into armed conflict between England and Spain. Spanish military commanders throughout the Americas feared that England might at any time retaliate anywhere in the hemisphere.[31] As a

29. O'Reilly to Arriaga, June 5, 1772, Arriaga to O'Reilly, May 28, 1772, both AGI, Santo Domingo 1211.
30. "Minuta," March 21, 1772, *ibid.*; Arriaga to Torre, June 20, 1772, royal order, Arriaga to Unzaga, June 20, 1772, royal order, both *ibid.*
31. Vera Lee Brown, "Anglo-Spanish Relations in America in the Closing Years of the Colonial Era," *Hispanic American Historical Review,* V (1922), 325–483; Octavo Gil Munilla, *Malvinas: El Conflicto anglo-español de 1770* (Seville, 1948).

defensive precaution, the captain general of Cuba increased his military strength and intensified the information gathering he oversaw. In late December, 1770, the minister of the Indies officially advised the captain general of a potential breach with Great Britain over the Malvinas incident. Nevertheless, he cautioned Bucareli not to initiate hostilities.[32]

The captain general therefore concentrated upon gathering information about military events in the nearby British colonies. He immediately notified his subordinate commanders of the situation and encouraged them to take heed of activity in British territories bordering their areas. In March, he dispatched a merchant from Havana to French Santo Domingo to gather news about the British navy and its movements in the Caribbean. That observer returned several weeks later with a report he had compiled from conversations with French and English traders. He also brought copies of the gazette published in El Guarico (Cap Français), which contained news from Europe about the diplomatic maneuvers over the Malvinas. Bucareli questioned the masters and captains of Spanish ships calling at Havana, in order to collect any information the crews might have acquired in their travels elsewhere in the Spanish Indies.[33] All the reports indicated that England and Spain still maintained peaceful relations.

Not satisfied with such efforts, the captain general had several local merchants, most of them of the Asiento, go to Jamaica on the pretext of trading in foodstuffs. The last of his observers returned during May, 1771, with a report on the number and class of English warships standing in the Kingston roadstead. To all appearances, the British did not contemplate a surprise attack on Spanish territories.[34]

Bucareli's term as captain general ended while he was superintending these observations. King Charles appointed him in 1771 as viceroy of New Spain, perhaps the highest and most prestigious position available to a Spanish colonial administrator. Because the king and his ministers realized that the change of personnel at Havana came at a critical time and during crucial observations of British settlements on the borders of the captain general's command area, they chose a proven commander and staff-level organizer as Bucareli's successor. The king had consulted General O'Reilly,

---

32. Bucareli to Arriaga, March 6, 1771, reserved, AGI, Santo Domingo 1214.
33. Bucareli to Arriaga, April 8, 1771, reserved, *ibid.*
34. "Diario de la navegación del surgidero del Batabano a montar la Isla de Jamaica por la parte del sur hasta entrar en Kingston," enclosed in Bucareli to Arriaga, May 8, 1771, no. 1792, *ibid.*

who recommended Don Felipe Fonsdeviela, the Marqués de la Torre, then serving as governor of Caracas, for his talent as a commander and administrator. Joining the Guardia Española as a cadet in 1735, Torre had risen through the ranks of the Regiment of Aragon to become its commander in 1750. He first arrived in the Indies as inspector general of the infantry in New Spain, during 1767. In 1770, he received a promotion to the rank of field marshal and assumed the governorship of Caracas.[35]

Torre arrived in Havana in November, 1771, taking formal possession of his office from Pasqual de Cisneros, who had been exercising interim command after Bucareli's departure for Mexico. Torre's tenure as captain general brought conspicuous improvements to the island. One historian has noted: "The Marqués de la Torre was without doubt one of the most efficient and successful governors that Cuba ever had. [He] was able to direct his attention to improvements which made for a higher standard of public health, and paved the way for a culture which, in spite of the wealth of the population, was still only in its beginnings."[36]

Cisneros briefed Torre about the intelligence gathering in progress, and the new captain general made the observation of neighboring British colonies one of his highest priorities. In December, 1771, he dispatched Antonio Marin, master of the fishing sloop *Nuestra Señora de la Concepción*, to the East Florida coast to deliver religious supplies to the Minorcan settlement on the Mosquito River.[37] Although the bishop of Cuba had decided that these Catholics resided outside his jurisdiction, the Spanish Council of Ministers granted permission for them to receive religious supplies from Havana. Since there still seemed a possibility of an English retaliation over the Malvinas incident, information that Marin might gather regarding British intentions held special interest for Torre. The captain general gave Marin a letter from the bishop of Cuba to Father Camps, requesting that the cleric monitor military affairs along the Florida coast in light of the international crisis.[38]

---

35. O'Reilly to Arriaga, May 13, 1771, Arriaga to O'Reilly, May 10, 1771, royal order, both *ibid.* 1211; "Noticias de las fechas de los empleos del Marqués de la Torre," October 15, 1776, *ibid.* See also Vicente Báez, *La enciclopedia de Cuba, historia* (4 vols.; San Juan, 1971), IV, 214–17.

36. "Decreto del Rey al Don Pedro Garcia Mayoral," June 6, 1771, AGI, Santo Domingo 1193; "Titulo del Marqués de la Torre," June 17, 1771, *ibid.*; Willis Fletcher Johnson, *The History of Cuba* (5 vols.; New York, 1920), II, 129–30.

37. Torre to Arriaga, February 23, 1772, no. 84, AGI, Cuba 1227.

38. Arriaga to the governor of Havana, December 20, 1771, royal order, AGI, Santo Domingo 1221.

Marin secretly arrived at New Smyrna on New Year's Day, unloaded the religious supplies, and remained long enough for Father Camps to draft a reply to the bishop's letter, agreeing to observe the British. Marin then set sail, but contrary winds impeded him from crossing the bar at the mouth of the river and forced him to stand to for almost three weeks. On the night of January 24, a Minorcan from the settlement came on board with startling news. The English lieutenant governor, whose Roman Catholic wife regularly took communion from Father Camps, had called at the vicarage to say that Great Britain might be declaring war on Spain in the very near future. Father Camps had also received a letter from Luciano de Herrera, a Spaniard living in Saint Augustine, that mentioned British troop increases there. Herrera, a Spanish Floridian, had remained in Saint Augustine, his lifelong home, when the British took control of East Florida, in order to represent various Spaniards who were leaving assets behind. He supervised, for example, the sale of property and real estate to Englishmen moving into the colony and associated with the Florida entrepreneur Jesse Fish and Juan Elegio de la Puente in such matters.[39] Herrera had asked Father Camps to give his letter to any of the Cuban fishing boats sailing along the East Florida coast, for forwarding to the authorities in Havana.

Marin set sail with his astounding news as soon as he could. Because Captain General Torre was away from Havana, on an inspection tour that had taken him to Matanzas, the master of the *Nuestra Señora de la Concepción* made his report to Juan Elegio de la Puente, another Spanish official. Puente, serving as *contador* of the royal treasury office in Havana, questioned Marin closely in order to gauge the validity of the information. The *contador* was a former resident of Saint Augustine who had arrived in Cuba after the territorial transfer in 1764. Because of his wide knowledge of the region, he often served the captain general in an advisory capacity regarding the British Floridas. He also enjoyed a personal relationship with the Florida Indians, especially the Yuchis, which made his services to the captaincy general even more valuable.[40]

39. Robert L. Gold, *Borderland Empires in Transition: The Triple-Nation Transfer of Florida* (Carbondale, Ill., 1969), 47.

40. "El Patrón Antonio Marin, que con la Goleta propia suya nombrada Nra. Señora de la Concepción, salio de este puerto de dia 13 de diciembre del año proximo pasado . . . ," February 15, 1772, AGI, Cuba 1227; Mark F. Boyd and José Navarro Latorre, "Spanish Interest in British Florida, and in the Progress of the American Revolution," *Florida Historical Quarterly*, XXXII (1953), 92, 115–16; Katherine S. Lawson, "Luciano de Herrera, Spanish Spy in British Saint Augustine," *Florida Historical Quarterly*, XXIII (1945), 170–76; Cummins, "Luci-

When Puente relayed Marin's information, the captain general hurried back to Havana, fearing that a communication from Madrid about war with England might be en route in the mail packet that had not yet arrived from Spain. The captain general lost no time in mobilizing the information-collecting network. In an urgent message to Governor Unzaga, he directed the Louisiana commander to use all available methods to observe events in West Florida. Unzaga talked with Englishmen passing through New Orleans and notified his outlying post commanders to monitor the situation as well. The Louisiana governor sent regular reports to Havana throughout the spring regarding British activities north of New Orleans.[41] Torre also apprised Viceroy Bucareli, in Mexico City, of the reports from New Smyrna and asked to be told of any information that might come to Veracruz or other Mexican ports.[42] The captain general alerted the Spanish naval commander at Havana, instructing him to canvass the captains of all vessels in port for news of British ship movements. He ordered, besides, that a sloop cruise the Tortuga Sound, watching the maritime lanes leading from Kingston to Havana.[43] None of these steps corroborated Marin's reports from New Smyrna.

Much to Torre's confusion, the monthly mail packet from Spain that arrived in Havana shortly thereafter contained no letters from the ministries about imminent hostilities between England and Spain. All appeared normal. Still, Marin's apparently erroneous reports unsettled the captain general, and he decided to continue collecting intelligence with a bearing on the matter.[44] He therefore implemented his earlier plan to send an observer to the upper seaboard of British North America. That person might be able to ferret out what lay behind the confusing reports brought from East Florida.

Governor Unzaga came up with a plan that would allow the observer to conceal his purposes. In looking into British activities in West Florida, the governor had learned that there were New Orleans merchants who had be-

---

ano de Herrera and Spanish Espionage in British Saint Augustine," *El Escribano*, XVI (1979), 43–57. For an autobiographical sketch of Puente, see "Informe de 1784," AGI, Santo Domingo 1160.

41. Unzaga to Torre, February 27, 1772, AGI, Santo Domingo 1211.

42. Torre to Bucareli, February 20, 1772, Torre to Unzaga, February 12, 1772, both AGI, Cuba 1227.

43. Torre to Arriaga, February 23, 1772, reserved, no. 84, *ibid.*

44. Unzaga to Torre, March 23, 1772, reserved, no. 12, *ibid.*

come involved in fraudulent business dealings with a British trader residing at New Orleans under dubious legality. That person, a Mr. Blouin, had in addition engaged in illegal land speculation in Spanish territory, and a rumor in the colony suggested that the English authorities on the Atlantic Coast also sought Blouin for illegal investment schemes in the Illinois country.[45] Unzaga decided that it was the perfect moment to send a messenger to General Gage, in New York, about Blouin's residence on the lower Mississippi and about Spanish dissatisfaction over the legal irregularities surrounding the trader.[46] The governor engaged the services of Juan de Surriret to deliver his letter of complaint to the British authorities in New York. In reality, Unzaga cared little about Blouin's defiance of legal norms. What was important was that Surriret had been tapped as an observer: the collection of information would be the true purpose of his voyage. Surriret was a French planter and merchant living at Pointe Coupee, across the river north of Baton Rouge. He had regular contact with the British, spoke fluent English, and was familiar with commercial practices on the Atlantic Coast. At Torre's instance, Unzaga briefed Surriret on the report Marin had brought from East Florida. He bid the planter gather any information in British America that had a bearing on the question of impending war, even if it appeared inaccurate. The two Spanish commanders also wanted Surriret to talk with as many Englishmen as he could, visit as many ports en route as possible, and gain as much firsthand knowledge of military and naval affairs as offered itself during his travels.[47]

The French planter did his job very successfully during 1772. He sailed for New York on board a private merchant vessel, telling everyone about his orders to deliver Unzaga's letter to General Gage, and, once at New York, he met with the general. On the whole, Surriret observed events closely, and his subsequent report provided a wealth of information. He learned that the court in London had sent dispatches to General Gage ordering the

45. Clarence E. Carter, ed., *The Correspondence of General Thomas Gage with the Secretaries of State and with the War Office and the Treasury, 1763–1775* (2 vols.; New Haven, 1931–33), II, 151.

46. Torre to Arriaga, March 23, 1772, AGI, Santo Domingo 1211; Stuart to Unzaga, September 1, 1773, AGI, Cuba 189-B; Thomas Gage to Unzaga, August 3, 1772, AGI, Cuba 2370; Unzaga to Arriaga, October 24, 1772, no. 76, AGI, Santo Domingo 1211.

47. Torre to Arriaga [February, 1772], draft, February 22, 1772, no. 81, both AGI, Santo Domingo 1211; Torre to Unzaga, March 20, 1772, no. 15, August 14, 1772, draft, both AGI, Cuba 1146.

consolidation of British forces in North America and that Gage had accordingly reorganized his command: the 2nd American Battalion had been reassigned from Canada to New York, and British troop strengths had been readjusted at Halifax, Boston, Philadelphia, and Saint Augustine as part of the consolidation. Those garrisons, Surriret reported, awaited orders either to join Gage at New York or to rendezvous with him once the expected troop deployments began. The observer ventured that this might explain the rumor of military preparations carried to Havana by Captain Marin. The Louisiana planter also learned that the garrisons at Providence Island had received similar orders.[48]

Surriret booked return passage to the Mississippi Valley on an English merchant vessel carrying munitions to Pensacola. During the voyage, he talked with a group of carpenters who had been ordered to the West Florida capital to construct army barracks large enough to house a thousand troops. Soon after his arrival in Pensacola, a second English ship made port there carrying additional supplies and munitions. Surriret apparently had free run of the town and observed at close range the building of a battery of seventy cannons on the bluffs overlooking the entrance to the bay. These fortifications had been constructed on orders from General Frederick Haldimand, he reported. The agent later provided Unzaga and Captain General Torre detailed plans showing the design and characteristics of the large fort, along with a description of a smaller emplacement for four cannons on Santa Rosa Island, across from the main battery.[49] In addition to preparing a written report, Surriret had several long discussions with Unzaga after his return to New Orleans. The Louisiana planter felt that much of the activity in Pensacola seemed directed not toward possible hostilities with Spain but toward the protection of normal English maritime routes to Jamaica. The new fortifications were defensive in nature, he believed, and not part of an offensive buildup against Spain.

Surriret was also able to enlarge on his explanation of Marin's inaccurate report from East Florida earlier in the year. A faction at the British court and in Parliament had indeed wished to strike against Spain without warning, in the hope that the attack would divert to a foreign enemy the atten-

---

48. "Noticias adquiridos de los vecinos colonias ingleses por Mr. Surriret vecino de Punta Cortado . . . ," October 2, 1772, AGI, Cuba 1146.
49. For the background on these activities, see J. Barton Starr, *Tories, Dons, and Rebels: The American Revolution in British West Florida* (Gainesville, Fla., 1976), 29.

tion of Atlantic Coast colonists dissatisfied with the London ministries, the observer reported. Public discussion of that strategy had apparently taken place in both England and the American colonies some months earlier. In London, the anti-Spanish group, however, had been branded as rash, and their ideas did not reflect official British policy.[50]

Well satisfied with Surriret's conduct of his mission, both Torre and Unzaga continued their efforts to collect information. Governor Unzaga questioned the crews of English ships passing through New Orleans and maintained watch on merchants in the city who had regular contact with West Florida. From the merchants, he learned that a British man-of-war had called at Pensacola shortly after Surriret's return to Louisiana. That ship carried word that the mobilization and consolidation of General Gage's troops had been in response to a supposed slave revolt on the island of Saint Vincent and to the possibility of English hostilities with Denmark.[51] Unzaga did not find the explanation completely convincing. Whatever the British motives were, reports coming to him at New Orleans clearly showed that England was engaged in bolstering military garrisons in many of its colonies. The captain general, who read all of those reports, tried independently to learn what lay behind the British operations, besides ordering Unzaga to continue his investigations.[52]

Dispatches from the Spanish court that arrived in Havana shortly thereafter confirmed that relations with Britain gave no indication of impending war between the two empires. Still, the captain general continued to observe the English in the ways he could. In early 1773, he was able to reassure Governor Unzaga that all attempts in Havana to collect data about British military operations had failed to uncover English activities that threatened Spanish interests.[53]

With the passing months, the reason for the British troop reassignments in North America became much clearer to the Spanish. From Spain's embassy in London, the chargé d'affaires, Francisco Escarano, began furnishing a great deal of information to King Charles and the court about the growing crisis in the governance of British America. Escarano suggested to the Spanish court that the military movements the captaincy general of

50. Unzaga to Torre, October 2, 1772, AGI, Santo Domingo 1211.
51. Unzaga to Torre, October 24, 1772, no. 76, *ibid.*
52. Torre to Unzaga, October 26, 1772, draft, AGI, Cuba 1146.
53. Torre to Unzaga, January 25, 1773, draft, *ibid.*

Cuba was aware of were a response to growing disorders in British North America. The Spanish envoy in London, in fact, told King Charles and his ministers that some at the British court feared the American colonists intended to use force in pressing their demands on the mother country. Great Britain had therefore increased troop levels in America and moved toward greater military preparedness all along the Atlantic Coast.[54]

Even so, Spain did not relax its efforts in Louisiana and Havana to collect information. Torre and his subordinate commanders, especially Governor Unzaga, maintained their vigilance throughout 1774 and 1775. Spain was still apprehensive of a surprise attack by the British against its colonial possessions, since Escarano continued to report on the noisy faction in London that favored a declaration of war against the Bourbon monarchies as a diversion to cool the crisis along the Atlantic Coast. Spain took that faction seriously. The court in any case believed that England would turn against Spanish America the moment problems in its North American colonies eased, if not before that.[55] Luckily for Spain, the bellicose group in London had no influence in Parliament. Their discussions and debates, nonetheless, explain why Charles and his ministers feared a surprise attack by England as late as 1778 and why the captain general of Cuba continued his efforts to observe at every turn the British colonies bordering on his command.

The fifteen years preceding Lexington and Concord were thus an important period for the captain general of Cuba as he developed, refined, and directed techniques to track events in the British colonies of North America. In addition to providing experience for the people who participated in the effort, the operations forced the creation of an administrative bureaucracy to collect, organize, and then transmit information to the Spanish court. For the most part, the observation efforts followed the lines of military command in the captaincy general. The captain general's office became the clearinghouse for intelligence gathered about the British, with the governor of Louisiana playing an important secondary role because of his physical proximity to a mainland British colony. What is as important as anything else is that the captain general began to assemble a group of observers. These included the Asiento merchants who traveled to Jamaica, the Minorcans in New Smyrna, the Saint Augustine resident Luciano de Herrera, and

54. Francisco Escarano to Grimaldi, January 18, September 2, 1774, both AGS, Estado 6988.
55. Juan Fernando Yela Utrilla, *España ante la independencia de los Estados Unidos* (2nd ed.; 2 vols.; Lerida, 1925), I, 54–56.

various Louisianians, including Juan de Surriret. With the coming of the American Revolution and Spain's desire to follow the progress of the revolt in connection with its own diplomatic policy, the Spanish court expanded the captain general's information-gathering assignment far beyond its original scope. Yet, later Spanish observation of the American Revolution was rooted firmly in intelligence practices devised at Havana and New Orleans between 1763 and 1775.

2

Watching the Revolution

1775–1776

The outbreak of fighting in Massachusetts did not surprise Charles and his ministers, since for years they had known of growing problems in the English colonies.[1] Their diplomatic envoys abroad had long been sending news of dramatic events in British America. Nevertheless, during 1775 the Spanish king and his advisers could not decide on the diplomatic response they wanted to make to the revolt at Lexington and Concord. Two royal ministers emerged as important leaders in the internal Spanish policy debates at court: Spain's ambassador to France, the Conde de Aranda; and the minister of state, the Marqués de Grimaldi.

Based in Paris, Aranda firmly believed that the Revolution presented Spain and France with a unique opportunity to advance their international standing at the expense of Great Britain. Aranda advocated joining the conflict immediately, with the combined forces of France and Spain attacking Great Britain as soon as events warranted. The ambassador went so far as to send Madrid a plan outlining the methods whereby the two Bourbon courts could join their naval forces to cut Great Britain's supply lines and disrupt its commerce. Aranda exercised greater influence at court than his diplomatic post in Paris might suggest. He had earlier served as president of the Council of Castille and still led an important court faction known as the *aragoneses*. Aranda's belligerent views during 1775 found a receptive au-

---

1. Luis Angel García Melero, *La independencia de los Estados Unidos de Norteamerica a través de la prensa española ("Gaceta de Madrid" y "Mercurio Histórico y Político")* (Madrid, 1977).

27

dience among his supporters at court. This has occasionally caused some students of the period to assign a more warlike stance to official Spanish policy during the first year or so of the American Revolution than was probably the case. For example, Samuel Flagg Bemis notes that during 1775, Spain desired to declare war against Great Britain and seemed even more bellicose in its reaction than France.[2]

On the other hand, Grimaldi, the minister of state, favored neutrality and noninvolvement. He seemed primarily preoccupied about the potential impact of the American Revolution on Spanish policy in South America.[3] At the time of Lexington and Concord, Spain was planning a military expedition to expel the Portuguese from the Río de la Plata, near Buenos Aires. In debate with his ministerial colleagues, Grimaldi pointed out that Great Britain was traditionally an ally of Portugal. The Revolution had brought a large number of British military forces to the Western Hemisphere that could easily be turned against Spain should Britain defeat the rebellious colonists, especially if the Spanish had already provoked hostilities with Portugal. Grimaldi took as proof of this that the Spanish ambassador in London had warned that some members of Parliament threatened war with Spain because of the Portuguese problem.[4] Moreover, the existence of the anti-Spanish viewpoint in Great Britain had been clearly substantiated by dispatches from the captain general of Cuba.

Grimaldi spent a great deal of time worrying about a possible surprise attack by the British on the Spanish Indies should the Revolution end quickly. He thought that the tidings of a British victory over the rebels in North America might first reach the Spanish Empire in the form of an attack. The American commissioners in Paris understood Grimaldi's reason-

2. Yela Utrilla, *España*, I, 41, 43; Samuel Flagg Bemis, *The Diplomacy of the American Revolution* (New York, 1935), 42–43. Although this interpretation accurately reflects the position of Aranda and his followers, it takes a rather monolithic view of the Council of Ministers as a royal advisory body in Spanish foreign policy. In fact, the Marqués de Grimaldi and his successor in the ministry of state, the Conde de Floridablanca, often found themselves in disagreement with the *aragoneses*. For an analysis of the Aranda group, see Rafael Olaechea, *El Conde de Aranda y el "partido aragones"* (Saragossa, 1967), and María Pilar Ruigómez de Hernández, *El gobierno español del despotismo ilustrado ante la independencia de los Estados Unidos de América* (Madrid, 1978), 158–69. Miguel Muzquiz, minister of finance, was the strongest supporter of Aranda in the Council of Ministers. The Conde de Ricla (minister of the army) and Julián de Arriaga (minister of the Indies) generally supported Grimaldi. See Vicente Rodríguez Casado, *La política marroquí de Carlos III* (Madrid, 1946), xiii–xvi.
3. Yela Utrilla, *España*, I, 44.
4. Escarano to Grimaldi, September 2, 1774, no. 354, AGS, Estado 6988.

ing. "Should Spain be disinclined to our cause from an apprehension of danger to her South American dominion," Benjamin Franklin noted, "cannot France be prevailed on at our request and assurances not to disturb theirs to guarantee [*sic*] to that Crown her Territories there against any molestation from us?"[5] Such suggestions had little result, and Grimaldi stood firm. His fears grew when reports from England made it seem that the revolt might be ending by negotiation. That idea—although subsequently proved inaccurate—arose because Spain's ambassador to Great Britain, the Principe de Masserano, related that several prominent figures in the Atlantic colonies had approached the British government seeking a reconciliation. In particular, Masserano had heard that influential voices in eight of the rebellious provinces had expressed a desire for peace if the home ministries would grant colonial requests regarding taxation and commerce.[6] Grimaldi feared that the British cabinet might do exactly that, especially since Masserano had reported throughout the early summer of 1775 that neither Parliament nor the cabinet had named a specific policy regarding the revolt.[7]

King Charles thus had to arrive at a diplomatic policy regarding Britain and its rebellious colonies on the basis of conflicting advice from his ministers. Discussion and debate took time. Further delay resulted from Spain's need to take French policy into account. As an allied Bourbon court under the terms of the Family Compact, France pledged to coordinate foreign policy with Spain.[8] Hence, the ministers of France and Spain maintained a lively exchange of opinion during 1775 regarding a coordinated response by their nations.[9] But little consensus emerged during the six months after Lexington and Concord. France and Spain realized that the colonial struggle placed Great Britain in a difficult position that could only result in the

---

5. Benjamin Franklin to William Temple Franklin, September 10, 1776, in *Letters of Delegates to Congress, 1774–1789,* ed. Paul Smith (16 vols. to date; Washington, D.C., 1976–), V, 132.

6. Principe de Masserano to Grimaldi, July 14, 1775, no. 38, AGS, Estado 6990.

7. Masserano to Grimaldi, July 24, 1775, no. 23, *ibid.*

8. The French viewpoint is discussed by Bemis in *The Diplomacy of the American Revolution,* 41–57, and by Jonathan R. Dull in *A Diplomatic History of the American Revolution* (New Haven, 1985), 57–65. See also James B. Perkins, *France in the American Revolution* (1911; rpr. Williamstown, Mass., 1970), 34–44; Elizabeth S. Kite, *Beaumarchais and the War of American Independence* (2 vols.; Boston, 1918), II, 31–55; and Edwin S. Corwin, *French Policy and the American Alliance of 1778* (1916; rpr. Gloucester, Mass., 1969), 49–53.

9. For a detailed recounting of these Franco-Spanish discussions during 1775 and 1776, see Yela Utrilla, *España,* I, 41–95.

deterioration of its international power. Beyond that rather obvious conclusion, however, the two courts could not agree on a unified plan of action. In mid-1775, Charles and his ministers settled for inertia, deciding to continue normal relations with Great Britain and to profess neutrality until events in North America recommended doing otherwise.

Grimaldi worried that England might attack Spain's American possessions despite the relative prudence of the decision at court, and his anxieties were heightened when he heard that France might be contemplating secret aid to the rebellious colonists. In a coded message from England, Ambassador Masserano had reported to him the British capture of a French frigate en route to North America. The vessel carried documents implying that an unnamed European power had already offered secret assistance and military support to the rebel cause. Although Masserano could not find out the identity of the nation involved, even if the British knew, he suspected that the captured papers had originated at the French court.[10] That possibility greatly disquieted Grimaldi, who feared that the anti-Bourbon faction in England would use French interference as an excuse for war against both France and Spain. Additional reports coming from Havana increased the minister of state's apprehensions. Observers working for the captain general of Cuba reported that two Spanish ships sailing from Central America had called at Charleston, South Carolina, and had sold gunpowder and supplies to the local rebel commander. Indeed, the incident later occasioned a formal diplomatic protest from the British ambassador in Madrid. Lord Weymouth furnished the Spanish ministry of state with letters of complaint written by the English blockade commander off the coast of South Carolina, against two Spanish ships that had arrived in October, 1775, passed the blockade, and unloaded their cargoes in Charleston. To impress the British with the sincerity of Spanish neutrality, Grimaldi ordered that one of the accused merchant captains be tried for violating the commercial laws that prohibited trade outside Spain's colonial system. The trial convened at Cádiz in June, 1776, but the judge acquitted the captain on the basis of his own testimony.[11]

France and Spain continued their discussions about a joint policy while Aranda counseled action and Grimaldi cautioned delay. The French foreign

10. Masserano to Grimaldi, September 1, 1775, no. 2, AGS, Estado 6991. Masserano dispatched this report in the rarely used Spanish diplomatic code, and Grimaldi apparently deciphered it personally.

11. Masserano to Grimaldi, December 15, 1775, no. 150, *ibid.* 6993; Juan de Meuda to Grimaldi, June 4, 1776, AGI, 881. See also "Minuta al President de la Casa de Contratación," June 4, 1776, AGI, Guatemala 881.

minister, Charles Gravier, the Comte de Vergennes, had views more in line with those of Aranda than of Grimaldi. Vergennes, a French aristocrat with experience in the diplomatic service, became secretary of state for foreign affairs in 1774. He favored war with England in an attempt to seize the role of arbiter of the European balance of power for France during the international crisis the American Revolution created. According to one commentator, for Vergennes "the American rebellion created . . . the opportunity to separate a major segment of the [British] empire from the mother country and establish an independent sovereignty under the guardianship of France. The end result, nevertheless, would be the weakening of the balance of power in Europe."[12] Vergennes believed that Britain would tie itself up in a costly and all-consuming war for as long as the American rebellion continued. Whatever the outcome, the British military would emerge so enfeebled that an attack on French or Spanish possessions in the Americas would be unthinkable. Grimaldi disagreed. He attempted to convince Vergennes of the pertinacity of those in England who advocated a move against Spanish colonies in the Americas. On several occasions in late December, 1775, and again in January, 1776, he wrote the French minister about this risk.[13] Vergennes was unpersuaded.

It soon became apparent that Spain felt far more threatened by the American Revolution than France did, since the French no longer had a large and extended colonial empire in the Western Hemisphere demanding protection. Vergennes saw himself in the enviable position of a detached bystander able to watch the British Empire spend itself with internal strife. Spain was not prone to a similar complacency, since it held territory contiguous to the struggle. Grimaldi clearly understood the dangers to which the American Revolution exposed the Spanish colonies and accordingly acted to reduce their vulnerability. He discussed his concern with King Charles, who agreed on the need for measures to protect and defend the possessions. As a result, the Conde de Ricla, Spain's minister of war and the former captain general of Havana, dispatched additional troops to Cuba and Puerto Rico in late 1775.[14]

12. Orville T. Murphy, "The View from Versailles: Charles Gravier, Comte de Vergennes's Perceptions of the American Revolution," in *Diplomacy and Revolution: The Franco-American Alliance of 1778*, ed. Ronald Hoffman and Peter J. Albert (Charlottesville, Va., 1981), 116. See also Murphy, "Charles Gravier de Vergennes, Profile of an Old Regime Diplomat," *Political Science Quarterly*, LXXXIII (1968), 400–418.
13. Yela Utrilla, *España*, I, 57–58.
14. *Ibid*, 50.

Grimaldi realized, however, that troop increases by themselves could not protect the Spanish Indies against a surprise English attack. He understood that Spain needed accurate information about both English and rebel military operations in the Americas. In addition, the king and his advisers needed regular reports about the rebels and their plans, in order to gauge the viability of the revolt. Consequently, Grimaldi decided to expand the observation responsibilities of the captain general of Cuba to include the monitoring of all events relating to the Revolution, even those not directly threatening to the Spanish colonies. He notified the French court in early 1776 that Spain would be creating a network of observers in North America to provide regular intelligence on the course of the Revolution. Grimaldi hoped France would adopt a similar line of action and that both courts could begin an exchange of information from their sources. He was not, however, sanguine about France's cooperating fully, since he suspected Vergennes of having already offered secret assistance to the rebellious colonists.[15]

Grimaldi knew, for example, that the French foreign minister had sent a Monsieur Bonvolour to Pennsylvania with instructions to investigate the intentions of the colonies and to provide the Paris ministries with information prospectively useful in formulating French policy. Bonvolour arrived in Philadelphia in November, 1775, and began sending reports to Vergennes soon after that. The French agent let his superior know that the colonies seemed to be in a state of extraordinary agitation. Philadelphia buzzed with rumors about military campaigns projected for the spring of 1776. Bonvolour talked with colonial leaders, who impressed him with their dedication and their ability to lead a revolt against the British. The information he provided the French court showed a strong will to resist on the part of the rebel colonists. Bonvolour did note, however, that the rebels lacked an adequate navy, proper supplies, and sufficient money.[16] The French foreign minister therefore, without telling the Spanish, dispatched the Caron de Beaumarchais to London to find clandestine methods of supplying the rebel colonies with arms and munitions.[17] The Caron de Beaumarchais most likely set in train activities that led to the captured letter that caused Grimaldi such concern.

15. *Ibid*, 62.
16. Enrique de Tapia Ozcariz, *Carlos III y su época* (Madrid, 1966), 317–18.
17. Kite, *Beaumarchais*, II, 37–43.

The reports Beaumarchais and Bonvolour provided only fired Vergennes' desire to exploit the American Revolution to weaken Great Britain by aiding the rebels. The French minister felt that the creation of a new nation in North America would serve as a counterbalance to English commercial power in the hemisphere and might permit France a larger share of world trade, thereby partly compensating for the colonial empire it had lost in the Seven Years' War.[18] Vergennes became increasingly bellicose during 1776 as he moved farther away from the cautious neutrality advocated by the Marqués de Grimaldi. The French foreign minister, however, decided to cooperate with Grimaldi up to a point. Let the Spanish gather all the information they wanted. In the meantime, France would independently and covertly press ahead with plans to assist the rebellious colonies. Vergennes saw little to be gained by informing the Spanish of this decision, especially since Grimaldi was averse to Spain's becoming involved.[19]

Unaware of Vergennes' efforts to collect intelligence in North America, Grimaldi during early 1776 set in motion the observation program he had described to the French foreign minister. The Spanish minister of state admired the means the captain general of Cuba had been employing to gather information about neighboring British colonies. In particular, Grimaldi had as foreign minister profited from the information sent to his office from Cuba during the Malvinas crisis of the early 1770s. The reports from Cuba had arrived at the ministry of state for analysis and correlation with information provided by the various Spanish diplomatic posts abroad. It was partly Grimaldi's successful experience then that had decided him on expanding the captain general's observer corps and charging it with the compilation of news about all aspects of the American Revolution. As minister of state, however, Grimaldi did not directly supervise any of Spain's colonial officials, and so did not directly supervise the captain general of Cuba. That superintendence fell to the minister of the Indies, the king's chief adviser for

18. Francisco Morales Padrón, *Participación de España en la independencia política de los Estados Unidos* (2nd ed.; Madrid, 1963), 4.
19. Information about the American Revolution continued to flow from Paris to the Spanish court throughout Spain's period of declared neutrality prior to 1779. Most of the reports did not, however, reflect the activities of the confidential French agents. The French foreign ministry provided the Spanish Council of Ministers primarily with information coming from French envoys abroad. For an example, see extracts of the letters written by Conrad Alexandre Gérard and the Chevalier de La Luzerne from Philadelphia that are contained in the Archivo Histórico Nacional, in Madrid, especially in Estado 3884 bis, expediente no. 6.

American matters and the royal official who administered the concerns of the Ministry of the Indies, Spain's colonial office.

The ministry of the Indies was in some disarray during late 1775, because its minister, Julián de Arriaga, suffered from a lingering and debilitating illness that incapacitated him for long periods. At his death, in early 1776, José de Gálvez assumed the post.[20] Arriaga had held dual portfolios at court, serving both as minister of the Indies and head of the ministry of the navy. Charles wished to continue that arrangement with Gálvez, but Grimaldi dissuaded him on the grounds that the possibility of warfare with the British would make it difficult for one person to fill both positions. When the king appointed the Marqués Gónzales de Castejón as the new minister of the navy, Gálvez was free to concentrate on the concerns of the colonial office.[21] Gálvez' appointment met with general approval at court, especially in view of his proven administrative abilities and his knowledge of the empire's colonies.[22] Grimaldi was optimistic about working with Gálvez in spite of the propensity of the new minister of the Indies toward a position like that of the Conde de Aranda on the question of Spain's proper reaction to the American Revolution.

Gálvez took vigorous direction of Spain's colonial empire in February, as soon as he entered office. Discussions with Grimaldi about the American Revolution were his first order of business. Both men agreed that Cuba and Louisiana should be bases for the orderly observation of the revolt and that the two colonies should become the first line of defense against a possible English attack. The new colonial minister wrote the captain general of Cuba that in case of war with Great Britain his command would have to play a prominent defensive role. To that end, he had Captain General Torre conduct a full-scale review of the military forces he commanded. Torre was to

---

20. Grimaldi to Masserano, January 29, 1776, draft, AGS, Estado 7016. Because of Arriaga's illness, José de Gálvez began functioning unofficially as minister of the Indies several months before his formal appointment to the position. He began signing royal orders to the Indies as early as December, 1775. See José de Gálvez to Torre for this month in AGI, Cuba 1214.

21. Angeles Rubio Argüelles, *Un ministro de Carlos III, D. José de Gálvez y Gallardo . . . Marqués de Sonora* (Málaga, 1949), 13. This study of José de Gálvez is antiquarian in nature, written to satisfy local historical interest about the Gálvez family. Gálvez' important tenure as minister of the Indies badly needs a complete scholarly analysis beyond that touched upon in Herbert I. Priestley's *José de Gálvez: Visitor General of New Spain, 1765–1771* (Berkeley, Calif., 1916).

22. Juan de Ureta to Torre, May 22, 1776, AGI, Cuba 1143; Grimaldi to Masserano, January 29, 1776, AGS, Estado 7016.

ascertain the exact number of battle-ready troops in his command districts, inventory the quantity of supplies and munitions in his warehouses, and form a plan of defense that would make clear any need for increases in regular troop strengths.[23] All of that, however, was to be accomplished in full realization that Spain remained neutral in the British colonial conflict. Grimaldi and Gálvez agreed, "We find it necessary to observe a perfect neutrality between the forces of the British crown and the Americans without conceding supplies to either side and by affording both the ordinary hospitality."[24]

Gálvez quickly implemented the enlargement of observation activities desired by Grimaldi. The minister of the Indies wrote Captain General Torre and Governor Unzaga that the Spanish court took a grave view of the considerable number of British forces arriving in the Americas to subdue the rebel Americans. Because Spain would eventually have to make a diplomatic response to the revolt, the court needed information, he said, and had decided to expand the scope and objectives of the observation already directed from Havana and New Orleans. The effort would be refocused from primarily gathering intelligence on specific British threats against Cuba and Louisiana to collecting news of any sort relating to the rebellion, including descriptions of military operations, British and colonial campaign plans, and the goals and objectives of the Americans.[25]

Gálvez empowered Torre to use whatever methods he had at his disposal. In particular, the minister authorized him to send observers to Pensacola, East Florida, Jamaica, or wherever else Torre thought they might obtain useful intelligence. The purpose of the missions, Gálvez cautioned, should be kept secret at all costs. The observers would perforce lack official status, and in all cases the involvement of the Spanish government should be obscured

23. J. de Gálvez to Unzaga, February 28, 1776, royal order, no. 199, AGI, Cuba 174-B. Torre also received a similar royal order of the same date, no. 483, which is mentioned repeatedly in other documents and is described as identical to the one sent to Unzaga. Efforts to locate it have been unsuccessful. The numerated order series that belonged to Torre remains intact as part of AGI, Cuba 1214, with a contemporaneous notation that royal order no. 483 was removed to another, unnamed file. Nevertheless, Torre made recurring references to this royal order as his basic authorization for directing espionage operations that focused on the American Revolution.

24. Torre to Unzaga, May 29, 1776, draft, no. 213, AGI, Cuba 1147. See also Kathryn Abbey [Hanna], "Spanish Projects for the Reoccupation of the Floridas During the American Revolution," *Hispanic American Historical Review*, IX (1929), 266.

25. J. de Gálvez to Torre, February 28, 1776, royal order, AGI, Cuba 1227.

completely. Gálvez suggested in this regard that the captain general continue to rely on the Asiento de Negros in his operations. The Asiento, as a Spanish government trade monopoly granted to the firm of Aguirre and Aristegui, based in Cádiz, enjoyed a monopoly for the importation of slaves into Cuba and held the privilege of trading in foodstuffs with foreign colonies in the Americas. Because it sent ships regularly to the French islands and upon occasion to English colonial ports, including Philadelphia, where the commercial house of Willing and Morris was its factor, its merchants would make useful observers. They had legitimate reasons for visiting British and rebel areas. Gálvez authorized Torre to dispatch special ships with important reports when he deemed the monthly packet service too slow.[26]

The minister of the Indies sent similar orders to Unzaga, in Louisiana, and Torre instructed the governor to communicate all the news reaching New Orleans about the revolt to Havana as well as to Spain. The minister of the Indies supported Torre and Unzaga by issuing a general order to colonial commanders requiring them to send directly to the captain general of Cuba any news coming to their attention about the Revolution.[27]

The months following the receipt in Cuba of Gálvez' instructions were busy for Torre and Unzaga as they scurried to augment their observer corps. As ranking commander, Torre took the lead, especially since Havana—the major Spanish port of the region—served as the center of a larger maritime network than New Orleans did. The captain general first concentrated on Gálvez' recommendation to use Asiento merchants as observers. Torre brought Gerónimo de Enrile, a Cuban merchant who directed the Asiento de Negros at Havana, into his confidence and discussed with him the possibility of the Asiento's lending itself to the collection of news about the Revolution. In addition, since for security reasons Torre did not wish to pay the costs of intelligence operations directly from the colonial treasury, he asked Enrile to advance money from the company's operating funds to cover them, promising reimbursement later. Enrile agreed, becoming both paymaster and supervisor for several major intelligence operations during the late 1770s.[28]

Legitimate commercial activities directed from Havana thus became a

26. J. de Gálvez to Unzaga, February 28, 1776, royal order, no. 200, *ibid.* 174-B.
27. An example copy of this "universal" royal order, dated February 28, 1776, may be found in AGI, Indiferente General 656.
28. Relación de los meritos y servicios del Marqués de Casa Enrile," March 1785, AGI, Santo Domingo 1214.

major opportunity for gathering news. As the need for information grew, so did the trade activities that enabled securing it. That meant the expansion of the authorized Spanish trade orbit to include the rebellious colonies in North America. Since Spain found these points of commercial contact difficult to control once the Revolution had run its course, however, the Spanish observation of the American Revolution had far-reaching commercial consequences for both Spain and the American rebels, creating new commercial patterns that lasted well into the nineteenth century.

Besides recruiting Enrile to the cause of intelligence, the captain general turned to Juan Elegio de la Puente, *contador* of the island and a former resident of East Florida. Puente was the unofficial leader of the *floridiano* community in Cuba—the community of Cuban residents who had lived in Florida prior to the transfer of the province to Great Britain in 1763. In exile, the *floridianos* desired above all the return of Florida and their beloved capital, Saint Augustine, to Spanish control so they could regain their former homes. Puente knew the Florida Coast well and continued to maintain contacts there among the Indians. It became his duty to oversee the gathering of information in East Florida, especially from the Yuchis Indians, who routinely sent trade delegations to Havana.[29] The information collected by the Indians of East Florida was often considered unreliable, however; it was not taken seriously without corroborative reports from other sources.[30]

The captain general mobilized various other people in his command structure to assist him in the effort. Having already notified the governor of Louisiana to begin investigating the revolt, Torre instructed the commander of the Spanish naval squadron based at Havana to provide regular reports on maritime movements in the Caribbean and Gulf of Mexico.[31] He also asked his lieutenant governors elsewhere on the island to forward any news they received about the revolt.[32] All Asiento ships received secret orders to report any information they might acquire on their regular voyages.[33] The

29. "Relación de los meritos y servicios de Juan Elegio de la Puente," February 3, 1780, *ibid.* 1217.
30. Torre to J. de Gálvez, June 4, 1776, no. 1102, *ibid.* 1225.
31. Torre to Juan Bautista Bonet, April 4, 1776, no. 1, AGI, Cuba 1227.
32. Torre to Ureta, April 21, 1776, *ibid.*
33. The Archivo General de Indias, in Seville, contains most of the extant records of almost four centuries of colonial administration in Spanish America. Many of the documents are found today according to a system of organization that reflects the administrative structure of the Council, and later the ministry, of the Indies paralleling the geographic locations of Spanish colonies. Many of the document groups bring together operational records of various historical commands. The modern researcher thus has the opportunity, in some cases, to examine

captain general decided, as well, to maintain closer contact with the Mosquito River settlement on the East Florida coast.[34]

In late May, Torre sent Joseph Carandi, an officer on his staff, to establish a coastal observation station at Cabo Corrientes—a high bluff overlooking waters at the northwestern tip of the island—in order to monitor maritime traffic passing through the Straits of Florida. Torre instructed Carandi to note the number, class, and nationality of all ships sailing the area and to report regularly to the lieutenant governor at Filipinas, the nearest settlement. This observer, and later his successor, Lucas Melero, had the additional task of collecting reports from the Spanish warships cruising the straits on picket duty. The Cabo Corrientes observation post eventually became quite an elaborate installation, complete with a tall wooden tower, quarters for the observers, and a staff of assistants to relay information between the Spanish picket ships and the captain general's office.[35]

Once Torre had made such preparations, he sent an observer to Jamaica in the guise of a trader for the Asiento. That merchant began reporting to Havana during late spring of 1776, with his dispatches continuing intermittently for the rest of the year. He kept regular count of the ships entering and leaving Kingston, described what the local population knew about English intentions regarding the Revolution, and briefed Asiento captains who called at the port. For the most part, his reports seemed to show that the British were more concerned with military developments along the Atlantic Coast than with a surprise attack against Spanish colonies. He also provided a full report on the rebel colonists' attack on Providence Island.[36]

Torre maintained regular contact with Viceroy Bucareli, in New Spain.

---

records of many eras organized according to a series of filing systems employed for information retrieval in the active administration of the Indies. As a result, it is sometimes appropriate to assume that certain officials of the past read specific documents. That sort of supposition, based on where the documents appear today in the archive is generally justified for the period of the American Revolution. Although there has been some loss and reshuffling of documents over the centuries, the files of the captaincy general of Cuba remain relatively intact for the 1770s and 1780s. An examination of those papers indicates that the document group known today as AGI, Cuba 1227, represents the special reserved file Torre maintained in connection with the initial years of surveillance regarding the American Revolution. Torre explicitly referred to this file when he relinquished his position in 1777 to Diego Joseph Navarro. See Torre to Diego Joseph Navarro, June 12, 1777, AGI, Santo Domingo 1217.

34. Torre to J. de Gálvez, May 10, 1776, AGI, Cuba 1227.
35. Torre to Gerónimo de Enrile, May 12, 1776, *ibid.;* "Instrucción a que se ha de arreglar Don Lucas Melero en la comisión que se pone a su cuydado," March 22, 1777, *ibid.* The coastal station continued in operation well into 1777.
36. Torre to J. de Gálvez, May 10, 1776, *ibid.*

He gave Bucareli an accounting of the various efforts being made in Cuba to observe the American rebellion. Bucareli seemed impressed and directed the governor of Veracruz promptly to relay to the captain general any news arriving in that port regarding the Revolution.[37]

During late 1776 the captain general decided to station an observer somewhere in the rebellious colonies in order to monitor the revolt firsthand. He approached Enrile in that connection, since the Asiento could provide the resources to sponsor the representative. Enrile agreed to cooperate and to organize the operation, recommending Miguel Antonio Eduardo, the public interpreter of Havana, as the person best suited for the task. On the colonial payroll since 1769, Eduardo spoke flawless English and had unquestioned loyalty to Spain.[38] He was recognized as a "most decent man of the highest qualities," and Torre characterized him as an "able citizen capable of taking correct action in any unforeseen situation."[39]

The captain general and Enrile deliberated how to arrange Eduardo's mission. They decided to send him to Philadelphia, where he would establish residence as an Asiento merchant, and they devised a complex scenario to make his arrival there seem a chance event. Eduardo would ostensibly take an Asiento cargo from Havana to Santo Domingo aboard one of the company's ships. At sea his vessel would develop problems and make for Philadelphia seeking repairs. Once there, he would decide to remain as a mer-

---

37. Torre to Bucareli, May 2, 1776, Bucareli to Torre, May 27, 1776, both *ibid*. This agreement between the captain general of Cuba and the viceroy of New Spain continued for the remainder of the Revolution. For other examples, see James A. Lewis, "New Spain and the American Revolution, 1779–1783: A Viceroyalty at War" (Ph.D. dissertation, Duke University, 1975), 41–44. See also Melvin Glascock, "New Spain and the War for American Independence, 1779–1783" (Ph.D. dissertation, Louisiana State University, 1969).

38. Little is known of Eduardo's career prior to his employment as public interpreter in 1769. It is possible that he was of English ancestry, since the surname Eduardo is not customarily found among people of Hispanic stock except as a Hispanization of Edwards. In addition, he seems never to have used a matrilineal surname as he would have if his family had had a Hispanic heritage. He was, however, almost certainly a native-born Spaniard or a Creole, since his title of appointment as public interpreter referred to him as a Spanish citizen. Many public interpreters were not native-born, but their commissions usually pointed out that they had been issued a *carta de naturaleza* in place of citizenship. (See "Minuta," December 8, 1768, AGI, Santo Domingo 1176; and Bucareli to Arriaga, June 4, 1769, no. 1105, Arriaga to Bucareli, March 12, 1769, royal order, both *ibid*.). Eduardo generally met the English ships arriving at Havana from 1769 to 1776, attended to the needs of their crews, helped arrange repairs when necessary, and certified official translations arising from relations at Havana with English-speaking visitors. He appears as well to have been considered a local authority on English maritime and trade practices. See William Hay to Bucareli, October 14, 1770, Bucareli to Arriaga, December 9, 1770, no. 1629, both *ibid*. 1151; and Torre to Arriaga, January 18, 1775, no. 821, *ibid*. 1520.

39. Bucareli to Arriaga, December 8, 1768, no. 858, *ibid*. 1176.

chant who had become interested in establishing a flour-purchasing operation in the Pennsylvania port.[40] That would provide a credible basis for Eduardo's residence in North America, and he would be able to send reports aboard the ships engaged in the flour trade. Enrile secured a cargo for Eduardo, gave him money to begin his commercial operations, and instructed him on the manner in which he should conduct his business dealings. The Asiento company furnished him a ship, the *Santa Barbara,* captained by Raphael Gonzalez, with a crew that did not know the voyage's true purpose. Enrile also gave Eduardo one thousand *pesos fuertes* from Asiento coffers to cover the expenses of the covert mission and cautioned him about problems he might encounter because of the English naval blockade. Meantime, Torre drafted secret instructions for the observer, charging him with determining the location and activities of troops, learning the plans and objectives of both sides, and reporting anything he heard about the course of the revolt. Torre urged Eduardo to avoid offending the British and to guard against taking rumors for fact. Torre cautioned him to collect information only among the most reliable people.[41]

The *Santa Barbara* sailed at sunrise on May 4, 1776.[42] When, according to plan, the vessel began to take on water and could not luff properly, the crew discovered that the mainmast had rotted at its base. Captain Gonzalez set a course for Philadelphia in order to secure repairs. On May 23, however, Eduardo suffered a reverse off the entrance to Delaware Bay when the English frigate *Liverpool,* cruising on blockade duty, stopped the Spanish vessel and sent a boarding party to question the captain. Although Torre's man

40. The arrangements regarding this operation are described in Torre to J. de Gálvez, May 11, 1776, no. 1090, *ibid.* 1522. The captain general's draft copy of this communication is dated May 10, 1776, and is located in AGI, Cuba 1227. Eduardo's mission is touched upon by Kathryn Abbey [Hanna] in "Efforts of Spain to Maintain Souces of Information in the British Colonies Before 1779," *Mississippi Valley Historical Review,* XV (1928), 59–60.

41. "Instrucciones reservadas que se dan a Don Miguel Antonio Eduardo que se embarca con titulo de sobrecargo en el paquebot *Santa Barbara* su captn. Don Raphael Gonzalez que sali del Puerto de la Havana con destino a el de Roseau en la Dominica," AGI, Cuba 1227.

42. "Diario de todo lo que ha ocurrido y experimentado al paquebot español nombrado *Santa Barbara* y propio del Real Asiento de Negros en America que salio de la Havana en 4 de mayo ultimo . . . ," October 28, 1776, AGI, Santo Domingo 1598-A. Duplicates of this diary may be found *ibid.* 1244 and in AGI, Cuba 1227. It is the journal of the voyage, apparently kept by Eduardo and upon his return to Havana presented to the captain general. Eduardo seemingly wrote it during the voyage, making entries by date, although not for every day. The journal does not reflect the secret aspects of the mission, thus adding weight to the supposition that its author compiled it during the voyage. The discussion of Eduardo's activities that follows is based on the diary.

had destroyed all documents relating to his secret mission and vigorously protested the ship's detention since it sailed for Philadelphia under emergency conditions, the suspicions of the British officer were aroused by a search of the Spanish vessel that revealed it to carry over twelve thousand *pesos fuertes* in bullion. That, of course, represented the funds marked for the flour-purchasing operation and Eduardo's expenses as an observer. After a discussion with Eduardo and Gonzalez, the boarding officer confiscated the ship's papers and escorted Eduardo and the captain to the *Liverpool* for questioning by the British captain, who, deciding that the Spaniards were delivering specie to the rebels, declared the *Santa Barbara* a prize and transferred all the money and the vessel's documents to the English ship. He ordered the Spaniards to sail on their honor for Hampton Roads, there to place themselves in the custody of the British fleet and await the *Liverpool's* return from blockade duty to begin admiralty proceedings. Eduardo had little choice but to obey. Moreover, he foresaw that this turn of events would at least give him an opportunity to observe British naval operations at close range.

The Spaniards entered Chesapeake Bay in late May, surrendered to the Royal Navy, and began their wait for the *Liverpool's* arrival. Eduardo observed the British navy carefully and set about compiling a secret diary of all he learned. The British officers on station apparently found a Spaniard fluent in English to be a pleasant diversion and frequently visited with him. Eduardo thus had an agreeable time with the British, full of relaxed dinners, smokers, convivial evenings over sherry, and a large portion of good conversation, much of which he eventually carried back to Havana. Eduardo even had several interviews with John Murray, earl of Dunmore, a royal governor of Virginia who had taken refuge on one of the British warships. Eduardo carefully noted the number, class, and armaments of the British ships lying off Virginia. He also witnessed several minor confrontations around Saint George Island between English and American troops. He talked at length about British war aims and the perceived views of the American rebels, drawing out of his hosts their opinions on what motivated the revolt. Eduardo came to the conclusion that the American Revolution would be a long military struggle.

A change in circumstances for the British navy made admiralty proceedings against the *Santa Barbara* moot during late August. When the British withdrew from Chesapeake Bay because of rebel successes in the region, they waived admiralty hearings and released the Spaniards. Eduardo, posting a promissory bond for the *Santa Barbara* and its remaining cargo, decided to return to Havana. Freed from British detention, the Spaniards cleared the Virginia capes with the departing fleet. En route home, the *Santa Barbara* called at Bermuda, where Eduardo learned some details about American and British privateers. He also stopped in French Santo Domingo and conferred with the local Asiento representative, collecting additional information about both British and rebel activities. Although Eduardo failed in the original aim of settling at Philadelphia, he returned to Cuba with a significant report on British naval operations, information of recent events concerning the revolt, and news that the Americans seemed to be persevering in their rebellion against Great Britain. He had made of his failed mission an intelligence-gathering success.

During the months of Eduardo's absence, the captain general was expanding his observation network. Torre continued to receive news from the observer in Jamaica, who notified him that almost all the warships and troops at Jamaica had departed to reinforce the continental British forces. Torre also collected information from the picket ships and observation station at Cabo Corrientes, met with the East Florida Indians coming to Havana, and provided regular reports to the minister of the Indies. He ordered the lieutenant governor at Barbacoa, in Cuba, to send ships from that port to French Santo Domingo to learn what merchants there might know about recent developments in the Revolution. Accounts coming to Torre from his various sources suggested that both sides in the struggle had resolved to fight on, with little chance of a peaceful resolution.[43]

One report did cause momentary excitement at Havana. The observer at Cabo Corrientes sent an express messenger to the captain general in late June to say that a large English convoy had been heading toward the Bay of Campeche. Torre immediately dispatched a ship to Veracruz with a warning for the viceroy of New Spain. On further investigation by a Spanish picket ship, however, the boats appeared to be a large flotilla of British merchantmen sailing together as protection against rebel privateers.[44] Span-

43. Torre to Señor Oloris, July 20, 1776, Torre to Unzaga, June 17, 1776, both AGI, Cuba 1227.
44. Torre to Bucareli, June 28, 1776, *ibid.;* Torre to J. de Gálvez, June 10, 1776, no. 1113, AGI, Santo Domingo 1522. This indeed proved to be the case. For the British side of the events, which confirms this Spanish assessment, see Vice Admiral Clark Grayson to Mr. Steppins, November 16, 1776, Public Record Office, London, Colonial Office 5, CLXII, 19.

ish officials at Havana had seen a general increase in American privateering in the waters around Cuba. During the early summer, English vessels began appearing at the Havana roadstead seeking refuge from it. In one case, a rebel ship entered the port and deposited a group of captured British sailors on the beach near Morro Castle. That June, Torre played host to twenty-two British seamen seeking sanctuary at Havana; another eighteen came the following month. The captain general allowed the British subjects refuge and permitted them to book passage aboard vessels going to Spain so that they could make their way back to England.[45] Such incidents convinced Torre that the American Revolution, at least for the time, had British naval forces in the region fully occupied, and he wrote Minister Gálvez that England and its colonies grew farther apart with each passing day and that the Americans resisted the British with great determination. Torre estimated for Gálvez that the British might have deployed as many as fifty thousand veteran and mercenary troops to meet the colonial resistance. The Americans seemed intent on continuing the struggle until the "last drop of blood."[46]

As time passed, Torre worried increasingly about the outcome of the scheme involving Miguel Eduardo. The captain general had received no word of the observer since his departure from Havana and by autumn had despaired of the success of the mission. Feeling it desirable to investigate Eduardo's whereabouts, he turned to sources in East Florida. Cuban fishing vessels continued to sail to the Florida Coast and to maintain watch on the British. During September, 1776, one of those boats returned from the Catholic settlement at New Smyrna with letters written to the bishop of Cuba by Luciano de Herrera, who still lived at Saint Augustine. Herrera's letters contained news about the colonial revolt and reported on British naval activities in Saint Augustine.[47] Upon receipt of the letters, Torre

45. Torre to J. de Gálvez, June 7, 1776, no. 1105, July 10, 1776, no. 1147, AGI, Cuba 1227; Torre to Captain Thomas Davey, August 14, 1776, AGI, Santo Domingo 1521; Torre to Unzaga, June 6, 1776, AGI, Cuba 1147.

46. Torre to J. de Gálvez, June 10, 1776, no. 1113, August 8, 1776, no. 1193, both AGI, Santo Domingo 1522. Draft copies of these letters are in AGI, Cuba 1227. The British stationed ships along the northern coasts of Jamaica in an effort to protect their maritime lanes from these American privateers. See Vice Admiral Grayson to Lord George Germain, January 11, 1777, Public Records Office, London, Colonial Office 5, CLXII, 112.

47. "Extracto de capítulos de varias cartas," enclosed in Torre to J. de Gálvez, n.d., no. 1235, AGI, Santo Domingo 1224. Included are summaries of Herrera's letters of July 16 and July 30, 1776, to the archbishop of Cuba.

sounded out the *floridianos* in Havana in an effort to assess Luciano de Herrera's character and his loyalty to Spain. Torre found and read the reports Herrera had written for Captain General Bucareli during the Malvinas crisis. The captain general decided to recruit Herrera as an observer.

Torre wrote Herrera, asking him to provide regular and secret reports about the American Revolution. The captain general explained that he especially wished to know the number and location of English naval and military forces in North America, particulars about the battles between the British and the rebels, and anything that might speak to the motives of either side. He admonished Herrera to watch for signs that Britain was about to launch a surprise attack against Spanish possessions. Torre emphasized the need to exercise great care with letters coming from Havana and suggested that Herrera burn them after reading them. In passing, the captain general asked that Herrera investigate the whereabouts of one Miguel Eduardo. Not yet fully convinced of the Floridian's trustworthiness, Torre did not declare the true nature of Eduardo's mission. Instead, he told Herrera that a merchant of the Asiento and his ship had been lost on a voyage to Santo Domingo and that according to rumor bad weather had forced the ship to make for a North American port, probably Philadelphia. The captain general bid Herrera find out what he could about this ship and to send on to Philadelphia a letter enclosed that was addressed to the firm of Willing and Morris seeking news of Eduardo.[48] A Havana fisherman, Miguel Chapuz, delivered Torre's letter to Herrera. The captain general stocked Chapuz' sloop with a supply of wine, olive oil, and fruit, serviceable both as gifts for the new observer and as props to mark Chapuz a trader in contraband if a British vessel stopped him.[49] After conversation with Chapuz, Herrera agreed to work for the captain general, and he soon became one of the most important Spanish observers along the Atlantic Coast. In 1781, however, the British commander in Saint Augustine discovered his activities.[50]

The questions about Eduardo received a full answer when the *Santa Barbara* returned to Havana on November 6, 1776. Although Eduardo's inability to establish the flour-purchasing operation disappointed the captain general, the observer's alert vigilance after being stopped by the *Liverpool* impressed him. Eduardo presented his secret diary to Torre and briefed

48. Torre to Luciano de Herrera, October 3, 1776, AGI, Cuba 1227.
49. Torre to Herrera, October 6, 1776, Torre to J. de Gálvez, October 12, 1776, both *ibid.;* Mowat, *East Florida*, 123–29.
50. Juan Cagigal to J. de Gálvez, September 25, 1782, no. 292, AGI, Santo Domingo 1527.

both the captain general and Enrile on all he had seen and learned. He brought important news of the colonies' declaration of independence under the name of the United States of America. Torre transmitted a comprehensive report to Gálvez, sending copies of the agent's journal along to Spain. The captain general lauded Eduardo's diligence, recommending him to the king as someone who showed ability and firmness in his efforts.[51] As Gálvez and the king read the diary, they came to concur in Torre's estimate of the observer. When the Marqués de Grimaldi analyzed Eduardo's reports, he joined in the opinion that they contained important information.[52]

Eduardo's diary arrived at Madrid during a critical period for Spain, as the king and his ministers attempted to maintain a position consistent with nominal neutrality and to coordinate foreign policy with France. Spain's response to the American Revolution during 1776 still rested on considerations not directly related to the revolt. In particular, fear of an English reprisal over Spain's territorial dispute with Portugal acted as a check on greater Spanish involvement in the Revolution, especially when events in South America did not go for Spain as it had hoped. Spanish military forces attacked the Río de la Plata in 1776, but Portuguese units subsequently captured Spanish strongholds at Río Grande and Santa Tecla. As a result, King Charles and his ministers found themselves that summer in the thick of organizing an expedition of nineteen hundred men and some one hundred fifty vessels at Cádiz for the purpose of regaining the South American settlements they had lost.[53] Grimaldi, moreover, held in reserve plans to attack Portugal directly, thus further complicating the balance that Spain had attempted to achieve in dealing with Great Britain and its American colonies. The South American expedition also created a drain on the operating capital of the court. In April, 1776, Gálvez directed the officials of the royal mint to support operations against the Portuguese by providing the governor of Buenos Aires with 500,000 *pesos fuertes;* in July, he directed them to send all uncommitted funds on hand and, if need be, any money already budgeted that could be diverted.[54] At least for the time, Great Britain's difficulties along the Atlantic Coast offered some assurance that it would not impede

51. Torre to J. de Gálvez, November 18, 1776, no. 1261, *ibid.* 1522.
52. J. de Gálvez to Torre, February 10, 1777, royal order, AGI, Cuba 1227; Grimaldi to J. de Gálvez, February 2, 1777, AGI, Santo Domingo 1522.
53. Luis Navarro García, *Hispanoamérica en el siglo XVIII* (Seville, 1975), 189; Octavio Gil Munilla, *El Río de la Plata en la política internacional: Génesis del virreinato* (Seville, 1949), 83.
54. J. de Gálvez to the governor and royal officials of the royal mint at Potosí, July 12, 1776, in Colección Mata Linares, CVII, 107, Real Academia de la Historia, Madrid.

Spain in its South American venture as long as Spain did not offend the British by siding too closely with the American rebels.

At this juncture, during the summer of 1776, an envoy from the Continental Congress, Silas Deane, of Connecticut, arrived in Paris seeking supplies and assistance. The French government provided Deane a sympathetic audience, and Vergennes proposed to Madrid a scheme whereby the two Bourbon courts would jointly furnish two million Portuguese pounds for the colonial cause. The rationale behind payment in Portuguese currency was that it would conceal the source of the aid. Ministers at the Spanish court agreed that limited, secret assistance to the rebels had a place in the general policy of keeping the British at bay in the Americas. So long as the aid remained minimal, it would help preserve Spain's option to support the rebellion more vigorously later on. Therefore Charles decided to cooperate, and Spain paid its share on the condition that its participation in the subsidy would not become known. Almost at once, France began efforts independent of Spain to furnish even more assistance to the colonies. The French court organized a fictitious trading company to front for its involvement with the revolutionaries. Headed by the Caron de Beaumarchais, the bogus firm began routing supplies to North America through French Santo Domingo.[55] Spanish ministers worried about the French assistance, both because the British might mistakenly believe Spain a party to it and because it signaled a growing inability to coordinate policy between Madrid and Paris.

More diplomatic problems arose for King Charles and his ministers when rebel vessels started arriving at Spanish ports, both in Europe and the Americas, seeking admittance under their own colors rather than the Union Jack. Spain had no policy on the matter, and its port commanders allowed them de facto entrance. But the British foreign office protested Spain's toleration of the rebel vessels, claiming that permitting the entrance of American ships under such circumstances constituted a violation of Spanish neutrality. Grimaldi temporized by promising a full investigation, though with the comment that little could be done since many port commanders had great difficulty distinguishing between rebel ships and those loyal to Great Britain.[56] Nevertheless, he issued a public warning to officials at all Spanish

55. Kite, *Beaumarchais*, II, 25–30; Yela Utrilla, *España*, I, 97–101.
56. J. de Gálvez to Unzaga, September 20, 1776, royal order, reserved, no. 16, AGI, Cuba 174-B.

ports on the Iberian peninsula and in the Indies against the admission of rebel ships. After discussion at court, however, Gálvez circulated a secret countermanding instruction—with Grimaldi's grudging approval—to commanders in the Indies. It reiterated that permission for the entrance of rebel vessels was to be in accordance with existing Spanish laws. That meant that rebel vessels flying their own colors could seek emergency anchorage in the Indies on an equal footing with shipping of other nations, so long as they did not attempt to sell their prizes or engage in commerce.[57]

By 1776, Captain General Torre felt his observation network had a weak link, in the Mississippi Valley. Most of his information-collecting efforts had been focused on East Florida and in the Caribbean. He decided that New Orleans would have to assume a greater role. Situated near the mouth of the Mississippi, the city played host to both Americans and Englishmen passing on the river. It could, he thought, become a key contact point between Spain and the rebellious colonies. Torre shared his opinion with the governor of Louisiana, who was in total agreement. When Unzaga ordered Spanish officials at outlying posts in the province to pay particular attention to news of the Revolution, he reaped quick dividends. The commander at Saint Louis, Francisco Cruzat, heard from a French trader that Montreal had apparently fallen to the rebels and that the "Bostonians" had unsuccessfully laid siege to Quebec.[58] The Spanish commandant at Saint Geneveve also mentioned this, adding that several families from Canada had recently passed through that post while en route to the English settlements in West Florida. The governor also undertook a program of systematic interviews with ship captains plying the Mississippi. He learned that Great Britain had approximately eighty warships in North American waters and some twenty-five thousand troops on the continent. He also sent word to Havana of increased military preparations in West Florida, where English garrisons feared a rebel attack.[59]

Unzaga informed the captain general that a Royal Navy frigate dispatched from Pensacola to cover the mouth of the Mississippi had entered the river and seized nine ships belonging to the rebels.[60] Although the in-

---

57. J. de Gálvez to Torre, September 20, 1776, royal order, October 23, 1776, royal order, Torre to J. de Gálvez, December 4, 1776, all *ibid.* 1227.
58. Francisco Cruzat to Unzaga, May 26, 1776, *ibid.* 81.
59. Silvio Francisco Castabona to Unzaga, June 12, 1776, *ibid.*
60. Unzaga to Torre, June 19, 1776, reserved, no. 193, *ibid.* 1227.

cident caused the Louisiana governor concern because of its proximity to New Orleans, he diplomatically refrained from becoming involved when the captain of the English frigate questioned him about rebel shipping on the river. The governor dissimulated, professing ignorance of such activity. He tactfully affected to suppose that all the foreign ships on the river belonged to loyal Englishmen.[61]

In June, Unzaga sent an observer to Pensacola to hear what he could there. The emissary became aware of many of the details of the rebel victories at Providence Island and Montreal,[62] and his success persuaded Torre and Unzaga once again to attempt sending an observer to Philadelphia. In organizing this mission Unzaga profited from his experiences during the Malvinas crisis in 1772, when he had dispatched Juan de Surriret to New York on a similar assignment. Surriret had traveled as a passenger on private vessels. This time the governor decided to outfit a boat for the purpose of buying flour, and to make its captain the observer. Unzaga selected an American resident and merchant of New Orleans, Oliver Pollock, as the person for the job.[63] At the last minute, however, he decided to substitute a loyal Spanish subject, choosing Bartolomé Beauregard. Captain Beauregard, brother of the powerful New Orleans merchant Santiago Toutant Beauregard, had been dealing with the Spanish government ever since the ill-fated Ulloa administration, often contracting his boat for official use.[64] In addition, the Beauregard family enjoyed a government-sponsored monopoly to export Louisiana lumber to Havana for the construction of the

61. Davey to Unzaga, June 4, 1776, Unzaga to Davey, June 12, 1776, both *ibid.* 188-C.

62. Unzaga to J. de Gálvez, June 19, 1776, no. 160, AGI, Santo Domingo 2547; J. de Gálvez to Unzaga, October 6, 1776, royal order, no. 21, AGI, Cuba 174-B; Unzaga to Torre, June 19, 1776, reserved, AGI, Cuba 1227. For examples of Unzaga's routine correspondence to the captain general regarding news of the Revolution, see "notas de indices" in Torre to Unzaga, April 26, August 1, September 14, September 24, September 25, November 9, 1776, AGI, Cuba 186-B.

63. Unzaga to J. de Gálvez, June 19, 1776, no. 160, AGI, Santo Domingo 2547.

64. Unzaga to J. de Gálvez, September 7, 1776, no. 180, *ibid.;* B. de Gálvez to J. de Gálvez, December 31, 1776, royal order, AGI, Cuba 174-B; Torre to Unzaga, March 8, 1772, AGI, Cuba 1147; Miguel de Altarriba to Unzaga, September 21, 1771, AGI, Cuba 82. Historians have long known of Beauregard's trip to Philadelphia, although few have considered it from the viewpoint of Spanish espionage. See: Gayarré, *The Spanish Domination,* 103. For information regarding the role of the Beauregard family in colonial Louisiana, see "History and Genealogy of the Toutant Family in Europe and Genealogy of the Beauregard Family in Louisiana," compiled by Captain Augustin Toutant Beauregard, Louis Toutant, and Joseph Emile Dueros (Typescript in Beauregard Family Papers, Special Collections Division, Howard-Tilton Memorial Library, Tulane University, New Orleans).

hogsheads used in the Cuban tobacco trade. Beauregard agreed to undertake the mission, feeling that cooperation with Unzaga would ensure the continuation of his family's preferential commercial operations with Havana. Besides, his agreement with Unzaga allowed him to keep any profits he made on his cargo.[65]

Beauregard left New Orleans in early September, 1776. In Philadelphia, he visited with members of Congress and other key officials. He returned to New Orleans with news that the Americans had a strong determination to gain their independence from Great Britain. Although he made detailed reports to Unzaga and Torre, his official papers and journal have apparently been lost to history. Nevertheless, related correspondence testifies that he reported on the notable military engagements of the year. He also gave his impression that the Americans were very confident and awaited the start of the spring campaigns of 1777.[66]

Contact between New Orleans and the Americans also occurred by way of the Mississippi about the time Beauregard departed for Philadelphia. A platoon of colonial troops commanded by Captain George Gibson arrived in the city from Fort Pitt, in western Pennsylvania. Ostensibly just one of a group of frontiersmen floating down the Ohio and Mississippi rivers, Gibson carried an intriguing proposal for the governor from General Charles Lee, Washington's subordinate. Lee wrote that the British naval blockade made the acquisition of supplies difficult for the Americans, and he asked that a systematic trade be opened between New Orleans and the colonies by way of the inland river system. He ventured that such commerce would prove advantageous for both Spain and the colonies.[67] Captain Gibson was also empowered to present orally an important matter to the governor regarding British West Florida. In a personal interview, Gibson explained to him, through Pollock as interpreter, that the Americans wished to send a military expedition down the Mississippi to capture the British settlements along the river and then to attack Pensacola. For that the rebels would need Spanish cooperation at New Orleans in addition to military supplies. Gib-

65. Torre to Unzaga, October 6, 1774, no. 150, December 3, 1774, no. 157, December 24, 1774, all in AGI, Cuba 1147; Torre to Bernardo de Gálvez, March 24, 1777, *ibid.* 186-B.

66. B. de Gálvez to J. de Gálvez, March 21, 1777, no. 26, AGI, Santo Domingo 2547.

67. Charles Lee to the governor of New Orleans, May 22, 1776, *ibid.* 2596. For background information on the Gibson mission to New Orleans, see Thomas Perkins Abernethy, *Western Lands and the American Revolution* (New York, 1937), 193–96. See also Abbey [Hanna], "Spanish Projects," 267–68.

son made clear that the Americans hoped, if successful, to cede West Florida to Spain as a protectorate for the duration of the struggle but that, when independence came for the colonies, they would expect Spain to return the former British province to American control.

Unzaga was surprised by the indelicate presumption upon official Spanish neutrality. At his request, Gibson committed the American proposal to writing: "I am instructed to propose the following queries to Your Excellency. 1st Wou'd the acquisition of the town and Harbor of Pensacola be a desirable object of His Catholic Majesty? Wou'd his Catholic Majesty receive possession of the same from the Americans?"[68] Since the Americans apparently did not understand that restrictions by the Spanish court closely circumscribed Unzaga's latitude to open commercial relations with them, Unzaga's reply to General Lee had to emphasize that a decision on the points Captain Gibson had broached lay beyond his authority as governor and required approval by the Spanish court. Unzaga promised to submit the American proposals directly to the king, for instructions from Madrid.[69]

While Unzaga prepared his dispatches to Spain on the matter, his immediate problem was the continued presence of the small rebel military detachment in his city. The British in West Florida maintained their own watch on events in Spanish Louisiana. They would certainly complain of any courtesies extended the Americans. Nevertheless, Unzaga decided to grant the rebels hospitality. Largely because of the intercession of Pollock, who was pro-American and who had been playing host to the detachment, Unzaga gave Gibson one hundred quintals of gunpowder from the royal stores for shipment to Fort Pitt.[70] Most of the powder left New Orleans with a traveling party under the command of a Lieutenant Linn, Gibson's executive officer. Linn and his detachment set out from New Orleans on September 23, passed the winter at the Spanish Arkansas post, and departed for Pennsylvania the following spring, after paying for their lodgings and supplies with a letter of credit drawn on Pollock. In October, Unzaga released

68. "Papelita firmada por Captain Gibson," n.d., AGI, Santo Domingo 2596.
69. Unzaga to Lee, September 4, 1776, *ibid.* A translated copy of this letter is in "Spanish Correspondence Concerning the American Revolution, 1779–1783," trans. and ed. James A. Robertson, *Hispanic American Historical Review,* I (1918), 305–306.
70. The British in West Florida quickly learned all the details of Gibson's proposals. See Davey to Peter Chester, November 27, 1776, Public Records Office, London, Colonial Office 5, CLXII, 114; and Stuart to Germain, October 26, 1776, no. 11, *ibid.,* LXXVIII, 55–62.

Gibson from the "arrest" he had placed the American captain under in case English suspicions should be aroused.[71] Gibson sailed to Philadelphia aboard one of Pollock's ships and carried a letter from Pollock to Robert Morris offering the New Orleans merchant's services in support of the revolutionary cause. "Permit me therefore," Pollock wrote, "to make tender my hearty services and to assure you that my conduct shall be ever as to merit Confidence and approbation of the Country to whom I owe everything but my birth."[72] Gibson's mission to New Orleans began Pollock's official association with the commerce committee of the Continental Congress, an affiliation that would ensure New Orleans' role as a vital supply center for the rebel troops operating in the Mississippi Valley from 1778 until the early 1780s.

The greatest impact of Gibson's journey for Louisiana, however, came through decisions made in Spain and Havana in response to Unzaga's dispatches about the mission. Unzaga laid out in great detail for his superiors the circumstances surrounding the American detachment's arrival in the city, and he forwarded translated copies of General Lee's letter, along with Gibson's written statement regarding a Spanish protectorate of West Florida. The governor told how Gibson had stressed the rebellious provinces' desire for the cooperation of Spain and France, especially since efforts to mediate a settlement with London had been fruitless. Unzaga also provided the court with a quaint description of the rebel military forces which he had gleaned from Gibson; he explained that the forces had two major divisions: "Continental" troops under the command of General Washington, and provincial forces known as "Minutemen" because of the speed with which they could be mobilized for battle.[73] In addition, the governor outlined the American plans to send a body of troops down the river the following spring to capture West Florida. The plan caused Unzaga some apprehension, since he felt it might make it difficult to uphold Spanish neutrality in the area. He requested additional troops and the implementation of regular mail service between New Orleans and Havana to provide quicker communication in the event of British and American military operations along

---

71. Caughey, *Bernardo de Gálvez*, 87.
72. James A. James, "Oliver Pollock, Financier of the Revolution in the West," *Mississippi Valley Historical Review*, XVI (1929), 71.
73. Torre to Unzaga, September 24, 1776, AGI, Cuba 186-B; Unzaga to J. de Gálvez, September 7, 1776, no. 181, AGI, Santo Domingo 2596. A translated copy of Unzaga's letter is in "Spanish Correspondence," trans. and ed. Robertson, 300.

the river. Whatever the future in this regard, Unzaga pledged to his superiors that the government at New Orleans would continue its neutrality.[74]

Gibson's visit created great interest at the Spanish court, since the American's request for supplies came when Spain and France had just decided to given additional assistance to the rebels. When, in Paris, Vergennes had informed Aranda that France would be shipping supplies and munitions to the colonies by way of its Caribbean ports,[75] the Spanish king and his advisers had debated what they should do. Reports arriving from the captain general of Cuba depicted the rebels as stubbornly persisting in their struggle against Great Britain although neither side could apparently gain a decisive victory. British successes near New York suggested to some Spanish ministers that the Americans might suffer additional reverses unless they received aid.[76] The discussions marked a turning point for Spain, because, for the first time since Lexington and Concord, the Marqués de Grimaldi did not play a significant role in the court debate regarding the Revolution. He had fallen into disfavor at the court because of his cautious policies and the military failure in South America. Although he remained minister of state for the time, he was shortly to be replaced. Grimaldi's rivals, especially Aranda and the *aragoneses,* saw their chance to implement a more aggressive policy regarding the American revolt. José de Gálvez was an influential member of Aranda's faction, and he particularly favored secret assistance to the colonies as a means of weakening the British in North America.[77] Aranda and Gálvez won the ear of the king. When Charles made his decision in early December, 1776, he instructed a reluctant Grimaldi that secret assistance to the colonies was "most urgent and necessary in order to animate the insurgents and keep them on the course they have adopted." The minister of state thus directed Aranda in Paris to tell the French court that Spain "was considering methods of furnishing direct assistance to the rebellious colonies."[78]

Unzaga's report of the Gibson mission to New Orleans arrived at court three weeks after Charles's decision to send secret supplies to the Americans.

74. Unzaga to J. de Gálvez, September 7, 1776, no. 181, September 30, 1776, no. 184, both AGI, Santo Domingo, Leg. 2596. See also "Spanish Correspondence," trans. and ed. Robertson, 300–304.
75. Aranda to Grimaldi, November 22, 1776, reserved, no. 12, in Yela Utrilla, *España,* II, 25.
76. *Ibid.,* I, 84–85.
77. "Dictamen de Gálvez," February 2, 1777, *ibid.,* II, 53–54.
78. Grimaldi to Aranda, December 9, 1776, reserved, no. 6, *ibid.,* 25–26.

It was especially welcome, since it presented Spain with a method of transferring supplies to the Americans. The king ordered the minister of the Indies to alert the captain general of Cuba and the governor of Louisiana that the items requested by Gibson would be sent to New Orleans. Charles and his advisers also decided that the captain general's observers would be the logical people to deliver the supplies to the Americans. Gálvez seemed excited about the possibilities that this turn of events had opened to Spain. Not only could New Orleans become an entrepôt to supply the rebels, he felt, but Spain's declared neutrality would enable it to accept custody of West Florida. The British, Gálvez reasoned, would probably prefer having the conquered province in the hands of an uncommitted power to seeing it under American control. For Spain, that would ease British pressures along the Gulf Coast and in the Caribbean. Gálvez discussed the situation with King Charles, who decided that Spain should indeed accept West Florida if the Americans conquered it.[79]

Gálvez drafted orders implementing the decisions on Christmas Eve of 1776. He realized that the success of the planned supply operation depended upon careful and secret execution. He thus wrote Captain General Torre that the secret network based at Havana that the captain general had organized to gather news of the revolt could serve as the agency to supervise the delivery of supplies to the Americans.[80] New Orleans thereby became a contact point between Americans and Spaniards, and news and information about the Revolution continued to flow from Cuba and Louisiana to Spain. The thrust of the information was that, barring a sudden and unexpected reconciliation, the colonial struggle would continue for some time. Largely because of reports furnished through the captain general, the Spanish court gradually began to view the American rebels as a serious force worthy of support. The following year, 1777, would bring an expansion of the captain general's efforts, an increased observation of British America, the continuing influence of information from Havana and New Orleans on policy at court, and the use of the observer corps as a supply service.

---

79. See marginal comment on Unzaga to J. de Gálvez, September 7, 1776, no. 181, AGI, Santo Domingo 2596. These comments are transcribed and translated in "Spanish Correspondence," trans. and ed. Robertson, 304–305.

80. J. de Gálvez to the governor of New Orleans, December 24, 1776, royal order, draft, J. de Gálvez to Torre, December 24, 1776, royal order, draft, both AGI, Santo Domingo 2596. Duplicates of these royal orders are respectively in AGI, Cuba 174-B, 1227.

3

A Benevolent Neutrality

1777

The Continental Congress decided in December, 1776, to send envoys to Europe in order to present its case for alliances and to seek assistance.[1] The emissaries it had appointed—Benjamin Franklin, Arthur Lee, and Silas Deane—had instructions to negotiate treaties of alliance with both France

---

1. Spanish policy makers were not alone in their desire for information. Intelligence gathering was a staple of the Revolution for all nations involved. See Carl Van Doren, *Secret History of the American Revolution* (New York, 1941). A complex espionage network developed in Paris, centered on the American envoys. All this has been well known to historians for generations and has been the object of a voluminous literature, including a nineteenth-century document collection: B. F. Stevens, ed., *B. F. Stevens' Facsimiles of Manuscripts in European Archives Relating to America, 1773–1783, with Descriptions, Editorial Notes, Collations, References, and Translations* (24 vols; London, 1889–1895). There is some historical evidence that Benjamin Franklin became involved as an informant for the British. One student of the matter has noted: "A cell of British intelligence was located in France, and Benjamin Franklin—covertly perhaps, tacitly at least, possibly deliberately—cooperated with and protected this spy cell operating out of his home in France shortly after his arrival in that country until the end of the war. Willingly or not, he made himself a party to treason to his own country while serving as its representative abroad" (Cecil B. Curry, *Code Number 72: Ben Franklin, Patriot or Spy?* [Englewood Cliffs, N.J., 1972], 12). For a perspective favorable to Franklin, see Samuel Flagg Bemis, "British Secret Service and the French-American Alliance," *American Historical Review*, XXIX (1924), 474–95. Another study contends that in passing the Declaration of Independence during the summer of 1776 the Congress was influenced by an agent, Pierre Roubaud, who intrigued in London on behalf of the French. As a double agent for the British, Roubaud created conditions that made it appear to leading members of Congress that the English might come to an accommodation with France and Spain in order to align the three European powers in an attempt to defeat the colonies and partition North America among themselves. The misimpression in Congress, according to this view, made the declaration seem urgent and was partly responsible for its being passed when it was. See James H. Hutson, "The Partition Treaty and the Declaration of American Independence," *Journal of American History*, LVIII (1972), 877–96.

and Spain.[2] Prior to formal appointment, Franklin had been in contact unofficially with the Spanish court in an effort to warm relations with Spain.
Don Gabriel Antonio de Bourbon, a member of the royal family, had translated into English Sallustius Crispus' *La conjuración de Catilina y la guerra
de jugurta* and had sent a copy to Franklin, who responded with profuse
thanks and reciprocated with a volume of the recently printed proceedings
of the Congress. Franklin also expressed his desire for an alliance with
Spain:

I therefore take the Liberty of sending your Highness a Copy, with some other
Papers which contain Accounts of the success wherewith Providence has lately favored us. Therein your wise Politicians may contemplate the first efforts of a rising
State. . . . I am very old and can scarce hope to see a powerful Dominion growing
up here, whose interest it will be to form a close and firm alliance with Spain (their
Territories bordering) and who being united, will be able, not only to preserve their
own people in peace, but to repel the Force of all the other powers in Europe.[3]

Upon receiving his appointment, Franklin sought an audience with the
Conde de Aranda, who received the American in his Paris lodgings on the
evening of January 4. The Conde de Lacy, Spain's ambassador to Russia,
who was then in Paris, assisted as translator when Aranda discovered that
Franklin could not express himself fluently in either French or Spanish. The
two Spaniards questioned the congressional envoy closely regarding American goals, the rebels' need for supplies, the military plans of Congress, and
the proposals the congressional representatives carried for alliances with the
Bourbon courts. In response, Franklin promised to send Aranda a packet of
documents detailing American desires for an alliance with Spain. Aranda
seemed impressed with Franklin. "The Americans," he reported to Madrid,
"propose only firm friendship and a reciprocal commerce."[4]

The king and his ministers weighed the ambassador's favorable recounting of the conference against the reports coming from the captain general's

2. Bemis, *The Diplomacy of the American Revolution*, 58–60.
3. Benjamin Franklin to Gabriel Antonio de Bourbon, December 12, 1775, in *Letters of Delegates to Congress*, ed. Smith, II, 478.
4. Aranda to Grimaldi, January 13, 1777, no. 939, in Yela Utrilla, *España*, II, 39–40; "Carta
de Franklin a Aranda," June 7, 1777, *ibid.*, II, 94. Franklin's offers greatly interested Aranda.
The American envoy affirmed that the United States would assist Spain in taking Pensacola
but that in return Congress desired free navigation of the Mississippi and use of the harbor at
Pensacola. Aware of the Spanish court's concern about a possible war with Portugal, Franklin
even suggested that the United States might agree to declare war against that nation. See
Gerald Stourzh, *Benjamin Franklin and American Foreign Policy* (2nd ed.; Chicago, 1969), 143.

observation system. By the time Aranda's memorandum occasioned a formal meeting of the Spanish Council of State,[5] Charles had appointed a new minister of state, José Moñino, Conde de Floridablanca. Previously the Spanish envoy to the Vatican, Floridablanca took several months to arrange for his move back to Spain, and during that time Grimaldi continued on the job.[6] The resulting "lame duck" incumbency at the ministry of state impeded any major changes in Spanish foreign policy in response to the congressional envoys. More important, the new minister of state, like his predecessor, advocated a cautious and temperate Spanish response to the revolt. In particular, Floridablanca was uneasy about the impact and influence an independent nation might have on Spanish possessions in the Indies. The new minister of state feared that if the colonists gained independence, the United States might replace England as a problem for Spain in the Americas. He hoped that the young "republic might remain in such division, with independence between the provinces and their interests so opposed to one another, that prudently there would not, in time, be the danger of a formidable power in the vicinity of [the Spanish colonies]."[7] Floridablanca advocated a diplomatic rather than military role for Spain in the struggle. Nevertheless, limited support for the rebels, in the form of supplies shipped through Havana and New Orleans, seemed to him a reasonable price for diplomatic leverage with the American Congress.[8]

5. Tapia, *Carlos III*, 310–13.
6. Grimaldi offered his resignation in November, 1776, but continued to direct the ministry until Floridablanca arrived at court on February 19, 1777. Floridablanca, a talented and proven diplomat, was eventually to become one of the outstanding Spanish ministers of the late eighteenth century, serving both Charles III and Charles IV. A lawyer by training, he began his government career as an attorney for the Council of Castile and quickly distinguished himself in a series of legal battles that placed him firmly in the ranks of the Bourbon reformers. He had a strong personality and was very much his own man rather than the follower of any court faction. Rewarded with a noble title for his adept negotiations with the pope in the aftermath of the Jesuit expulsion from the Indies, he became minister of state at age forty-five. A man of moderation, Floridablanca seldom strayed from the main chance to advance Spain on the international front. Although his service as minister of state lasted over two decades, there is no complete biography of him. His memoirs as minister are held in manuscript form by the Real Academia de Historia, in Madrid, and have been published in several editions, the most complete of which is Antonio Rumeu de Armas' *El testamento político del Conde de Floridablanca* (Madrid, 1962). For biographical data, *see* Cayetano Alcázar Molina, "Ideas políticas de Floridablanca: Del despotismo ilustrado a la revolución francesa y Napoleón, 1766–1801," *Revista de estudios políticos*, DXXIX (1955), 35–66; Alcázar Molina, *El Conde de Floridablanca: Notas para su estudio* (Madrid, 1929); and Alcázar Molina, *El Conde de Floridablanca: Su vida y su obra* (Múrcia, 1934).
7. Yela Utrilla, *España*, I, 184.
8. *Ibid.*, 183.

Meeting at Madrid in late January, 1777, the Council of State reviewed its policy regarding the revolt. It examined implications that might arise from the open relations proposed by the Continental Congress. Owing to the urgency of these questions, the king and his ministers decided to meet even though Floridablanca had not yet arrived from the Vatican to take up his post. Gálvez made available to his fellow ministers summary extracts of information collected by the captain general at Havana that led most ministers to feel that war with Great Britain would be the immediate result of cooperating with the Americans, at least along the lines suggested by Franklin. King Charles and his ministers decided that during 1777 such cooperation would be prejudicial to Spain and that the Spanish military needed to be brought to better preparedness before they could risk conflict with Great Britain. Some of the ministers estimated that Spanish land and naval forces could not be ready for war until the spring of 1778 at the earliest. On that supposition, any treaty of alliance with the Americans seemed a dangerous step. The Marqués de Grimaldi felt that "formation of a treaty with the colonies at present would be inopportune and indiscreet,"[9] and the other ministers on the council shared in this sentiment.

The king and his ministers did arrive at two conclusions about the American Revolution: first, that the ability of the Americans to win a victory from the British had not yet been proved, and second, that it would be foolhardy for Spain to rule out the possibility of the rebellious colonies' negotiating a peace settlement with England, with both sides thereafter uniting to attack Spanish and French colonies in the Americas. The Council of Ministers accordingly decided to take additional time to prepare for what appeared to be the certainty of a war with Great Britain. "It seems consistent with all the rules of prudence," Grimaldi wrote to Aranda after the council meeting, "that additional time be gained in order to see if the colonies better their condition during the coming summer."[10] In the meantime, Spain could accelerate her military preparations, both in Europe and in the Indies. The ministers decided that the American envoys in Paris should be played along by Aranda and given the impression that closer relations with Spain might eventually be a possibility.[11] Spain would continue to watch and wait.

In late February, 1777, however, Arthur Lee precipitated a potential crisis that threatened this policy when he decided to travel to Madrid and present

9. "Dictamen de Grimaldi," February 1, 1777, *ibid.*, II, 51.
10. "Despacho de Grimaldi a Aranda," February 4, 1777, no. 1, *ibid.*, 63.
11. *Ibid.*, I, 64.

the propositions of the American envoys directly to the Spanish court. His design was to force the king to confront directly American proposals to which he did not want to make explicit responses. From Paris, Aranda alerted Grimaldi, still the minister of state, as soon as he heard of the American envoy's impending trip. King Charles and his ministers felt that deliberations on Spanish soil with a congressional representative would strain relations with Great Britain. At the same time, they did not want to offend the Americans, anticipating a time when Spain might want closer relations with them. After hurried discussion, they decided that Lee should not be permitted to appear at the Spanish court.[12]

The Marqués de Grimaldi, expecting Floridablanca's imminent succession to his office, reluctantly took charge of dealing with Lee. He enlisted as an ally the Bilbao merchant Diego de Gardoqui, whose family's commercial firm had long traded with Englishmen.[13] Joseph Gardoqui and Sons had also served as corresponding agent for Elbridge Gerry, the Massachusetts merchant. Starting in 1775, Gerry began to use the Gardoquis as a source of supplies for the state of Massachusetts, and he sometimes wrote Gardoqui long, news-filled letters about the progress of the revolt, presenting a favorable account of the American cause.[14] Thus, Gardoqui already had some understanding of the Revolution. Upon learning that Lee's trip could not be stopped because he had already departed from Paris, Grimaldi and Gardoqui decided to meet with the American secretly before he could arrive at Madrid. Grimaldi dictated a letter for Lee that Gardoqui translated into numerous English copies and dispatched by express riders to Spanish officials along the roads to France. His note implored Lee to stop at the small town of Vitoria, where the minister of state would make contact.[15] Grimaldi notified royal officials along the way that the American envoy

12. "Carta de Diego Gardoqui a Arthur Lee," February 17, 1777, *ibid.,* II, 68. For a complete assessment of Lee's career in Europe, see Louis W. Potts, *Arthur Lee: A Virtuous Revolutionary* (Baton Rouge, 1981).

13. George A. Billias, *Elbridge Gerry: Founding Father and Republican Statesman* (New York, 1976), 125–29. For a letter from Gerry to Gardoqui providing news of the Revolution, see Elbridge Gerry to Joseph Gardoqui and Sons, September 1, 1777, in *Letters of Delegates to Congress,* ed. Smith, VII, 582–84.

14. The Bilbao firm of Joseph Gardoqui and Sons had already been dealing with the Americans, who needed war materials. See Gerry to Joseph Gardoqui, July 15, 1775, and Gardoqui and Sons to Jeremiah Lee, n.d., in *Naval Documents of the American Revolution,* ed. William B. Clark *et al.* (9 vols. to date; Washington, D.C., 1964–), I 401, 818.

15. "Carta de Diego de Gardoqui a Arthur Lee," February 17, 1777, in Yela Utrilla, *España,* II, 68.

would probably be easy to recognize since he did not speak Spanish and had no knowledge of the country.[16] Indeed, the administrator of the royal mails at Burgos easily picked Lee out at a local inn where he delivered copies of Grimaldi's message. The Spanish postal official had Lee remain in Burgos and notified Madrid of the American's whereabouts by return express.

Grimaldi and Gardoqui hastened to Burgos, where they had meetings with the congressional representative which they hoped might remain completely unknown to the British. The American made a thorough presentation of congressional proposals for European alliances. Grimaldi found the conferences difficult, since the congressional envoy insisted that the Spanish minister speak to him only in French, the accepted language of formal diplomacy, but it appeared that Lee lacked fluency in that tongue. Although he apparently understood most of what the Spanish minister said, he had difficulty responding. Grimaldi talked in slow and simple French, but Lee could give only rudimentary responses in that language. For more complicated statements, Lee spoke English to Gardoqui, who translated the answer into Spanish for Grimaldi. The cumbrousness of the exchange nettled the minister of state, who had brought Gardoqui along as a Spanish-English translator but instead had been coerced into a complicated three-way discussion in which each spoke a language different from those employed by the other two.[17]

Lee presented his proposals in that awkward atmosphere. He told Grimaldi that alliances with France and Spain were objectives of the first importance for the Congress, and he argued that the fate of the rebellion rested in the hands of the Bourbon courts, in that the materials and supplies they could furnish would be the key to American success. In view of how badly the Congress needed money and lines of credit in Europe in order to continue the struggle, Lee requested immediate material assistance.[18] Though the American desire for an alliance with Spain did not impress Grimaldi, who refused even to consider the possibility or to discuss it further with Lee, he did permit the emissary to submit a written memorial setting forth arguments in support of an alliance between the Americans

16. "Carta de Grimaldi al regente de Pamplona y al administrador de correos del Burgos," February 17, 1777, reserved, *ibid.*
17. "Minuta de los various efectos que el diputado Arthur Lee, Esquire, dice que necesitan las colonias, Marzo, 1777," *ibid.*, 72.
18. "Memorial de Lee a las Cortes Expañolas," March 4, 1777, *ibid.*, 72–74.

and Spain. Grimaldi gathered that Lee was unaware of the request for supplies General Charles Lee had sent several months earlier by way of George Gibson to Governor Unzaga at New Orleans. Lee's lack of knowledge on that point puzzled the Spanish minister but also gave him the upper hand, since he negotiated with Lee knowing that King Charles had already approved secret assistance for the Americans as a result of Gibson's mission. The Spanish minister received from Lee a list of the supplies the Americans desired, and was able to assure him that the Spanish government could immediately provide most of the items. Grimaldi, in addition, informed a very pleased Lee that lines of credit for the Continental Congress would be opened in European banking houses, with the backing of the Spanish court. American ships would be allowed secretly to purchase war materials and supplies from the firm of Joseph Gardoqui and Sons, in Bilbao. Diego de Gardoqui left the meeting directly for Bilbao to arrange to have blankets loaded aboard two American vessels then in the harbor of that northern Spanish port.[19] During the conferences with the Spaniards, Lee repeatedly sought permission to continue his journey and make his proposals before the Spanish court, but Grimaldi consistently declined the petition. At Grimaldi's adamant insistence, Lee reluctantly returned to France to await further communications from Madrid.

The Spanish monarch approved the results Grimaldi reported to him in connection with the discussions with Lee. The Conde de Floridablanca, who had arrived in Madrid during Grimaldi's absence and assumed office as minister of state, wrote Aranda in Paris that "the [requested] material has been sent to various places so it can be remitted without delay to the colonies." The new minister of state also let Aranda know that Spain had issued secret letters of credit to several Dutch banking houses so that the Americans could purchase supplies through private merchants in Holland.[20] Word of Spain's favorable decision traveled quickly to the revolutionaries. "By a letter from Dr. Lee dated at Burgos in Spain . . . ," William Whipple related with satisfaction in Philadelphia, "large quantities of clothing are preparing in that Kingdom for this Country. Some are already sent to the Havanna."[21] The decision committed Spain to a benevolent neutrality in its dealings with

---

19. "Despacho de Grimaldi a Floridablanca," March 14, 1777, *ibid.*, 88.
20. "Despacho de Floridablanca a Aranda," March 24, 1777, *ibid.*, 92.
21. William Whipple to Josiah Bartlett, May 19, 1777, in *Letters of Delegates to Congress*, ed. Smith, VII, 91.

the Americans. Captain General Torre's observers played an important part in the new policy, since in addition to collecting news about the revolt, they became involved in transferring supplies to the Americans.

Personnel changes accompanied the policy shift, as new occupants assumed the offices of captain general of Cuba and governor of Louisiana during 1777, the five-year terms of both Torre and Unzaga having expired. Diego Joseph Navarro y Valladares was appointed captain general; Bernardo de Gálvez replaced Unzaga in the governorship of Louisiana. Diego Navarro, however, took almost a year to assume his new post after Charles named him to it in August, 1776. He spent the fall in Barcelona settling his personal affairs, finally embarking from Cádiz in the early spring of 1777. But bad weather forced additional delays, and he did not arrive in Havana until summer.[22] As a result, Torre continued as captain general for much of the year.

The new governor of Louisiana, Bernardo de Gálvez, was just entering his prime. He had served honorably as a field commander on the northern frontiers of New Spain while his uncle José had been visitor general. For the new governor, the post at New Orleans was not only the badge of a rapid advancement in Spain's military hierarchy but also a sterling opportunity to prove his leadership talents and advance his career. Louisiana would be an advantageous assignment should Spain go to war with Great Britain, since military exploits on the western frontiers of English America could furnish an astute commander with the makings of a record of service that might lead to the highest levels of Spain's government. José de Gálvez perhaps had that in mind when he supported his nephew's selection as governor in 1776. One resident of New Orleans later recalled that the minister of the Indies realized that "Louisiana was destined to be the siege of war, and the place where his nephew could make his mark. . . . He planned everything so advantageously that an officer with any ordinary capacity should have succeeded within a year."[23]

Whatever his personal motives, Bernardo de Gálvez never failed to pursue what was best for his nation in the Gulf Coast region.[24] His decisions in Louisiana prior to Spain's entrance into the war in 1779 reflected his per-

---

22. Torre to Navarro, June 12, 1777, Torre to J. de Gálvez, June 13, 1777, both AGI, Santo Domingo 1217.
23. Du Fossat, *Synopsis of the History of Louisiana*, 34.
24. Oliver Pollock to the Continental Congress, March 8, 1780, AGI, Cuba 2370.

sonal desire to inconvenience the British at every opportunity. As a result, he sometimes tolerated rebel activity in the Mississippi Valley and made judgments in favor of the Americans beyond the limits of Spanish neutrality, especially in choices not specifically covered by instructions from Spain. But his activities generally reflected the spirit of Spanish policy as formulated at court, and he arrived in Louisiana at the very time King Charles had decided to supply the Americans through New Orleans. During the month of October, 1776, Bernardo de Gálvez was in Havana, conferring with Torre.[25] The new governor arrived at the Balize post in the Mississippi River delta in late November and made his entrance into New Orleans early the following month. He spent several weeks in conferences with Unzaga, formally taking command of the province on New Year's Day, 1777, although Unzaga did not depart until late March.[26]

Governor Gálvez became an active sponsor of the collection of intelligence shortly after taking office, when he arranged for an observer to be sent to Pensacola. The governor ordered the agent to report on the state of fortifications, survey English positions along the Gulf Coast, and study the military works at Pensacola itself. According to established practice, Gálvez arranged to pay for the operation out of secret funds placed at his disposal by the captain general for "matters of the royal service." The governor kept the mission secret to the extent that none of the confidential reports on it contained the observer's name or anything that might give away his identity.[27]

The observer made his trip and returned to New Orleans in July, 1777, reporting on the state of the fortifications at Pensacola, the number and class of troops in the garrison, and what he could uncover concerning British plans. He told Gálvez that the West Florida garrison counted just over eight hundred soldiers, with by far the majority at Pensacola. Of these, some sixty had been declared unfit for duty. About one hundred of the troops had arrived recently from England as reinforcements. The observer also had intelligence of British relations with the Indians of the region. He learned that the British superintendent of Indian affairs, John Stuart, had talked

25. Unzaga to Torre, November 1776, no. 1278, AGI, Santo Domingo 1224.
26. Caughey, *Bernardo de Gálvez*, 34; Casa Mena, *Españoles in Nueva Orleans*, 31–34.
27. Robert L. Gold, "Governor Bernardo de Gálvez and Spanish Espionage in Pensacola, 1777," in *The Spanish in the Mississippi Valley, 1762–1784*, ed. John F. McDermott (Urbana, Ill., 1974), 87–99; "Relación de las cantidades . . . ," October 24, 1774, AGI, Santo Domingo 2547.

with various tribes in an effort to ensure their neutrality in the event that Britain should go to war against Spain. The observer became aware that many of the inhabitants of Pensacola expected France and Spain to enter the war soon. Many residents seemed to know about the assistance France was providing the Americans. The agent also learned that some in West Florida worried about an American attack by way of the Mississippi River.[28]

Much to Gálvez' consternation, his observer also learned that the British had agents in Louisiana, particularly at New Orleans, who fed regular reports about events in the Spanish territory to West Florida's governor, Peter Chester. The observer told Gálvez that "in New Orleans there are some individuals who collect and write to Pensacola all the news and intelligence they can gather relative to the Spanish government. They also correspond concerning the friendly treatment and favors that the Spanish and French government conceded to the Americans. The powder that went up the Mississippi last fall is said to have been by permission and consent of Governor Unzaga's administration under the direction of Mr. Pollock, a suspected agent of the Congress."[29]

Upon investigating, Gálvez during early 1778 expelled two British traders for providing news to the British.[30] In the meantime, he sent a summary of his agent's report to the captain general and also directly to court. The minister of the Indies and the king commended Governor Gálvez and encouraged him to undertake similar operations when he could.[31]

During the yearlong interval between Navarro's appointment as captain general and his arrival at Havana, the Marqués de la Torre continued to superintend observation of the Revolution, and he kept the minister of the Indies abreast of what came to Havana from his sources. For example, soon after the beginning of the new year, a ship of the Asiento returned to Havana after being in contact with Torre's observer in Jamaica, who sent the captain general copies of the Kingston gazette, which contained reports of

28. Gold, "Governor Bernardo de Gálvez and Spanish Espionage," 94–95.

29. *Ibid.*, 95.

30. These two traders, Robert Ross and John Campbell, were arrested for spying by Governor Gálvez and eventually banished from Louisiana. Having lost most of their property, they pressed for a settlement with the Spanish government from their new homes in Pensacola. For information about their claims, see their correspondence in AGI, Cuba 190. For British efforts to secure a settlement for lost property, see Chester to Germain, September 11, 1778, no. 60, Public Records Office, London, Colonial Office 5, DXCV, 14–186.

31. J. de Gálvez to B. de. Gálvez, October 10, 1777, royal order, AGI, Cuba 174-B.

fighting in the vicinity of New York. Miguel Eduardo, once again performing translation services for Torre, prepared extracts for the captain general to transmit to Spain.[32]

In reports from Kingston during the following weeks, Torre learned that the British naval forces there had been reduced to fewer than a dozen ships, including small vessels, and that the garrison consisted of little more than five companies of poorly disciplined troops. Torre notified José de Gálvez that Kingston suffered from a lack of provisions and that, in an unusual turn of events, its population depended largely on smugglers for supplies. He mentioned, moreover, that the Asiento's ships had brought word of English concern about the supplies being shipped to the rebels through French Santo Domingo. Because of the assistance, many Jamaicans manifested a healthy repugnance toward their French neighbors at Cap Français.[33]

Most of the reports from the Spanish observer at Jamaica reached Torre through his lieutenant at Santiago, Joseph Tenton, who used his city's location near the British island to supervise the Asiento company's contact with Kingston. Tenton issued passports for the ships making the run to the British colonial port and upon their return collected intelligence for transmission to Havana. He also maintained contact with Spanish officials in the city of Santo Domingo.[34]

While Torre waited for Navarro, he resolved to improve the efficiency of maritime surveillance in the region. The number of picket ships on station had been reduced to a minimum during the winter, and with the return of spring weather the captain general reassigned vessels to augment them. In particular, Torre decided to place two brigantines along the eastern coast of Cuba, dispatch an additional ship to cruise the Florida Straits, and retain the vessels working in conjunction with the observation post at Cabo Corrientes. Later in the spring, he moved that post to a higher location farther down the beach. In addition, the commander of the naval squadron stationed an armed launch at the Isla de Pinos to provide better coverage of the English sea-lanes to Jamaica.[35] Torre designated a fast vessel at Havana

32. Torre to J. de Gálvez, January 15, 1777, reserved, AGI, Santo Domingo 1598-A; J. de Gálvez to Torre, March 22, 1777, royal order, AGI, Cuba 1227.

33. Torre to J. de Gálvez, April 5, 1777, reserved, AGI, Santo Domingo 1227.

34. For examples of such activities, see Joseph Tenton to Torre, March 8, April 15, April 19, 1777, all AGI, Cuba 1143; and Tenton to J. de Gálvez, April 18, 1777, AGI, Santo Domingo 1227.

35. Torre to J. de Gálvez, March 28, 1777, AGI, Santo Domingo 1598-A; Torre to Bonet, March 21, 1777, Bonet to Torre, March 24, 1777, both AGI, Cuba 1227.

to stand on alert in case urgent messages needed to be dispatched to Spain or to the viceroy in Mexico.[36]

Torre routinely provided Viceroy Bucareli, in Mexico City, with copies of most reports about the American Revolution. Juan Ignacio de Urriza, the intendant of Cuba and a personal friend of the viceroy from his years in Havana, also supplied Bucareli with information received in Cuba.[37] The two Cuban officials assured the viceroy that, according to everything they heard, both sides in the revolt remained fully occupied, neither having made appreciable gains during the winter. Perhaps expressing the feelings of many government officials at Havana, Urriza considered the lack of definitive success by either side highly agreeable. "This is what we want," he wrote Bucareli, "inasmuch as they may destroy each other and thus not create a situation that will worry us."[38]

Reports from the observers during the early spring indicated a relative inactivity in the fighting between the British and the rebels on all fronts. Bernardo de Gálvez informed Torre from New Orleans that he had been unable to learn anything of consequence.[39] From Saint Augustine, Luciano de Herrera furnished the captain general with details on developments in Philadelphia through the end of January. Herrera said that the Americans persisted in their rebellious attitude, and he cautioned that the British seemed to be making Saint Augustine into a primary defensive position. The Spanish observer's opinion was that this would have serious consequences for Spain because of the English city's proximity to Cuba.[40] Later information Herrera provided continued perhaps to overemphasize the military role of East Florida in the revolt. He thereby helped create a somewhat misleading impression at Havana that the area of Georgia and Florida constituted a significant arena of confrontation between the rebels and the English during 1777.[41]

Contradictory and dubious assertions from sources and observers at times contended for Torre's attention. In late March, the captain general received a report that a British man-of-war had seized a Spanish ship and taken its

36. Bonet to Torre, March 20, 1777, no. 1, AGI, Cuba 1227.
37. For routine reports, see Torre to Bucareli, March 7, April 6, April 25, 1777, all AGI, Santo Domingo 1214.
38. Juan Ignacio de Urriza to Bucareli, January 31, 1777, *ibid.*
39. B. de Gálvez to Torre, March 21, 1777, no. 6, AGI, Cuba 1146.
40. Torre to J. de Gálvez, April 5, 1777, reserved, *ibid.* 1227.
41. Abbey [Hanna], "Efforts of Spain to Maintain Sources of Information," 61.

crew to Jamaica, where, before escaping, the captured men had observed a large British naval force. An official at Trinidad to whom the men had given testimony quickly informed Torre. But upon investigation, Torre discovered that the seamen involved had reputations as notorious smugglers of doubtful veracity. They apparently sought favors from the Spanish government in exchange for information. Word from the observer stationed at Jamaica explained that the story the captured sailors told had no basis in fact.[42] In the main, though, most of the information the captaincy general received mirrored the situation in English America accurately despite its occasional distortion and exaggeration because of misunderstandings, language difficulties, and rumor.

Because Navarro's arrival at Havana was delayed, it also fell to Torre to implement the secret royal order of the previous fall authorizing the admission of American ships into ports under his jurisdiction. Torre welcomed the new policy, since he realized that the masters and crews of the rebel vessels would bring knowledge about the revolt. Nonetheless, he understood that the vessels could be extended no courtesies or privileges beyond what Spanish regulations permitted regarding all foreigners. The Laws of the Indies, for example, allowed the entrance of foreign ships only in proven emergencies and, even then, severely limited contact between their crews and Spanish subjects. The procedures at Havana seem to have been fairly typical in this regard. The captain general's office maintained a special quarantined anchorage for foreign vessels near the main batteries of Morro Castle. There the port commander inspected foreign vessels seeking refuge in order to determine the validity of their claims and approve the necessary repairs. The battery officers at Morro Castle monitored activities on the ships and reported suspicious behavior to the captain general. The crews of the visiting ships were not allowed to set foot on land except by special permission, and when that was granted, armed guards from the local garrison accompanied them. In no case were foreigners to be given freedom of the city. Conversely, local residents were not permitted free contact with the vessel. The port commander always assigned guards to the ship when workmen might be aboard. When careening or major repairs demanded that the boat be brought into the dock area, the crew was to be placed under guard and the cargo was to be sealed for storage in the royal customs warehouse.

42. Torre to J. de Gálvez, March 20, 1777, reserved, AGI, Cuba 1227.

The harbor master was expected to attend to the vessel's needs and send it on its way as soon as possible.[43] José de Gálvez' orders of September and October, 1776, extended the procedures to American ships arriving under the colors of the United States. Since the colonies did not have access to normal lines of British credit, rebel captains had to pay for repairs and purchase supplies with cash, letters of exchange on recognized commercial houses, or barter slaves—who were badly needed on the island. Under no circumstances were they authorized to trade their cargoes, except for the slaves, to raise money for repairs.[44] Torre promised to admit American ships only in cases of true emergency and to "extend them the same hospitality as if they were European English or French."[45] He instructed his subordinate commanders that the regulations applied equally to ships obviously engaged in privateering, and he cautioned about the need for special care to ensure that privateers did not attempt to sell their prizes.[46] Awareness of the change in Spanish policy, although it was supposedly confidential, spread quickly, and American ships began arriving almost at once, thus opening a new channel of information. The Havana harbor master, as part of the investigation to determine the validity of a boat's claimed emergency, always questioned the captain and crew about the rebellion. Then, as a rule, the captain general's office took extracts from the statements for submission to the minister of the Indies.[47]

Accounts given by many of the rebel vessels convinced Torre that he should maintain closer contact with the French colonial port of Cap Français, since large quantities of supplies destined for North America seemed to be passing through that harbor. The captain general knew that someone who apparently served as the Continental Congress' commercial representative in French Santo Domingo resided there. Torre had the previous November learned of this man, Stephen Ceronio, from Miguel Eduardo, who had talked with the merchant during his layover in Santo Domingo on the way back from Chesapeake Bay. The American had shortly thereafter writ-

43. Torre to J. de Gálvez, August 3, 1776, AGI, Santo Domingo 1521.
44. J. de Gálvez to Torre, September 20, 1776, royal order, Torre to J. de Gálvez, January 31, 1777, reserved, both AGI, Cuba 1227.
45. Torre to J. de Gálvez, December 11, 1776, reserved, *ibid.*
46. Torre to Juan Ignacio Urriza, December 8, 1776, *ibid.*
47. Reports of foreign vessels calling at Havana during 1777 are in AGI, Santo Domingo 1217. For an example of information collection concerning the American Revolution, see Navarro to J. de Gálvez, June 14, 1777, reserved, *ibid.* 1598-A.

ten Enrile a hopeful proposal outlining the benefits of trade between Havana and his commercial agency at Cap Français.[48] Ceronio told Enrile that he served as an accredited representative for both the firm of Willing and Morris and the American Congress. Philadelphia merchants wanted him to open commercial relations with Cuba and, in particular, to offer foodstuffs for the Havana market. Ceronio requested permission for American merchantmen to call regularly at Havana and engage in that trade.[49]

Enrile discussed the matter with the captain general, who, understandably, initially denied the American's request. Once Spain moved toward a benevolent neutrality, however, Torre suggested to Enrile that Ceronio might be a good source of information about events in North America. The captain general decided to inaugurate the trade Ceronio proposed, but only in the Asiento's ships. Vessels of Spanish registry would make the voyage to Cap Français.[50]

Ceronio had been tendering unsolicited information about the Revolution before the captain general acted to recruit him. One dispatch from the American by way of rebel seamen was a long letter in early 1777 describing events in Pennsylvania and New Jersey. His communication was translated and excerpted in the captain general's office for transmittal by express to José de Gálvez. Ceronio reported that military events had lately favored the rebels. Although the English had made some gains after taking New York, American forces had stopped the British at Trenton, northeast of Philadelphia. The English, Ceronio added, had experienced heavy losses in engagements with colonial troops at Trenton and New Brunswick. The rebels had, besides, retaken the forts above New York along the Hudson River and planned to move directly against the city. Ceronio, partisan and even biased in his reporting, told Enrile that British forces had been guilty of extreme

48. Stephen Ceronio to Enrile, October 27, 1776, AGI, Cuba 1227. Stephen Ceronio, known to the American Congress under that name, was a merchant who had been engaged as a commercial agent to receive goods delivered to Santo Domingo by the Beaumarchais firm of Rodrique y Hortalez. He supervised the transshipment of those supplies from the French island to Philadelphia and other ports along the Atlantic Coast. See committee of secret correspondence to Ceronio, October 23, 1776, in Papers of the Continental Congress, item 37, fol. 79, National Archives. Ceronio advanced the Congress large sums of money from his personal resources and later had some difficulty in securing repayment. In the end, he received some recompense. See "Report of the Commerce Committee on Stephen Ceronio, May 8, 1781" (*Ibid.*, item 31, 209). See also *Letters of Delegates to Congress*, ed. Smith, V, 367n.

49. Torre to J. de Gálvez, March 7, 1777, reserved, AGI, Cuba 1227.

50. Torre to J. de Gálvez, January 26, 1777, reserved, no. 1355, AGI, Santo Domingo 1598-A; J. de Gálvez to Torre, April 7, 1777, royal order, AGI, Cuba 1227.

cruelty during the campaigns in New Jersey. They had rifled and burned much colonial property, generally leaving devastation in their path. The Americans had pledged retaliation for the harsh English behavior.[51]

This letter helped persuade Torre to open regular correspondence with Ceronio. The captain general also decided to send an observer to confer secretly with him at Cap Français. Antonio Raffelin, a colonel in the Cuban dragoon regiment, was the representative Torre appointed to establish contact with the American merchant. A Frenchman by birth, Raffelin had joined the Spanish army as a youth and served honorably in several European campaigns. He had executed important secret commissions for the Spanish court in his service during the Italian wars and had come to the Indies in 1762, where he had gained wide experience in Caribbean matters. He impressed the Spanish king with his dedication and efficiency. King Charles had considered him as a replacement for Governor Unzaga in Louisiana before deciding upon Bernardo de Gálvez.[52]

A reason for Torre's wish to keep Raffelin's visit with Ceronio secret was that, at a time when France seemed to be cooperating openly with the Americans, the captain general did not want to give Ceronio the misimpression that providing reports about the Revolution constituted an official relationship with the Spanish government. Raffelin went to Cap Français supposedly as a private citizen arranging personal matters on the island. Torre provided him a letter of introduction to the French governor there and confidentially alerted Spanish officials in the city of Santo Domingo about Raffelin's mission, requesting their assistance should he need it.[53] The royal treasury disbursed five hundred *pesos fuertes* to meet Raffelin's expenses, and the captain general drafted both a letter for Ceronio and detailed instructions for the colonel, many of them about collecting information on his own.

Raffelin's written instructions spelled out the kind of intelligence the captain general wanted regarding the American revolt. Torre left no doubt that the most important objective of the journey was to gather general news about recent events. If Ceronio seemed trustworthy, Raffelin was to deliver

---

51. "Copia del capítulo de la carta que en 5 de mayo del presente año de 1777 escribió en el cabo frances Don Esteban Ceronio," AGI, Cuba 1227.

52. "Instancia de Raffelin," March 1, 1776, *ibid.*

53. Torre to Jean-Baptiste d'Liancour, February 21, 1777, d'Liancour to Torre, April 14, 1777, both *ibid.*

the captain general's letter asking for regular reports. Under no circumstances, however, was Raffelin to divulge the full nature of his commission or identify himself as on official business. If anyone questioned the colonel's interest in the American rebellion, he was to plead only personal curiosity. Torre enumerated eighteen specific questions that Raffelin was to seek answers to in his conversations with Ceronio. Many related to the status of the English and American troops in North America and concerned their number, location, condition, and armaments. In addition, Raffelin was to determine how the rebels received their provisions at Cap Français, and he was to look for any estimates that might be available regarding future needs. He was also to ascertain the goals and objectives of the rebels, and he was especially to try to find out whether the Americans planned to continue the revolt or to negotiate with Great Britain. The colonel was to observe as well the treatment the French afforded the American vessels at Cap Français in order to see if there was open favoritism toward the rebels.[54]

Traveling with four personal servants and voluminous baggage, Raffelin appeared at Cap Français to be a successful man coming from Cuba to transact personal business relating to his family in France. Raffelin soon located Ceronio and spent several days evaluating the American merchant's suitability as a source. The colonel learned that the merchant was not in as close touch with Philadelphia as he implied in the letter to Enrile. Privateers flying both the English and rebel flags made communication difficult between Cap Français and the Atlantic coast, he learned. An American privateer in the area had recently captured a British prize carrying over four hundred slaves and had called at the French colonial port to sell them. Although the French did not normally allow sales by privateers, Ceronio had persuaded the local authorities to permit the disposal of the captured slaves and cargo. Much of the information he shared with Raffelin during their conversation came from the crew of that single privateer. Apart from that contact, it had been months since the American merchant had received news from North America. Nevertheless, the colonel believed it advisable for the captain general to maintain contact with Ceronio, since he would surely from time to time come upon information that the Spanish court desired.[55]

---

54. "Instrucción reservada a que se ha de arreglar el Señor D. Antonio Raffelin . . . en la comisión que lleva a Puerto Principe de la colonia francesa de la isla de Santo Domingo," February 21, 1777, *ibid.*

55. Antonio Raffelin to Torre, March 19, April 6, April 25, April 27, 1777, all *ibid.*

Raffelin therefore delivered the confidential letter in which Torre explained the need for reports about the revolt. People of all nations, the captain general wrote, had a consuming interest in the events of the American rebellion. The interest was especially strong in Cuba, because of the island's proximity to North America. The captain general lamented that he had to depend upon rumor and hearsay. Torre, saying he believed Ceronio could remedy the lack of solid information, and citing the American merchant's "honor and veracity," requested him to furnish regular reports by means of ships of the Asiento sailing to Cuba. Torre told Ceronio that his desire for information was personal in nature and did not involve the Spanish colonial government in Cuba.[56]

Ceronio seemed delighted and flattered by the unexpected Spanish attention. He readily consented to the proposal and immediately drafted for Raffelin a short synopsis that included all the information about the revolt that he then had at hand.[57] The colonel explained to the American that two channels existed for secure transmission of future reports to the captain general. First, the Asiento's vessels sailing for Cuba could forward information. Second, Spanish officials in neighboring Santo Domingo would be made aware of Ceronio's activities and could send dispatches to Havana, though communication through them would not be as quick.[58]

While engaged in discussion with the American merchant, Raffelin also collected news and information on his own. He discovered that French officials merely tolerated Ceronio's activities. They showed him no favoritism, though French supply of the colonies did involve regular shipments handled by him. On sailing into the harbor, Raffelin had observed two French navy frigates carrying engineers, artillery officers, and munitions. He also learned that French merchantmen sailed directly from France to Philadelphia in delivering munitions to the Americans.

At the completion of his mission, he returned to Havana aboard a private vessel outfitted by merchants at Cap Français. Trade with the French colonial port had been rendered so difficult by privateers that local traders chartered shares in Raffelin's ship to sail for France by way of Havana under the protection of the Spanish flag. Torre seemed pleased with Raffelin's accomplishments, especially since he brought some assurance that the British army

56. Torre to Ceronio, February 21, 1777, *ibid.*
57. "Papelita de Ceronio," March 19, 1777, *ibid.;* Torre to Tenton, April 6, 1777, *ibid.*
58. Raffelin to José Solano, March 18, 1777, Torre to Tenton, April 3, 1777, both *ibid.*

commanded by General William Howe was fully occupied by the Continentals. That meant that the English would have little margin for attacking Spanish possessions. The captain general wrote the minister of the Indies that, as a result of Raffelin's mission, it appeared almost certain that the British forces in North America "ought not to cause us concern for our principal establishments."[59] Torre also relayed this opinion to Viceroy Bucareli, in Mexico City.[60]

The delay of Navarro's arrival in Havana was a great worry for Torre. Colonel Raffelin had sought news in Santo Domingo of the Spanish vessel carrying Navarro from Cádiz, but without result. Much to Torre's relief, the ship appeared at Havana on June 9, after an exhausting eighty-day voyage from Spain. Bad weather had forced delays en route, and although Navarro arrived safely, he suffered from exhaustion.[61] He received an abrupt introduction to some of the problems he would experience in his new command when, on the very day of his arrival, he saw Torre circumspectly play host to five American privateers anchored in the roadstead of Havana. The ships had been cruising the area to prey on an English merchant flotilla expected in the Straits of Florida. Running low on provisions, they were calling at Havana with the allegation of an emergency so that they could replenish their food, water, and firewood. Torre conferred with Navarro, and the two Spanish officers decided to sell the Americans the supplies they needed on the understanding that they would depart at once to prevent the English from learning of their presence.[62]

After that, Navarro began conferences with Torre concerning the transfer of the captaincy general to his command. José de Gálvez had written in the formal instructions for the new captain general that "the Marqués de la Torre will personally inform you of the observations and opportune methods that he has secretly undertaken to investigate the events" of the English colonial revolt. The minister of the Indies had been clear that Navarro should make it a high priority to continue Torre's efforts.[63] The retiring captain general therefore gave Navarro an oral briefing concerning the ob-

59. Torre to J. de Gálvez, April 29, 1777, reserved, no. 1429, AGI, Santo Domingo 1598-A.
60. Torre to Bucareli, April 6, April 25, 1777, both *ibid.* 1214.
61. Navarro to J. de Gálvez, June 13, 1777, no. 1, *ibid.* 1217.
62. See the report of Rafael de la Luz, June 10, 1777, enclosed in Torre to J. de Gálvez, June 12, 1777, *ibid.*; and Navarro to J. de Gálvez, June 14, 1777, reserved, no. 1, *ibid.* 1598-A.
63. "Instrucción que V. M. manda guardar y observar a Don Diego Josef Navarro, Mariscal del Campo . . . ," January 6, 1777, *ibid.* 1214.

servation network. He also prepared a written summary outlining the major activities and observers of the summer of 1777.[64] Having assembled and cataloged all the reports, correspondence, and documents relating to the network, he counseled Navarro, "You will be able to see from this secret file, which I have marked as Number Two in the archives, the measures taken as a result of the large number of British forces now in American waters for the purpose of subjugating their northern colonies, and of the methods which I have used to acquire news of what happens between the two sides."[65]

Navarro took office formally on June 11, 1777. An experienced and mature commander who placed great faith in military etiquette and obedience to superiors in his conduct of affairs of state, Navarro brought a measured prudence to his new position. First and foremost, he was a soldier who lived according to the regulations. His desire to serve the king, as commanded from Spain, functioned at times as a judicious check on what seemed to be a degree of impetuousness on the part of Bernardo de Gálvez, his subordinate in Louisiana. Navarro's tenure as captain general was to be his first major assignment in the Spanish Indies; his previous posting had been as military governor of Tarragona, on the peninsula.[66]

Unlike Torre, Navarro was not an innovator. Instead, he showed himself to be a careful and deliberate commander. He relied heavily on staff organization and freely consulted with officials in Havana before making decisions. In particular, Juan Elegio de la Puente, along with Juan Bautista Bonet, the commander of the Cuban naval squadron, worked closely with Navarro in the operation of the observation network. Navarro brought a talented assistant, Antonio Ramón del Valle, from Spain to serve as secretary to the captaincy general. Valle reorganized the administrative practices of the Havana offices along more efficient lines. He also became an important figure in the day-to-day direction of the observers from Havana.[67]

64. Torre to J. de Gálvez, June 13, 1777, no. 1458, *ibid.*
65. Torre to Navarro, June 12, 1777, *ibid.*
66. "Minuta," August 15, 1776, *ibid.* 1217.
67. For a discussion of Puente's relationship to the American Revolution, see J. Leitch Wright, *Florida in the American Revolution* (Gainesville, Fla., 1975), 67–69. See also Boyd and Latorre, "Spanish Interest in British Florida," 92. No full study has been attempted regarding Puente's portion in Spanish reaction to the Revolution. His major contribution, which consisted of consulting on surveillance of East Florida, overseeing Indian relations in the region, and attempting to return the Floridas to Spanish control, may be gathered from reading his "Merits and Services," July 17, 1782, AGI, Santo Domingo 1526.

Within a week of taking office, Captain General Navarro sent the minister of the Indies a detailed outline of new measures he planned to use in collecting information. In particular, he wanted to expand the number of observers in order to increase regular contact with the rebel Americans.[68] Navarro thus pressed ahead with closer observation of the revolt at the same time that he continued all the operations under way at Torre's departure. He relied upon the governor of Louisiana as his most important subordinate in that regard. The new captain general wrote Bernardo de Gálvez soon after arriving in Havana, and the two officials began a regular correspondence concerning English activities in the Mississippi Valley.[69]

Perhaps because of the influence of Puente, Navarro increasingly used the Indians of Florida as sources of information. The Yuchis, always close to their former colonial masters, preferred a return to Spanish control. The officials at Havana, however, had exercised extreme care with the tribe in order to avoid creating an incident with the English. Nevertheless, during 1775 and 1776, the Yuchis had occasionally provided Torre with data about British military garrisons along the Gulf Coast. Soon after Navarro's arrival in Havana, a group of the Yuchis made the crossing to Cuba in order to confer with Spanish authorities. To a greater extent than his predecessor, Navarro considered the Indians worthy of confidence as sources about the revolt. The captain general interviewed them, encouraged them to provide information, and sent their reports to José de Gálvez.[70]

As Navarro surveyed the observer organization created by his predecessor, he concluded that Luciano de Herrera was one of the most vital and important parts of the network. The new captain general wrote Herrera to compliment him on the "fidelity and ardent zeal" with which he had provided reports to Captain General Torre. He urged Herrera to continue his reports and suggested additional ways the *floridiano* could send news to Havana. Navarro arranged for certain Cuban fishing boats to call along the East Florida coast on a regular schedule so that Herrera could send his dispatches through them.[71] Herrera replied to Navarro's letter with a renewed pledge to serve the Spanish king. The Floridian recommended in

---

68. Navarro to J. de Gálvez, June 20, 1777, reserved, AGI, Santo Domingo 1598-A.
69. Navarro to B. de Gálvez, June 17, 1777, AGI, Cuba 1232; Navarro to J. de Gálvez, October 14, 1777, AGI, Santo Domingo 1217.
70. Navarro to J. de Gálvez, September 19, 1777, AGI, Santo Domingo 1598-A.
71. Navarro to Herrera, August 12, 1777, AGI, Cuba 1290.

addition that the new captain general consult frequently with Puente—something he was already doing—since the *contador* had an extensive knowledge of the area and could offer counsel on the best methods for collecting information.[72]

Herrera proved to be a regular and fruitful source for Navarro, who drew extracts from the news originating in Saint Augustine which he forwarded to José de Gálvez.[73] The East Florida observer's reports held interest for the Spanish court. A fishing boat brought to Havana a dispatch from Herrera that outlined British plans for future campaigns. According to it, the British army planned to split New England from the rest of the colonies by sending an expedition down from Canada through Lake Champlain and the Hudson River to New York City, where it would join the English army at Manhattan. Herrera had knowledge that such an operation had already begun, with the Canadian force commanded by General John Burgoyne moving southward. But General Howe did not seem to be cooperating. Instead, his army had moved southwest, as his troops headed for an attack on either the Carolinas or Philadelphia. The report of Howe's movements confused Navarro, who felt that it would be most logical for the British commander in chief to support the advance of Burgoyne's forces as they moved toward New York City. The captain general wondered why Howe did not open a theater of operations in southern New York or northern New Jersey in order to create a second front of fighting at the opposite end of the Hudson River. He mulled this over in discussions with his staff in Havana and came to the conclusion that, whatever the British general's intentions, he had no plans to attack Spanish possessions. Navarro agreed with Puente, who felt that General Howe eventually hoped to create a British buffer area between the rebellious colonies and Saint Augustine by conquering the province of Georgia.[74]

The conversations in Havana about General Howe's intentions highlighted the growing importance of Puente as an adviser to Navarro on the American Revolution. A former resident of East Florida, Puente had a burning desire to see that province returned to Spanish control. He saw the Revolution as presenting the possibility of the result he sought. As his influ-

---

72. Herrera to Navarro, September 17, 1777, *ibid.*
73. Navarro to J. de Gálvez, October 4, November 18, 1777, both AGI, Santo Domingo 1598-A.
74. "Noticias de un residente de la Florida," October 5, 1777, AGI, Cuba 1290.

ence in Havana grew after Navarro's arrival, he used every chance available to recommend that the return of East Florida to Spanish control become a primary object of Spain's foreign policy. In fact, during late 1777 he proposed such a scheme directly to the minister of the Indies. Puente argued that Spanish interests in the Gulf of Mexico and northern Caribbean would suffer if the British or the Americans retained authority over the Floridas.[75]

He converted Navarro to his conviction by preparing a map and compiling a detailed jurisdictional history of East Florida that attempted to show that it had formed an important Spanish territory from the very beginning of the colonial era. Impressed, Navarro conveyed his memorial to Spain, along with his map. The map was one of the most accurate charts of the region then in Spanish possession. It proved extraordinarily useful to the ministers at court, especially since it displayed the entire south Atlantic and northern Gulf coasts. Puente's influence on Navarro worked a subtle change regarding the nature of information furnished by the captain general after the summer of 1777. From then on, many of the reports arriving at court from Havana reflected a tendency to focus upon the strategic importance of Saint Augustine and to cultivate the impression that the area played a larger role in the revolt than it did.

Stephen Ceronio did not meet Captain General Navarro's expectations as an observer at Cap Français. He appeared to report only rebel successes. During the late summer of 1777, he wrote Havana that several vessels had arrived from the Atlantic Coast but that little purpose would be served by reporting the accounts they bore since they only told of tenuous British gains. Much of the information he did send included long diatribes against the Quaker population of Pennsylvania. Ceronio maintained that this religious sect fostered great division and discord. According to him, Philadelphia fell to Howe's army because of the Quakers, who assisted the British navy by lending pilots for navigating Chesapeake Bay and who spied for Howe, delivering information that enabled the capture of the city.[76] The captain general did not believe that the collapse of the American capital was a direct result of the activities of the Quakers. Even though he first learned of Howe's successes in Pennsylvania from Ceronio, he decided to terminate his correspondence with the American.

75. Yela Utrilla, *España*, I, 327–73.
76. Ceronio to Navarro, September 15, 1777, AGI, Cuba 1227.

Navarro decided to replace the sacked Ceronio with a loyal Spaniard who would formally establish a trading branch of the Asiento at the French colonial port. In July, he dispatched Josef Melchor Acosta, a naval officer stationed in Cuba, to Cap Français to do that. Acosta was to substantiate information earlier sent to Havana by the American merchant and to file additional reports. Having signed on with Enrile as a merchant of the Asiento, he devoted much of his time to visiting with other merchants and ship captains in order to gather news. He periodically shipped cargoes to Havana, with the vessels carrying secret dispatches for Navarro.[77] For the most part, Acosta's secret reports revealed that Ceronio's information about the fall of Philadelphia had been generally accurate notwithstanding his overblown rhetoric against the Quakers. Acosta also provided details about the notable American victory at Saratoga, where the rebels had defeated General Burgoyne's army as it moved south toward New York City. The British, however, did not appear as debilitated as Ceronio pictured them. Acosta learned that the English army at New York gave every sign of being able to hold that key port against attacks from General Washington's forces. The observer reported as well that the English at New York expected reinforcements from Europe that would increase troop strengths. Acosta also became convinced that the rebel plans for capturing Canada could probably never be brought off since the British retained firm control there despite the occasional rumors that the former French province had decided to join the rebel cause.[78]

The captain general in addition enlisted the assistance of the Asiento in sponsoring an operation by one of its regular merchants, Lorenzo Tomati. In late October, 1777, the captain general dispatched Tomati on an inspection tour on the Caribbean for the supposed purpose of assessing commercial practices of the Asiento. In truth, Tomati was to collect news of the revolt, especially at Jamaica. Navarro charged him with the task of finding additional men in the ports of the area who might be willing to furnish information about the revolt to the Asiento's traders.[79] Tomati embarked on his trip, arriving first at Cap Français, where he visited with Acosta. Sailing

---

77. Navarro to J. de Gálvez, October 14, 1777, reserved, no. 12, *ibid.* 1290.
78. "Reportaje de Josef Melchor Acosta," October 31, 1777, *ibid.;* Navarro to J. de Gálvez, October 8, 1777, *ibid.*
79. "Instrucción reservada para el regimen de Don Lorenzo de Tomati en la acuisitión de noticias," November 6, 1777, *ibid.;* Navarro to J. de Gálvez, November 8, 1777, *ibid.*

on to Jamaica, he spent several weeks in Kingston assessing British naval affairs. He found that the English had become increasingly upset over French support for the rebel cause, especially since additional soldiers had begun arriving from Europe in France's West Indian colonies. He learned that partisans of both the loyalists and the rebels existed among the inhabitants at Kingston. Bad feelings between the two factions had created problems in the Jamaican port, with the divisions between them worsening as the island increasingly suffered from rebel privateers. Tomati observed that British naval strength appeared to be minimal at Kingston and that American privateers appeared to be intercepting the better part of English shipping bound for Kingston. But in spite of the presence of rebel sympathizers in Jamaica, Tomati wrote Navarro that he had been unable to locate trustworthy people who he felt could be enlisted for the continuing collection of information. In a full report Tomati drafted on his voyage when he returned to Havana in February, 1778, he summarized all he had learned. Navarro gave a full accounting to the minister of the Indies and expressed his satisfaction with Tomati's efforts.[80]

Once the Acosta and Tomati missions were arranged, the captain general concentrated on shipping to New Orleans the supplies destined for the Americans. José de Gálvez had already devised the basic plan for the supply effort, modeling it on the French court's arrangements with Beaumarchais. The Spanish naval commander at La Coruña received instructions in January, 1777, to begin transporting supplies on the monthly mail packets to Havana, while port officials at Cádiz started assembling consignments to be carried aboard merchant vessels bound for Cuba.[81] The minister of the Indies decided to select one of the observers at Havana to pose as a private merchant, go to New Orleans, and deal directly with the rebels, so as to give the impression of a private business transaction not involving the Spanish government, especially since the English would surely learn of the assistance when the rebels appeared at New Orleans to take delivery, if they did not hear of it before.

Ideally the observer would accompany the first shipment to New Orleans, supervise receipt of later cargoes, and remain in Louisiana to negotiate de-

80. Lorenzo de Tomati to Navarro, February 7, 1777, *ibid.*
81. J. de Gálvez to the governor of New Orleans, December 24, 1776, royal order, draft, AGI, Santo Domingo 2596; J. de Gálvez to the president of the Casa de Contratación, January 14, 1777, AGI, Cuba 1227.

livery when the American forces came down the Mississippi. The minister of the Indies left the selection of a person for this mission to the captain general, who chose Miguel Antonio Eduardo, of the ill-fated attempt to get a foothold at Philadelphia the year before. José de Gálvez drafted secret instructions for Eduardo, sent them on to Havana, ordered the captain general to organize the cargoes for transfer to New Orleans, and told him to make the necessary local arrangements for Eduardo's departure.[82]

Events moved so quickly, however, that the shipments from Spain began arriving in Havana before the captain general received these instructions from the court. Nevertheless, Navarro realized that the consignments were those destined for the American army and placed them under guard in the customs warehouse.[83] The captain general added to them the surplus gunpowder and rifles in the Havana arsenal. After receiving the ministry's instructions, conferring with Eduardo, and passing along copies of the secret orders from Spain, the captain general wrote a letter to Governor Gálvez. Eduardo was, he said, to take special care to ensure the secrecy of his mission, and even the captain and crew of the boat taking him and the supplies to Louisiana did not know of the Spanish government's involvement in the project. In addition, Eduardo was not to board the boat until it cleared Havana harbor, so as not to excite the suspicions of inhabitants who knew that the public interpreter occasionally performed sensitive missions for the captain general. Eduardo had instructions to carry all correspondence regarding the mission in a heavily weighted pouch that could be cast overboard should his ship be stopped by the British.[84]

The royal treasury paid Eduardo four hundred *pesos fuertes* to meet his personal expenses. The observer sailed for New Orleans on May 1 aboard the *San Joseph y las Animas*, which carried a cargo of clothing, gunpowder, ammunition, rifles, and medicine. Upon arriving in New Orleans, he met secretly with Governor Bernardo de Gálvez and briefed him about the supply effort. He reviewed the decisions made in Spain to supply the rebels through New Orleans and gave the governor a packet of letters that contained various royal orders, instructions from the minister of the Indies, and recommendations from the captain general on how best to accomplish the

82. J. de Gálvez to Torre, January 4, 1777, royal order, no. 5, AGI, Cuba 1227.
83. Torre to J. de Gálvez, April 5, 1777, reserved, no. 8, *ibid.*
84. Torre to J. de Gálvez, May 9, 1777, no. 1455, AGI, Santo Domingo 1598-A. See also Torre to B. de Gálvez, April 3, April 21, 1777, both AGI, Cuba 1227.

mission. The plan appeared to be clear and direct.[85] Unanticipated problems, however, developed soon after Eduardo's initial conference with Governor Gálvez. Several residents of New Orleans recognized the observer as the former public interpreter at Havana and were skeptical about his claim to be in Louisiana as a private merchant. Moreover, Spain's restrictive commercial regulations—designed to prevent smuggling—dashed the well-laid plans of the operation. According to anticontraband laws, bills of lading for all legal imports into Louisiana had to be presented for tax assessment and certification. Only government property enjoyed duty-free entry. No one had informed the customs officials at New Orleans about the mission, and before Governor Gálvez could take measures to have the shipment treated as personal property Eduardo was importing for private sale, customs officials acted upon the true bills of lading, which listed the government as owner and certified the ship's cargo to be royal property. They sent the supplies to the royal warehouse to be stored with similar effects belonging to the Louisiana garrison.[86] Although a consignment of military supplies arriving from Havana hardly constituted a rare or suspicious occurrence, its subsequent removal from the royal stores and transfer to rebel Americans coming down the Mississippi would have been likely to attract attention.

Gálvez quickly modified the plans in a way that he hoped would rectify the error. He enlisted the assistance of Santiago Toutant Beauregard, a New Orleans merchant and the brother of the observer Bartolomé Beauregard. Gálvez thereupon declared that the royal warehouse contained supplies beyond the need of the military garrison at New Orleans. Following established policy in such situations, he offered to sell the excess at public auction—the excess in this case being the supplies destined for the rebels. Beauregard bought them all with funds secretly provided by the governor, and he confidentially agreed to replace Eduardo in negotiating delivery with the Americans. The secret supply operation consequently shifted to the Beauregard warehouse in New Orleans.[87] Subsequent shipments from Spain were loaded aboard Beauregard's vessels, which routinely called at Havana. Governor Gálvez also made confidential arrangements for the car-

85. B. de Gálvez to J. de Gálvez, May 13, 1777, no. 52, AGI, Santo Domingo 1598-A; J. de Gálvez to B. de Gálvez, February 20, 1777, royal order, no. 49, J. de Gálvez to B. de Gálvez, February 22, 1777, royal order, no. 50, both AGI, Cuba 174-B. See also "Instrucción dada a Don Miguel Eduardo quando fue remitado a la Luysiana," April 24, 1777, AGI, Cuba 1227.
86. B. de Gálvez to Torre, June 21, 1777, no. 8, AGI, Cuba 1232.
87. *Ibid.*

goes to bypass Louisiana customs for transfer directly to Beauregard's private storehouse in the city.[88]

Given the recognition of Eduardo by several New Orleanians and the problems at customs, both the captain general and the minister of the Indies had to concur in Governor Gálvez' new plan. The Beauregard family's earlier performance in the observation network satisfied their concerns about maintaining the secrecy of the operation. Once the new arrangements had been made, however, Miguel Eduardo's continued presence at New Orleans became a matter of disagreement between Gálvez and Navarro. Governor Gálvez believed that the mission to supply the Americans would have a greater chance of success if the Cuban returned to Havana.[89] Captain General Navarro decided not to deviate radically from the royal orders that assigned Eduardo to New Orleans. The observer could use the Louisiana port as a base to collect information about the revolt, he concluded, especially since the Americans would probably come down the river and attack British West Florida. Miguel Eduardo was thus to remain in New Orleans, listed vaguely on the Louisiana government payroll as a "commissioner" residing in New Orleans under "royal disposition."[90] In the meantime, Governor Gálvez, Beauregard, and Eduardo began what was to become a long wait for the arrival of a rebel detachment to take delivery of the supplies.

88. *Ibid.*
89. Navarro to B. de Gálvez, , November 1, 1777, *ibid.*
90. "Partido de Nueva Orleans," June 15, 1778, *ibid.* 191.

4

Observers and Spanish Involvement

1778

All the supplies sent to Louisiana for the Americans had arrived by the summer of 1777, and they languished in Santiago Beauregard's warehouse at New Orleans. Governor Gálvez envisaged the sequence of events connected with their delivery: an American expedition would come down the Mississippi, receive the supplies, conquer West Florida, and then offer the province to Spain. The governor believed his part in this would be twofold. First, he would secretly give the supplies to the Americans, and second, he would ensure Spanish neutrality between the warring sides once the rebels attacked West Florida. "In case the colonies take the English posts along the river," José de Gálvez had written his nephew, "and they wish to deliver them to His Majesty, you may receive them in deposit, always taking care to see this will not cause violence with the British." The minister of the Indies recommended that young Gálvez establish a Spanish protectorate in West Florida since the British would probably find that preferable to having rebels control the conquered territory.[1] Providing military supplies to the Americans would be a cheap price to pay in laying the groundwork for such a turn of events.

As time passed, however, no American expedition presented itself on the river, though rumors of an invasion circulated in West Florida.[2] During the summer, Governor Gálvez wrote his uncle, "According to reports from Pen-

1. J. de Gálvez to B. de Gálvez, August 15, 1777, royal order, AGI, Cuba 191.
2. These rumors even came to the attention of the British cabinet. See Lord Sandwich to Germain, January 28, 1777, Public Records Office, London, Colonial Office 5, CLXII, 170.

sacola and the repeated rumors given by the English on this river, it looks as though the Americans are disposed to come down the river this summer, numbering four to six thousand men, with the intention of dislodging them from their posts and take Pensacola."[3] Once the reports of an impending American expedition on the Mississippi reached Spain, they passed from José de Gálvez to Floridablanca. When the minister of state asked Aranda to query the congressional envoys in Paris about American intentions, the American representatives gave the Spanish ambassador strong assurances that there was indeed the intention to send a force to conquer Pensacola in return for Spain's promise to hold the area in trust.[4]

Nevertheless, the year 1777 wore on, and still there was no glimpse of the Americans on the river. The Continental Congress had on several occasions discussed such an expedition but for a variety of reasons had decided not to approve it. "It was vain," Henry Laurens remarked, "to hope for Secrecy of an enterprise which had been often talked of in different states & long suspected by the enemy." Furthermore, the troops needed for the campaign could not be spared. Others who opposed the venture worried that Spain would not cooperate fully.[5] Governor Gálvez, however, was unaware of Congress' decision. His worry was that no Americans had come to collect the supplies and that some of them might spoil in Louisiana's subtropical climate. He and the observer Eduardo also wondered if rebel commanders on the Atlantic Coast might be unaware that the shipments of the cloth, gunpowder, rifles, and medicine they had requested had arrived at New Orleans. Deciding to write the Continental Congress and inform them about the supplies, the governor carefully composed an oblique letter that would not implicate Spain if it fell into British hands. With measured circumspection, he informed the Congress that the articles mentioned in its earlier communication to his predecessor had arrived at New Orleans and that these effects would be delivered to representatives who carried appropriate accreditation. He added that until then, concerned parties in New Orleans had arranged for the goods' safe storage. The governor dispatched

3. B. de Gálvez to J. de Gálvez, June 2, 1777, no. 57, in "Confidential Dispatches of Don Bernardo de Gálvez to his Uncle José de Gálvez" (Typescript in Correspondence of the Governors of Louisiana, Special Collections Division, Howard-Tilton Memorial Library, Tulane University, New Orleans).

4. "Carta de Franklin a Aranda," April 7, 1777, in Yela Utrilla, *España,* II, 94–95.

5. Henry Laurens to John Rutledge, August 12, 1777, in *Letters of Delegates to Congress,* ed. Smith, VII, 466–68.

his letter to Philadelphia in the hands of a "citizen of confidence" who sailed to the Atlantic Coast under the cover of buying a cargo of flour for the Louisiana garrison.[6]

Congress did not need to be reminded about the supplies by governor Gálvez. Some of its members had already received word of the shipments from two other sources. In early June, 1777, Oliver Pollock wrote the commerce committee of the Congress and told them about supplies arriving at New Orleans from Spain. Pollock probably knew about them because of his many merchant contacts in the city.[7] Congress had also received word of the shipments from Arthur Lee, who informed the commerce committee that a person of consequence in Spain had assured him that "supplies of Blankets, & clothing as well as Military Stores would be ordered out to Havanah and New Orleans, there to be lodged for our use & to remain until we should send for them."[8] The commerce committee of the Congress had taken action to secure these supplies at New Orleans before it received the letter from Governor Gálvez. It appointed Oliver Pollock congressional agent at New Orleans and organized an expedition to claim the goods. By its action, it legitimized Pollock as its official representative in Louisiana, agreeing to guarantee any debts he might contract in New Orleans in support of the American cause. The committee wrote Governor Gálvez:

We have employed Mr. Oliver Pollock who resides at New Orleans for our Agent; and have Instructed him to charter or buy suitable Vessels to Transport these stores Coastwise until they can get into some of our Ports or Inlets to land them. He is instructed to consult your Excellency in this business, and we pray your favourable attention to this business—that you will advise in all things needful—and Protect the Ships, Cargoes & Mr. Pollock if occasion shall so require. . . . We are compelled to go farther in our requests and beg that you will also supply him with money if it becomes necessary to defray the charges and Expenses that will accrue on the transshipping of the Stores. He must grant receipts for what you supply and we will repay the amount by our Agent at the court of Spain.[9]

A former West Florida planter, James Willing, became the commander of the troops organized in the United States to convey the letter and take delivery of the supplies. A brother of the powerful Philadelphia merchant

6. B. de Gálvez to J. de Gálvez, August 9, 1777, no. 76, AGI, Santo Domingo 2547.
7. Commerce committee of the Congress to the governor of Louisiana, June 12, 1777, AGI, Cuba 112.
8. *Ibid.*
9. *Ibid.*

Thomas Willing, who was one of Robert Morris' partners, he seemed a natural choice to lead the expedition. He had lived near Natchez during the early 1770s and had had business dealings with Pollock at New Orleans. Young Willing met with the commerce committee to discuss plans for the mission.[10] The committee furnished him an introduction to Bernardo de Gálvez and Oliver Pollock's letter of appointment as commercial agent.[11] Beyond those communications to Gálvez and Pollock, record of the committee's specific instructions to James Willing have been lost. It appears, however, that Congress did not authorize an attack on West Florida as part of the expedition's assignment.

After meetings with the commerce committee, Willing, armed with a Continental captain's commission, left for Fort Pitt, on the Pennsylvania frontier, with permission from Congress to recruit his men.[12] He gathered thirty or so volunteers, secured the flatboat *Rattletrap*, and began his journey down the Ohio River on January 10, 1778. News of the expedition preceded it, alarming British commanders all along the Mississippi. Gálvez heard about Willing's progress, as well, and assumed that the expedition was to secure the supplies and attack West Florida. It certainly appeared that the expedition planned to conquer West Florida, since Willing's men began plundering as soon as they reached British settlements on the Mississippi. On February 16, an advance guard arrived at the plantation of Anthony Hutchins, took the planter prisoner, and seized some of his property.[13] As Willing and his men continued down the river, they engaged in similar raids against individual British residents.[14] Willing also took the small English settlement of Concord, near the Arkansas River on the British

10. Regarding the Willing family and its part in the American Revolution, see Thomas Willing Balch, ed., *Willing Letters and Papers, Edited with a Biographical Essay of Thomas Willing of Philadelphia, 1731–1821* (Philadelphia, 1922), and Burton Alva Konkle, *Thomas Willing and the First Financial System* (Philadelphia, 1937).
11. Commerce committee of the Congress to the governor of New Orleans, November 7, 1777, AGI, Cuba 112.
12. At Fort Pitt, George Morgan supplied Willing with enough provisions to last thirty men approximately 180 days. See George Morgan to James Willing, January 17, 1778, in General Edward Hand Papers, Historical Society of Pennsylvania, Philadelphia.
13. For studies of Willing's raid, see John W. Caughey, "Willing's Raid down the Mississippi, 1778," *Louisiana Historical Quarterly*, XV (1932), 5–36; Robert V. Haynes, *The Natchez District and the American Revolution* (Jackson, Miss., 1976), 51–75; José Rodulfo Boeta, *Bernardo de Gálvez* (Madrid, 1976), 65–69; and Starr, *Tories, Dons, and Rebels*, 78–121.
14. Willing in fact apparently issued written passes to some rebel sympathizers which offered them protection from the marauding of his men. See Pass Signed by James Willing, March 3, 1778 (Gratz Collection, Historical Society of Pennsylvania).

side of the Mississippi. Upon their arrival at Natchez, the Americans forced a bloodless surrender from the local British commander. Willing coerced the inhabitants at Natchez into oaths of fidelity to the Continental Congress, which many swore with reluctance.[15]

Willing's expedition created chaos for the British along the Mississippi River. Governor Gálvez received numerous reports of the expedition's advance as it approached New Orleans. These confirmed his opinion that Willing's force intended to take West Florida, although it puzzled Gálvez that the attack had apparently begun before the supplies had been delivered. Nonetheless, he knew his duty and began to discharge it. Gálvez' instructions bid him cooperate with any rebel force sent to receive the supplies and conquer the neighboring English province. In early March, he therefore initiated actions designed to facilitate the Americans' arrival in New Orleans while protecting Spanish neutrality.

Governor Gálvez issued a formal proclamation of neutrality and publicly instructed his upriver commanders to provide refuge for British citizens escaping from the American expedition. The governor also secretly wrote his subordinate commander at Spanish Manchac, Juan de la Villebeuvre, and told him that if the Americans asked to turn over to Spain the territory they were conquering, Villebeuvre could accept it as a Spanish protectorate. "As it might happen that the American who is found in command there," the governor wrote Villebeuvre, "might wish to cede to His Majesty those territories they have conquered from the English along the river, I ought to inform you that you should accept the cession."[16] Gálvez wrote his uncle José that the American expedition that planned to attack West Florida had apparently arrived on the Mississippi. He promised to follow his instructions regarding the transfer of the supplies and accept control of West Florida when the rebels offered it.[17]

Gálvez also permitted Oliver Pollock to prepare for Willing's arrival at New Orleans. Pollock had learned from several American partisans coming down the river that Willing carried his formal appointment as the congressional agent in Spanish Louisiana. That emboldened him, and he made

15. "Capitulación de Natchez," February 21, 1778, AGI, Santo Domingo 2547.

16. B. de Gálvez to Juan de la Villebeuvre, March 20, 1778, no. 133, *ibid*. For information on Villebeuvre's career as a post commander, see Jack D. L. Holmes, "Juan de la Villebeuvre and Spanish Indian Policy in West Florida, 1784–1797," *Florida Historical Quarterly*, LVIII (1980) 387–99.

17. B. de Gálvez to J. de Gálvez, March 24, 1778, no. 133, AGI, Santo Domingo 2547.

ready for the American captain's arrival at New Orleans. Pollock later re-called, "In February, 1778, I receiv'd intelligence of Capt. Willing's approach, & immediately I waited on his Excellency the Governor & took ev'ry necessary arrangement with him. I was therefore extremely solicitous to comply with the Orders I had received from the Honorable Mr. Laurens, Mr. Morris, & Mr. Smith a secret Committee of Congress to Charter Vessels & Transport a large quantity of Merchandise by Sea & also to send as much as possible up the River, for the use of the United States."[18] Gálvez most likely welcomed Pollock's sponsorship of Willing and his men, since that removed the Spanish governor from direct contact with the Americans. Such might soften the anticipated British charges of favoritism that Governor Chester would probably level at Gálvez.

While arrangements went forward at New Orleans, the American expedition continued to move south, ravaging British settlements along the way. Near Manchac, Willing's advance party captured the British frigate *Rebecca,* a sixteen-gun vessel, which the Americans quickly appropriated for their own use. They also raided British plantations along the Mississippi and Amite rivers, although they spared those belonging to rebel sympathizers.[19] Excess and wanton destruction marked many of the seizures. Gálvez received reports "that the Americans shot hogs, killed cattle, broke bottled wine, burned dwellings and in other ways laid waste" to many individual plantations.[20] Thrown into turmoil, many British citizens along the river took advantage of Gálvez' invitation of sanctuary. They fled by the hundreds, and Spanish posts all along the west bank of the Mississippi overflowed with refugees.

Once at New Orleans, Willing met with Governor Gálvez, with Pollock as translator. To the governor's surprise, the American captain did not offer Spain any of the territories conquered by his expedition nor did he express an interest in attacking Mobile or Pensacola. What is more, he seemed unaware of any such plan on the part of the Congress. To Gálvez, Willing's chief motivation appeared revenge against particular British residents along the river, owing to personal differences that arose from his residence in West Florida before the Revolution. The American commander had apparently

---

18. Oliver Pollock, "Events in the Public Career of Oliver Pollock, 1776–1782, as Related by Himself," September 18, 1782, in James's *Oliver Pollock,* 348–49.

19. Caughey, *Bernardo de Gálvez,* 122.

20. *Ibid.,* 121.

acted on his own initiative in ordering his men's attacks and had no instructions to conquer West Florida. Willing wanted two things from the governor: the supplies sent from Spain and official permission to sell his plunder at New Orleans. Pollock echoed Willing in these petitions. Armed with the letter appointing him congressional agent, Pollock agreed in wanting to move ahead promptly with liquidating the spoils of the expedition in the name of the Congress.[21] Gálvez carefully considered the developments in view of his orders from Spain specifically requesting him to cooperate with any Americans sent to receive the supplies. A review of his instructions convinced him that the conquering of West Florida might have been a secondary American objective. Since his instructions did not cover the selling of prizes, he gave liberal interpretation to the standing directive from the court on such matters and decided to allow the Americans to sell what they had seized. In addition, he permitted Pollock use of port facilities to outfit the captured British frigate *Rebecca* as a privateer.

Pollock's appointment as congressional agent brought a change to the governor's plan to deliver the supplies to the Americans. He had intended for Santiago Toutant Beauregard to deal directly with the American troops. Such matters could be handled directly and personally by Pollock. Beauregard therefore "sold" the supplies to Pollock soon after the American expedition's arrival at New Orleans. These transactions took place without problems. In late March, Gálvez wrote his uncle, "Having arrived in this city a Captain Willing, commissioned to receive here the effects that were sent to me from the mother country with destination to the English colonies, I ought to inform Your Excellency that the major part of these effects have already left the city, and as soon as all of them have been delivered, I will inform Your Excellency."[22] Pollock chartered several vessels to transport the supplies to the Atlantic Coast. His sloop *Virgo* quickly left New Orleans, followed several weeks later by other vessels, "with more Goods for the United States." Throughout the fall, Pollock dispatched additional ships and bateaux to the colonies.[23]

While Willing and his men enjoyed the freedom of the city, Pollock or-

21. "Disposition of Pollock," in James Wilkinson's *Memoirs of My Own Time* (3 vols.; Philadelphia, 1816), III, Appendix A.
22. B. de Gálvez to J. de Gálvez, March 24, 1778, no. 136, AGI, Santo Domingo 2547.
23. Pollock, "Events in the Public Career of Oliver Pollock," in James's *Oliver Pollock*, 350–51.

ganized a public auction of articles and slaves captured by the expedition. The sale attracted a large crowd of New Orleanians, and spirited bidding brought considerable profit to the American cause. It also prompted a strident protest from Governor Chester, of West Florida, who sent a British warship to New Orleans with a formal letter of complaint. Chester expressed shock and indignation at the hospitality afforded Willing and the American troops at New Orleans, arguing that this could only be interpreted as a violation of Spanish neutrality. The British governor warned Gálvez that he would attack Louisiana if Spain departed further from its proclaimed neutrality. "I have judged it proper to inform your Excellency," he wrote, "that I sent a Detachment of Troops to Manchak in order to establish a base for the protection of that area." Chester also began to augment British troop strength elsewhere along the Mississippi.[24]

Gálvez politely refused to be intimidated by three additional British warships calling separately at New Orleans during the several months following. Their captains demanded a full restoration of captured British property and an immediate end to the refuge provided the Americans.[25] In the end, the governor compromised and did return some of the seized English goods not yet sold by Pollock, although he allowed the Americans to remain. He explained to the British that he had extended exactly the same privileges to loyal British subjects when they wanted to sell prizes at New Orleans. Nonetheless, the behavior of the Willing expedition gravely concerned Governor Gálvez, because he recognized the critical circumstance the raid had created, namely, bad relations with the British in West Florida. In this regard, he promised his uncle José that he would "take whatever measures and precautions necessary" to defend Louisiana "against any invasion the English might attempt."[26] But though the British reacted vocally to Willing's raid, they did nothing more than complain.

The residents of Louisiana hailed Governor Gálvez for the stern manner and calm strength he exhibited in standing up to the British in the crisis. What they did not know, however, was that he had never been very worried about a British attack during the tense months after Willing's arrival at New Orleans, since he had had an observer at Pensacola during the time the American was conducting his raids in West Florida and the information he

24. Chester to B. de Gálvez, May 28, 1778, AGI, Santo Domingo 2547.
25. Caughey, *Bernardo de Gálvez*, 123.
26. B. de Gálvez to J. de Gálvez, June 9, 1778, no. 166, AGI, Santo Domingo 2547.

got from the agent convinced him that the British would not deliver on their threats. The observer mission had been arranged in early 1778, before news of Willing's expedition reached New Orleans. The observer, Captain Jacinto Panis, of the Louisiana Regiment, had left for West Florida in February, 1778, on a seemingly routine voyage. The ostensible purpose of his visit to Pensacola was to discuss with Governor Chester the problem of runaway slaves from the colonies who took refuge in neighboring territory. In reality, Panis had instructions to gather as much information as possible about the British army and navy in West Florida.[27]

Captain Panis traveled to both Mobile and Pensacola, remaining in the British colony for several months. He carried a letter of recommendation to Chester from Bernardo de Gálvez, along with a "box of white sugar and a cask of wine" as gifts to the Englishman. Panis was well received by the inhabitants of the British province during his travels, although news of the raid by Willing placed him in the unexpected position of having to vouch continually for Spanish neutrality. Nonetheless, at the very time Chester wrote his strongly worded complaint to Gálvez regarding the American raid, the British governor also played host to Panis at Pensacola. Even with the strained relations, Chester afforded Panis every courtesy as his guest. Panis responded with an eloquent profession of Spanish neutrality. "I cannot entertain the least doubt of the Sincerity of his last assurances which I have received from him," Chester wrote the Louisiana governor, "but I flatter myself, that His Excellency will continue the Same friendly disposition whenever occasions offer." The series of discussions Chester and Panis held about the problems facing the two colonies resulted in an agreement for the return of runaway slaves.

While away from New Orleans, Panis compiled a report on the status of English military defenses in West Florida. He also talked with numerous residents about the revolt, gaining a fuller understanding of British intentions regarding both the Spanish in Louisiana and the American rebels. He drafted a proposed plan of attack on Pensacola should Spain enter the war. He submitted a valuable description of the British post at Mobile:

The fortifications are, as you know, in very bad condition; they consist of a regular square, built of brick, and flanked with breastworks, trench, and glacis, as before,

27. John W. Caughey, "The Panis Mission to Pensacola," *Hispanic American Historical Review*, X (1930), 480–89.

situated very near the barracks and at the shore of the bay for defense by sea, as on land by Indians. Its walls are going to ruin. Almost all of the artillery is dismounted, and the trenches in some places are choked up. The barracks are in equally bad repair; in the front and side sections are housed the small garrison of forty-five soldiers, commanded by a captain, lieutenant, and sergeant; the other side, the northeast, is uninhabitable, for nothing but its walls remain, the rest having been consumed by a fire.[28]

Panis provided similar descriptions of the English military works at Pensacola, in even greater detail. Panis reported that passage of the American expedition down the Mississippi had caused a full-scale mobilization of British troops in the province and a commitment from Governor Chester to remedy the weaknesses of all his garrisons in order to bring them to fighting readiness. That suggested to Governor Gálvez that Chester would be unable to make good on his threats to deal harshly with Louisiana. In addition, once war between Spain and Great Britain came in 1779, Panis' reports became the blueprint for a Spanish attack on West Florida.

The Willing expedition marked a turning point for Louisiana in the American Revolution. It exacted an immediate price for Spain: the end of all possibility of good relations between British West Florida and Spanish Louisiana. Many West Florida residents, along with the entire British government at Pensacola, thereafter viewed the Spanish in Louisiana as the enemy in an immediate sense. A gap existed in the lower Mississippi Valley between Spain's rhetoric as a neutral and the reality of its role in the revolt. In particular, Governor Chester reacted to the Willing raid by redoubling his military defenses in the western part of his province, especially at garrisons on the Mississippi River.

The period between the American raid in the early spring of 1778 and Spain's entry into the war during 1779 became a time of constant tension as both Bernardo de Gálvez and Peter Chester increased their defenses, prepared for conflict, and carefully watched each other's activities. The pressures greatly decreased Louisiana's ability to participate in the captain general's observation network based at Havana. Instead, Bernardo de Gálvez focused his attention on West Florida and worried about British military affairs in the region that had a direct, local impact on Spanish Louisiana. After late 1778, emphasis on collecting general information about the Ameri-

28. *Ibid.*, 486–87.

can Revolution moved away from New Orleans and became the concern almost exclusively of the captain general at Havana.

While Willing and his men were beginning their trip down the Mississippi during early 1778, momentous events in France altered the nature of Spanish participation in the American Revolution. France recognized the independence of the United States and declared war on Great Britain. The American victory at Saratoga in October, 1777, caused this shift in policy at the French court. Vergennes feared that the British might sue for peace in the face of Burgoyne's resounding defeat, and he began negotiations with the American representatives in Paris soon after news of the battle arrived in France.[29] The French foreign minister gave Spain the opportunity to join with France in recognizing the independence of the American colonies.[30] Still favoring war, the Conde de Aranda gave Vergennes the impression that Spain might agree to such a course of action. The French ambassador in Madrid, aware of the influence of the *aragoneses* at the Spanish court, reported to Vergennes that Aranda might be correct in this case. In particular, the Spanish king realized the inevitability of a Franco-American alliance.[31] Vergennes drafted a long memorial for King Charles and his ministers in early January that explained why France wanted an alliance with the rebellious colonies.[32]

Floridablanca, the minister of state, carefully reviewed the French proposals but, after discussion with Charles, found them to be incompatible with Spanish policy. The minister of state felt that the time to recognize the colonies as an independent nation had not yet arrived. "Our court," Floridablanca wrote Aranda in Paris, "must reflect on protecting our vast possessions in the Indies from insult, sending enough competent troops, and there must be circumspection. On the contrary, France has few possessions to protect, and it has already dispatched troops in sufficient numbers, it believes, for the security of its islands."[33] Floridablanca saw only danger

29. See Lawrence Kinnaird, "The Western Fringe of Revolution," *Western Historical Quarterly,* VII (1976), 253–70.

30. For a discussion of this offer and subsequent Spanish refusals to join with France, see Jonathan R. Dull, *The French Navy and American Independence: A Study of Arms and Diplomacy, 1774–1787* (Princeton, 1975), 86–87, 91–94, 100–101.

31. William C. Stinchcombe, *The American Revolution and the French Alliance* (Syracuse, N.Y., 1969), 10.

32. Bemis, *The Diplomacy of the American Revolution,* 60–61.

33. "Memoria remitada a la Corte de España por la de Francia, 8 de enero de 1778," in Yela Utrilla's *España,* II, 173.

for Spain if it followed France into an alliance with the Americans. He believed that Spanish colonies in the Americas needed stronger defenses before embarking on a war with Great Britain. He also feared for the safety of Spain's annual treasure fleet, the *flota*, then preparing to leave Mexico for Spain. Joining with France in the war with the British would give the British navy license to attack the *flota* and thereby ruin Spain's economy for 1778 and 1779.[34]

Faced with the impending French alliance, King Charles called a meeting of the Council of Ministers in January, 1778. It reviewed the implications of France's decision to join with the Americans. The majority of ministers agreed with Floridablanca and recommended continued neutrality. The king echoed the sentiments of the minster of state, who told the council that joining France would provoke immediate war with England, for which Spain lacked complete readiness. The minister of state instead proposed that Spain sponsor an international peace negotiation.[35] In a formal vote, the council unanimously agreed upon continued neutrality. For the time, Spain would refuse either to enter the war or recognize the independence of the United States.[36]

Suspecting all along that Spain would not become a partner to the American alliance, Vergennes had begun negotiations with the congressional envoys before he learned of the Spanish court's decision not to participate. The French minister notified the Continental Congress on January 8, 1778, that Louis XVI had decided to enter into a treaty of recognition and alliance with the Americans. On February 6, Vergennes and the American commissioners signed two treaties. One outlined the terms of Franco-American friendship and commerce and the rights of belligerents and defined "most favored nation" status for the two powers. The second established a "conditional and defensive alliance" between them. It provided for a "common cause" between France and the United States, created a firm military alliance, and committed both nations to seek a joint peace with England at the conclusion of hostilities.[37] These treaties would be activated when France

34. Conde de Floridablanca to Aranda, January 13, 1778, reserved, no. 2, *ibid.*, II, 192–93.
35. *Ibid.*, 193.
36. "Dictamen de Floridablanca, 22 de enero de 1778," *ibid.* This effort at mediation came to nothing, although for a time England and France agreed to cooperate with Spain. Their demands, however, were unrealistic, and George III of England remained solidly opposed to any compromise with either France or Spain. See Dull, *The French Navy*, 126–35.
37. Yela Utrilla, *España*, I, 302.

and England entered into a formal state of war soon thereafter. The war in North America spread to Europe with their signing.[38]

The Franco-American alliance had an immediate impact on Spanish policy regarding the American Revolution. José de Gálvez, for one, realized that the French alliance meant an expanded role for the captaincy general of Cuba. Captain General Navarro commanded Spain's first line of defense against the British as they fought the French. During the January meeting of the Council of State, Gálvez told his colleagues that the naval squadron at Havana should be reinforced immediately with at least two ships of the line. In addition, a minimum of two regiments would have to be added to the island's garrison, along with one new regiment for Puerto Rico and several others for the viceroyalty of New Spain. Gálvez recommended that short-term defensive measures be taken to protect the treasure fleet when it passed through Havana en route to Spain.

Gálvez also told the king and the Council of Ministers during the January meeting that he planned to expand the observation network commanded by the captain general of Cuba. The minister of state voiced strong agreement with this decision and suggested sending new Spanish observers to permanent posts in North America, where they could observe the Revolution at close range. In particular, Floridablanca wanted an observer to establish residence at Philadelphia in order to provide regular reports on congressional activities. He also saw benefits from another observer's living in proximity to a major British army operating in North America. José de Gálvez agreed enthusiastically with these suggestions and, after the meeting, quickly implemented them.[39] He drew up special instructions for Captain General Navarro requesting that observers be recruited for the new missions to the meeting place of the Congress and to a posting near one of the major English armies in North America.[40] The two observers would gather information about the struggle according to the guidelines already in force for the captain general's observation network. Should Spain eventually decide to take a more active role in the revolt, the observer sent to the meeting

38. For a complete discussion of these treaties, see Bemis, *The Diplomacy of the American Revolution,* 61–69.
39. "Dictamen de D. J. de Gálvez, 23 de enero de 1778," in Yela Utrilla's *España,* II, 204.
40. "Minuta de Floridablanca," n.d., AHN, Estado 3885, expediente 17, fol. 1. Although this note bears no date, the captain general of Cuba and the governor of Louisiana received instructions based on it during August, 1777. That implies that Floridablanca wrote the memo between February and August, 1777.

place of the Congress could easily become an unofficial or official representative, depending upon Spain's eventual decision regarding the opening of
formal relations with the United States.[41]

José de Gálvez also took steps to ensure continued Spanish neutrality. He
wrote Navarro that war between the British and the French would soon be
a reality. When that happened, he said, the captain general should exercise
special care not to become involved in the "quarrels and insults" between
the two powers. He should maintain the "same good harmony in all cases"
with both sides.[42] Navarro relayed the directive to his subordinate commanders and cautioned them that Spain would remain impartial.[43] Minister
Gálvez also instructed Navarro to strengthen the defenses of Cuba: "The
king commands me to order you . . . to take what measures and precautions
may be appropriate for the certain defense of the garrisons and territories
of your command, and to repel whatever invasion the English may in-
tend."[44] Navarro complied by conducting a formal inspection of all defenses
in the Havana area. Finding full protection of the harbor lacking, he ordered the construction of batteries near Morro Castle. He also instructed
his subordinate governors at Santiago de Cuba and New Orleans to conduct
similar inspections of their defenses.[45] Captain General Navarro by the summer of 1778 understood that the French alliance with the Americans and the
increasing tensions with the English in West Florida placed Spain in difficult
circumstances that created additional demands on the observation network.
According to instructions, he therefore expanded his information-collecting
operations, bypassing Bernardo de Gálvez, in Louisiana, since the Willing
expedition had made for troublesome relations with West Florida.

Navarro reviewed the observation network during the late spring of 1778
and decided to make two important changes: first, he would use the Florida
Indians as significant sources of information, and second, he would dispatch
the two new observers to North America as requested by José de Gálvez.
He turned first to the recruitment of the Indians, since an unexpected opportunity arose in that regard. Shortly after the Willing raid, a group of
Yuchis, led by their chief, Tunapé, came to Havana from the Appalachee

41. J. de Gálvez to the governor of Havana, August 26, 1777, royal order, reserved, AGI,
174-B.
42. Navarro to B. de Gálvez, December 3, 1777, *ibid.* 1232.
43. J. de Gálvez to Navarro, March 22, 1778, royal order, reserved, no. 21, *ibid.*
44. J. de Gálvez to Navarro, March 3, 1778, *ibid.*
45. J. de Gálvez to Navarro, January 24, 1778, royal order, reserved, no. 18, *ibid.* 1290.

region to discuss renewing close relations with the Spanish. Since many of the Florida Indians had converted to Roman Catholicism during the Spanish period prior to the Peace of Paris in 1763, Tunapé asked that a priest be sent to the abandoned fort at San Marcos in order to baptize children and hold periodic mass. The chief also suggested that the captain general occasionally send a commercial vessel along the Florida Gulf coast to trade with the Yuchis. It could carry goods and supplies for the Indians and bring some of their trade items back to Havana.[46]

Juan Elegio de la Puente took part in these discussions and enthusiastically supported the Indians. He pointed out to Navarro the information-gathering benefits of contact with the Yuchis and reminded the captain general that ships from Havana could covertly rendezvous at the site of old Fort San Marcos on the Appalachicola River, long abandoned by the British.[47] Convinced, Navarro set about organizing regular contact. Tunapé and his party returned to the Florida Coast as passengers on the first of the vessels, which carried a priest and supplies for the Indians. The captain general also informed the minister of the Indies that he would be "sending aboard this ship, under cover of returning the Indians, an observer to reconnoiter Pensacola and Saint Joseph bays in order to observe English ships there."[48]

By the end of 1778, Navarro had made permanent arrangements to send an observer to the abandoned former Spanish fort at San Marcos in order to collect information from the Indians about other tribes and about events in English America and in order to ensure the Indians' continued loyalty.[49] In selecting this person, Navarro followed the advice of Puente, who recommended a *floridiano*, Francisco Ruiz del Canto, as best qualified for the mission. Canto had extensive experience with the tribe and spoke several Indian languages.[50] The captain general gave explicit instructions governing the agent's conduct among the Indians. He cautioned him that the British must never learn of his activities. He should reside in Havana but travel regularly to Florida to meet with the Yuchis. In particular, he should use the abandoned fort at San Marcos as his base, profess Spanish affection and

46. Navarro to J. de Gálvez, April 11, 1778, reserved, no. 232, *ibid.*
47. J. de Gálvez to Navarro, March 3, 1778, Navarro to J. de Gálvez, January 17, 1778, both *ibid.*
48. *Ibid.*
49. *Ibid.*
50. Navarro to J. de Gálvez, January 15, 1778, reserved, no. 171, AGI, Santo Domingo 1598-A.

friendship for the Yuchis, and promise them a continuing supply of gifts. His most important objective, however, would be to learn "the manner in which the war between the English and the colonists progressed, the numbers of the garrisons at Pensacola and Saint Augustine, and the events that occurred in Georgia."[51]

Canto made numerous clandestine trips into East Florida, camping at San Marcos and talking with the Indians. On his first voyage, he spent over a month living in the ruins of the fort, where he met with delegations from the Yuchis. He learned that the major chiefs of the Yuchis, including Tunapé, Tolope, and Nitafatique, all favored a close alliance with Spain. The Indians saw no difference between the two sides in the revolt, preferring to remain neutral in the revolutionary struggle. The two parties in the conflict, they told Canto, were "brothers" who could join against the tribes of the region at any moment. The chiefs reported, however, that other tribes of the region did not share their opinion and many took sides with the British or the rebels. Canto found that some four hundred warriors in the region had cast their lot with the British and were actively fighting against the Americans. Canto also learned a great deal about the state of British military affairs at Pensacola. The Indians told him that the garrison there needed provisions. In addition, the majority of the troops and provisions in the West Florida capital had been shifted to the Mississippi River posts as a reaction to the American raid the previous year. Canto continued his observations at Fort San Marcos for the remainder of the American Revolution, although his trips became increasingly infrequent once Spain entered the war.[52] The observer regularly encouraged the Indians to watch the British at Pensacola and Saint Augustine, distributed gifts to them, and promised continued Spanish support.[53]

51. Navarro to J. de Gálvez, January 15, July 26, 1779, reserved, both AGI, Cuba 1290. Ruiz del Canto appeared before the *junta de floridianos*, the government resettlement commission in Cuba in October, 1777, in order to ask for a position in the Spanish colonial government of the island. Canto's friendship with the Puente family seems to have been the chief motivation behind his selection as agent to the Yuchis in 1779. See Navarro to J. de Gálvez, October 10, 1777, AGI, Santo Domingo 1227.

52. "Relación de lo acaecido in la expedición que acabo de executar al castillo del San Marcos de Appalache para donde sali de este puerto de 24 de julio ultimo le regresado hoy dia de la fecha," September 26, 1779, AGI, Cuba 1290.

53. "Ynstrucción de lo que ha de observar y executar Don Francisco Ruiz del Canto en la commisión a que se le destina en la Goleta *Nra. Sra. del Regla* del Patrón Lorenzo Rodriguez," July 20, 1779, *ibid.*

Canto's success in recruiting Florida Indians as sources encouraged Navarro as he began arrangements for the more complex project of sending two permanent observers to North America. "The general objects of these commissions," José de Gálvez noted, "must be informing on the state of the war, of its progress and of the general success of each side, of their respective forces and their disposition, and of whatever prejudicial designs either might have toward Spain and its colonial possessions."[54]

In setting things up, however, the captain general and the ministers in Spain altered the role the governor of Louisiana would play.[55] The original plan considered by the ministries in Spain called for the observer posted to the Continental Congress to be the responsibility of the governor of Louisiana, who was to choose an appropriate person for the job. The agent would sail up the Mississippi from New Orleans to Fort Pitt. There he would make contact with the Americans and travel to Philadelphia, where he would establish his residence as a private merchant. He would maintain communication with Spain through his commercial shipments to New Orleans by way of the Ohio and Mississippi rivers. The other observer, to reside near a major British army in North America, would be sent from Havana to an appropriate place along the Atlantic Coast. He would communicate with Havana through the observer Luciano de Herrera in Saint Augustine.

The increased tensions between the British in West Florida and the Spanish in Louisiana in the months after the Willing raid, however, made such arrangements inadvisable. Navarro reasoned that Spain's congressional observer could become isolated if the Mississippi Valley became an area of confrontation. In addition, the captain general and the minister of the Indies agreed that the governor of Louisiana had to give primary attention to dealing with local problems in the wake of the Willing raid. Supervision of the congressional observer in such circumstances would be difficult. Navarro therefore decided to dispatch both observers from Havana.[56] The minister of the Indies authorized him to select both the persons, draft their instructions, and superintend their activities. They would communicate with Spain through Havana. That decision effectively removed the governor

---

54. J. de Gálvez to Navarro, January 10, 1780, royal order, no. 73, April 23, 1780, royal order, no. 86, both *ibid*.

55. J. de Gálvez to the governor of Havana, August 26, 1777, *ibid*.

56. Navarro to B. de Gálvez, December 3, 1777, *ibid*. 1232.

of Louisiana from a major role in the collection of information about the American Revolution after 1778.

The captain general thus assumed control of what would become the major observer operation for Spain during the remainder of the Revolution. With Puente, Navarro discussed who might be drafted for the assignments. The persons selected, he specified, should have the "sagacity, zeal, and prudence" to accomplish the objectives of the operations. As usual, Puente's opinion influenced him: both the observers he selected were members of the Puente family. The captain general chose Juan de Miralles y Trajan, a merchant of Havana and a brother-in-law of Puente's, to be the congressional observer. Miralles had participated in information operations during the Seven Years' War, when he furnished news to the Spanish governors of Puerto Rico, Santo Domingo, Cartagena de Indias, and Havana about British naval movements in the region.[57] Navarro appointed Joseph Elegio de la Puente, brother of his adviser, to be the observer settling near a major British army in North America. A former resident of East Florida, the younger Puente had familiarity with the Atlantic Coast and its Indian tribes.

José de Gálvez approved Navarro's selection of observers.[58] The captain general charged his personal secretary, Antonio Ramón del Valle, with supervising day-to-day administrative matters at Havana relative to the two secret missions. Several months earlier, King Charles had formally created the position of "secretary of the government of Havana and captaincy general of Cuba," elevating Valle to the office as its first occupant.[59] Valle proved himself a trustworthy and able administrator, reorganizing the captain general's offices in Havana along more efficient lines. He assumed an immediate role in arranging for the transportation of the new observers to North America, in securing secret funds from the government treasury, and in organizing the specific details of both missions.

The captain general decided that Joseph Elegio de la Puente should be the first to embark for his post since his activities had military implications for the defense of Havana. Puente's mission to the region of East Florida and Georgia also conformed to the hidden agenda of the exiled *floridianos*

57. Navarro to J. de Gálvez, November 11, 1777, reserved, no. 197, *ibid.* 1290; Navarro to J. de Gálvez, n.d., reserved, no. 124, AGI, Santo Domingo 1598-A.

58. J. de Gálvez to Navarro, January 21, 1778, royal order, no. 16, AGI, Cuba 1290.

59. Navarro to J. de Gálvez, December 17, 1777, reserved, no. 148, AGI, Santo Domingo 1598-A; "Nombramiento de Don Antonio Ramón del Valle, Secretario del Govierno de la Havana y Capitania General de Isla de Cuba," May 13, 1779, reserved, AGI, *ibid.* 1193.

in Cuba, who had already proposed to the minister of the Indies that the Spanish attempt an invasion of East Florida in the event that Spain entered the war.[60] Since Joseph's sojourn in this area would therefore be important if the time came to advocate the invasion at court, *contador* Puente encouraged Navarro to make haste in arranging for his younger brother's departure from Cuba. Although Navarro did not fully share the convictions of the *floridianos,* he acceded out of his friendship for his colleague.

The captain general decided to ask Luciano de Herrera, in Saint Augustine, to assist young Puente. Once Navarro made up his mind that Joseph would travel first to the East Florida capital, where Herrera would brief him on the region and help him select a final destination, he sent Herrera a secret dispatch describing minutely the proposed mission. Plans called for Puente to leave Havana aboard a fishing vessel for the Florida keys. Every attempt would be made to create the appearance of a normal voyage. Once under way, the ship carrying the observer would call at Saint Augustine, where Herrera would extend the necessary protection and hospitality to the young man. What he did would probably not arouse British suspicions, since Herrera had been friendly with the Puente family since their years in Florida.[61]

Navarro also put instructions for Puente in writing and briefed him on the mission. The observer was to follow Herrera's advice in all local matters. With the Floridian's assistance, Puente would eventually travel to "Georgia, Carolina, or where the British army is said to be." There, he would assume an occupation as a cover for collecting information about the revolt. All his letters to Cuba were to be sent to Herrera, who would forward them to the captain general by the Cuban fishing vessels that worked the coast. "The principal object of the mission," Navarro told Puente, "must be truthfully informing about the progress of the war and its current state, about the principal gains of both sides and their respective forces, about the plans both sides wish to follow, and about any prejudicial designs they might have toward France or Spain."[62] Navarro especially wanted to know the number and type of British troops in the region, their location, and their future plans.[63]

60. For Puente's proposals to J. de Gálvez, see *ibid.* 1598-A.

61. Navarro to J. de Gálvez, December 17, 1777, reserved, no. 128, *ibid.*

62. "Ynstrucción reservada para el regimen y govierno de Don Josef Elegio de la Puente y Don Luciano de Herrera en la importante comisión que se les fia," December 10, 1777, AGI, Cuba 1290.

63. J. de Gálvez to the governor of Havana, August 26, 1777, J. de Gálvez to Navarro, January 21, 1778, royal order, no. 16, both *ibid.* 174-B.

While Navarro briefed the new observer, Valle made ready to send him to East Florida. He hired Miguel Chapuz, master of the *Divina Pastora*, to carry young Puente to Saint Augustine. The royal treasury secretly delivered four hundred *pesos fuertes* to the observer in order to defray the costs of the operation. Meanwhile, the Puente family circulated the story about town that Joseph would be traveling to Florida for reasons of family business: several British residents still owed him money for the sale of real estate at the time of the territorial transfer of the mid-1760s. Armed with his secret instructions and his money, Puente sailed on December 15, 1777.[64] At Saint Augustine, the British allowed the Spaniard freedom of the city when he explained that he came to settle family business stemming from the Spanish era. Puente quickly made contact with Herrera, who had been expecting him, and remained at Saint Augustine for several months while Herrera secured him introductions to the leading inhabitants and British officers of the town. The observer used this period as a seasoning time, practicing his English and learning British social customs. He got along well with his British neighbors, and it surprised no one when he decided to tarry in East Florida.[65]

The two Spaniards also began laying plans for sending Puente northward to Georgia. They decided that he should go in the guise of a private entrepreneur engaged in contraband with Cuba. That would give him some credibility with the locals while permitting him to communicate with Herrera, the Cuban fishing fleet, and the Minorcans. During April, Puente purchased a small boat to relay messages to the Roman Catholics at New Smyrna and to the Cuban fishing vessels. Herrera and Puente also "secured at a good price" the services of a "friend" living at Saint Marys on the border between East Florida and Georgia, who promised to collect information for them.[66]

Puente had hoped to leave for Savannah by May at the latest, but unanticipated conditions delayed his departure. The increased number of rebel privateer attacks in the area worried him. The privateers plagued shipping along the East Florida coast and had rendered communication with British areas to the north difficult and infrequent. Herrera and young Puente also learned that British military officials in Saint Augustine censored all incoming letters and gazettes from Georgia, making it very risky for Puente to

64. Navarro to J. de Gálvez, December 17, 1777, no. 148, AGI, Santo Domingo 1598-A.
65. Herrera to Navarro, April 23, 1778, AGI, Cuba 1290.
66. Herrera to Josef Elegio de la Puente, May 4, 1778, *ibid.*

send his dispatches to Cuba through Herrera. They decided to adjust their plans: for the time, Puente would remain at Saint Augustine.[67]

During all the preparations, Miguel Chapuz had waited aboard his vessel in the vicinity of Cape Canaveral on the pretext of fishing, so that he could return to Cuba with a report for the captain general on the arrangements made to send Puente northward. Chapuz had been there most of the spring and was becoming restive. In May, Herrera reluctantly decided that Chapuz should return to Havana and tell Navarro that settling the final details of Puente's operation seemed to be taking much longer than expected. Herrera and Puente wrote a long letter for the captain general that included an explanation of what they had already accomplished and enlarged on the difficulties that had presented themselves. Chapuz departed for Havana during May with the letter safely in hand, but bad weather delayed his arrival in Cuba for almost three months.[68]

In the meantime, Navarro had heard nothing from Puente, and becoming increasingly anxious for news, he had decided to send a messenger to Florida in order to inquire about him and find out what had happened to Chapuz. The captain general engaged Lorenzo Rodríguez, captain of the fishing boat *Nuestro Señora de la Regla,* for that purpose.[69] Rodríguez sailed to the Minorcan settlement at New Smyrna, arriving under the pretense of being a fisherman who had experienced difficulty with his vessel. He left his small ship in the care of a trusted settler there and stole away to Saint Augustine in the company of two of his sailors. They traveled under cover of darkness in a canoe, reaching Saint Augustine late in the night so that they would not be observed. Rodríguez carefully made his way to Herrera's home, where he found the two Spaniards sitting in the parlor playing cards. His arrival greatly surprised them, especially since they had just the week before sent Miguel Chapuz back to Havana with their letter to the captain general. Rodríguez urged them to make another report immediately; Herrera correctly surmised that the bad weather plaguing the region had delayed Chapuz' arrival in Cuba.[70]

Puente and Herrera spent most of the night preparing another report for the captain general, Rodríguez worrying all the while that they would not

67. Herrera and Puente to Navarro, May 12, 1778, *ibid.*
68. Navarro to J. de Gálvez, August 4, 1778, reserved, no. 48, *ibid.*
69. Navarro to J. de Gálvez, June 16, 1778, reserved, no. 43, *ibid.*
70. "Relación de lo acaecido a Lorenzo Rodriguez, Patrón y Dueno de la Goleta Nuestra Señora de la Regla desde el dia primero pasado, que en diligencia del Real Servicio, partio de este Puerto, hasta ayer que regreso a el," June 15, 1778, *ibid.*

finish by sunrise. The two observers were clearly conscious that the captain general was not happy with them, so they took special pains to include in their report all the recent intelligence they had about the Revolution —something they had neglected to do in Chapuz' letter. They recorded that news of open warfare between Great Britain and France had arrived in Saint Augustine and reported on a naval engagement that had occurred off the coast of Normandy. That, they considered, marked the start of fighting between the two powers. Herrera also described at length rumors from New York that referred to the Carlisle Commission, an instrument for a possible peace negotiation between England and the rebels. He explained that reports arriving in East Florida indicated the British Parliament had suspended all the punitive colonial acts passed since 1763 and had dispatched members of the commission to New York empowered to discuss peace. At the same time, it appeared that the Continental Congress would reject the British overtures. Instead, the Congress demanded nothing less than the total withdrawal of British troops from the continent and full independence from Great Britain. Herrera also mentioned that he had talked with the captain of a ship sent by Governor Chester, of West Florida, to London for the purpose of delivering reports on James Willing's raid on the Mississippi. "By a packet from Pensacola," he wrote, "we are informed that the Americans have arrived in those parts by land and sea, and have destroyed different plantations and taken more than two hundred Negroes, which they have carried to New Orleans, and that the Spanish Governor there permitted them to be sold, and he welcomed them with friendship."[71]

Returning to Havana with the report, Rodríguez offered to the captain general yet another explanation of why Puente had not gone to his appointed destination. The large British army the Spanish supposed to be in the southern part of Georgia apparently did not exist, and Herrera had been wrong in this regard. Rodríguez learned from the Minorcans and Father Camps that English forces along the Saint Johns River numbered only about eight hundred while the garrison at Saint Augustine totaled little more than one hundred. On the other hand, an American force of some three thousand men was stationed nearby on the Altamaha River in Georgia.[72] In late July, Chapuz finally made it back to Havana bearing the first letter sent by Herrera and Puente. Navarro studied the two communica-

71. "Papelita de Herrera y Puente," June 15, 1778, *ibid.*
72. "Relación de lo acaecido a Lorenzo Rodriguez," June 15, 1778, *ibid.*

tions and realized that he had probably been duped by the *floridianos*. Their desire to regain East Florida had led him into a venture that he should have avoided. The *contador* Puente apparently foresaw that sending an observer to the region would make it seem more important than it was to the Spanish court.

Navarro understood, however, that he would have to continue working with Puente and the *floridianos,* many of whom were persons of power and importance at Havana. Conscious that there was little he could do but end the mission, he informed the minister of the Indies, "Reflecting that there does not exist in Georgia, nor in neighboring Florida, the primary objective of Don Joseph Elegio de la Puente's commission, I have decided to retire him, leaving only Don Luciano de Herrera (who was previously there) for the submission of such news that might occur or be known in Saint Augustine."[73] Navarro resolved to offer young Puente a choice: if it appeared that the British might begin large-scale military operations in Georgia, he should continue his activities; if not, he should return to Havana.[74]

The captain general sent Chapuz back to Saint Augustine to discuss the matter with Puente and to bring him home should he decide to return.[75] Just getting to Saint Augustine, however, proved harder than anyone anticipated. Chapuz departed for the capital of East Florida in September, but once again he encountered bad weather, to the damage of his ship. When Chapuz put four men overboard in a skiff to make repairs, a sudden squall blew them away. Unable to rescue them, he limped back to the safety of Havana. After securing repairs there, he sailed once more for Saint Augustine in early January, 1779. He finally made contact with Herrera and Puente after sneaking into the town at night. When he reviewed with them the captain general's reservations about continuing the operation and offered to take the young observer back to Havana, Puente acquiesced and returned.

Puente brought some useful information from Saint Augustine. He reported that the British officials there believed that war between England and Spain could not be avoided. Some fifteen hundred veteran troops had gone to Pensacola in order to spring an attack on New Orleans as soon as confirmation of war with Spain reached them.[76] Navarro transmitted this

73. Navarro to J. de Gálvez, August 4, 1778, reserved, no. 48, *ibid.*
74. Navarro to Puente, September 9, 1778, *ibid.*
75. Navarro to J. de Gálvez, September 15, 1778, reserved, no. 53, *ibid.*
76. Navarro to J. de Gálvez, January 10, 1779, reserved, no. 60, *ibid.*; Navarro to J. de Gálvez, April 15, 1779, reserved, no. 65, AGI, Santo Domingo 1598-A; "Noticias y demas que bajo la

intelligence to José de Gálvez, who issued instructions to his nephew Bernardo for the defense of Louisiana. The decision to cancel Puente's mission met with the entire approval of the court in Madrid. Both the king and his ministers agreed that Joseph Elegio de la Puente had to be recalled since he did not meet the objectives of his commission.[77]

Despite Puente's recall, the captain general continued to use East Florida as a base from which to gather information. Herrera remained at Saint Augustine and provided reports into the early 1780s. Ship captains from Havana also maintained contact with Spanish sympathizers, especially the Minorcans and the Indians. Indeed, both Lorenzo Rodríguez and Miguel Chapuz could regularly be found along the coast on "fishing" trips. In the spring of 1779, for example, Rodríguez put together for Navarro a thorough assessment of military strength in Georgia. He reported that the Americans would be victorious in holding most of the colony even though the British had been recruiting Indian allies to take up arms against the rebels. Herrera substantiated this information and predicted that the Americans would drive the British from Georgia.[78] As the months passed, however, reports coming to Havana from Saint Augustine indicated that East Florida played a progressively smaller and more isolated role in the American Revolution.

Diego Navarro realized that the failure of the Puente mission to Georgia made Miralles' operation all the more crucial for Spain, and the ministers at court concurred. The captain general had wanted to delay sending Miralles to North America until Puente had become established in Georgia. But when he decided to order Puente's return to Cuba, he began planning Miralles' mission. Navarro had full confidence in Miralles and worked with him closely in planning the operation. From one of the most powerful commercial families in Cuba, Miralles had married the sister of the *contador* Puente. His father, Manuel de Miralles, had secured official approval to trade with the English in the early 1700s and had earned a substantial fortune. Juan continued the family tradition of successful commercial operations. He had a network of contacts that extended through the Caribbean to the Atlantic Coast of North America. Fluent in English, he had numerous business dealings with Philadelphia merchants, including Robert Morris. As one histo-

---

maior confianza se me comunican en la Plaza de San Augustin de Florida," signed by Joseph Elegio de la Puente, April 10, 1779, AGI, Cuba 1290.

77. J. de Gálvez to Navarro, February 15, 1779, royal order, reserved, no. 38, AGI, Cuba 1290.

78. Navarro to J. de Gálvez, June 18, 1779, reserved, no. 73, *ibid.*; "Papelita de Herrera," June 18, 1779, no. 73, *ibid.*

rian has noted, he was "one of the Havana traders most active with the thirteen colonies."[79]

The captain general had a series of conferences with Miralles in which they discussed the major objectives of his mission. These would be "informing about the state of the war, and its progress, of the gains of each party, of their respective forces, of the dispositions of both sides, and whether or not they might follow them, and learning of any prejudicial designs against Spain and its American colonies."[80] Miralles was to accomplish these goals "without suspicion or the danger of being seen as a spy," so that he could "communicate the news he acquired" to the captain general. Navarro also told Miralles to be especially watchful for any signs that the Americans might negotiate a peace settlement with Great Britain. In that case, he was to make every attempt to notify the captain general without delay.[81]

Navarro told Miralles that he was never to implicate the government of Spain in connection with his surveillance. Instead, he was to act in all appearances and representations only as a private citizen. Navarro and Miralles also devised a scheme to make the observer's arrival in North American appear the result of happenstance. The Asiento contract held by the firm of Aguirre, Aristegui, and Company would be expiring at the end of the year. Miralles would announce that he wanted the contract for himself, and he would plan a trip to Spain to lobby for the concession. The trip would be the Cuban merchant's excuse for leaving Havana. In reality, he would never head there. The ship carrying the observer would make for Charleston under the pretext of having experienced an emergency at sea. The captain general conspired with the master of the vessel to sabotage the ship so that its arrival in South Carolina would seem legitimate. Miralles would then decide to remain in North America rather than risk continuing to Spain on a vessel that had already floundered. After staying awhile in South Carolina, Miralles was to travel to Philadelphia, ostensibly to open a flour trading business.[82]

79. Navarro to J. de Gálvez, November 11, 1777, no. 197, *ibid.;* Amalia A. Rodríguez, ed., *Cinco diarios del sitio de la Havana* (Havana, 1963), 250; Manuel Conrotte, *La intervención de España en la independencia de la América del Norte* (Madrid, 1920), 25.

80. J. de Gálvez to Navarro, August 26, 1777, AGI, Cuba 1290.

81. *Ibid.*

82. J. de Gálvez to Torre, February 22, 1776, *ibid.* 1214; "Petición de Juan de Miralles," October 12, 1776, *ibid.* 1281. During 1776, Miralles had applied to the court for the Asiento contract. That made his story all the more credible.

The flour trade between the United States and Cuba was to provide Miralles with a cover for his information gathering. Still, that posed a problem with respect to the port authorities at Havana, for Spain's commercial regulations placed strict prohibitions on foreign trade. Since Miralles could not be allowed openly to flout the restrictions once his commerce began, Navarro found it necessary to arrange confidential procedures allowing him to trade legally between a North American port and Cuba. The captain general instructed his secretary, Antonio del Valle, to handle all the administrative matters regarding this commerce so that ships dispatched by Miralles could enter Havana harbor and not be mistaken for contrabanders. According to Spanish law, foreign goods and merchandise could be legally landed in Cuba only after formal certification that an emergency need for the cargo existed in the colony. Valle routinely served as the government official who furnished such certifications, and vessels involved with the Miralles mission always received them automatically. Navarro had quietly instructed the Havana harbormaster to admit all Miralles' ships under these conditions, doing his best not to arouse suspicion. Navarro and Juan Elegio de la Puente also made confidential arrangements to reimburse Valle from funds in the royal treasury for any expenses incurred by Miralles' operation. Valle was to remit to Miralles reimbursements for all official expenditures made by the observer in North America.[83]

Commercial restrictions aside, Miralles' mission raised a delicate problem for Spanish policy makers in Madrid. Spain had carefully avoided recognizing Congress as the legitimate governing body of an independent state. The possibility existed that, should Miralles' connection with the Spanish government be discovered, his residence in the town where Congress met might seem to some Americans—or the British—as the first step in Spain's recognition of the United States.[84] According to one historian, the minister of state, Floridablanca, "resolved that Spain should not follow blindly and implicitly in the wake of French policy, and was determined that any move made on the part of his government during this war was to be primarily for

---

83. "Ynstrucción reservada para el regimen y govierno de D. Juan de Miralles en la importante comisión del Real Servicio que se le fia," December 17, 1777, *ibid.* 1290.

84. Special diplomatic agents acting in semi-official capacity had traditionally been used to open diplomatic relations with previously unrecognized powers. See Henry M. Wriston, *Executive Agents in American Foreign Relations* (1929; rpr. Gloucester, Mass., 1967), 406; Yela Utrilla, *España*, I, 387; and José Martínez Ortiz, "Un valenciano en la independencia de los Estados Unidos," *Revista de Historia de América*, L (1960), 492.

the advantage of Spain."[85] He worried that Miralles' operation coincided with the dispatch of a formal French envoy to the Continental Congress. Indeed, Conrad Alexandre Gérard arrived in Philadelphia as France's first accredited representative several weeks after Miralles established residence in the town. King Charles and his ministers therefore carefully refrained from conferring upon Miralles any diplomatic responsibilities. Miralles was absolutely to admit no connection with the Spanish government unless specifically instructed to do so at a later date. The captain general stressed to Miralles that he served only as an observer in the secret information network based in Havana.[86] Before leaving, Miralles nonetheless took the unprecedented step of writing a confidential, personal letter to Gálvez, the minister of the Indies. In it he outlined the instructions given by Navarro and promised to furnish all news he might acquire both to the captain general and to the ministry of the Indies. Miralles promised that he would dispatch special ships immediately if something of extraordinary importance occurred at the Congress. "In cases that might occur of advising Your Excellency about something very important and in major secrecy," Miralles melodramatically wrote, "I will avail myself of the protection of signing my letters with the fictitious name Pedro Payas."[87]

Miralles set sail from Havana in late December, 1777, ostensibly bound for Cádiz aboard the merchant vessel *Nuestra Señora del Carmen*. According to plan, the captain noticed that the ship had begun to take on water. He therefore made for Charleston and the closest repair yard. The Spaniards could not cross the bar for several days, because of contrary winds, so an American official came on board and arranged for the ship to enter port when the weather cleared. The Spaniards finally landed on December 12, and Miralles paid an immediate courtesy call on Edward Rutledge, president of the South Carolina Assembly. Rutledge received the Spaniard cordially and offered complete cooperation in securing repairs for the damaged vessel.[88]

During the following days, Miralles also met other "principal citizens" of Charleston, all of whom welcomed him into their homes for dinners and

85. Samuel Flagg Bemis, *The Hussey-Cumberland Mission and American Independence: An Essay in the Diplomacy of the American Revolution* (1931; rpr. Gloucester, Mass., 1968), 6.
86. Bemis, *The Diplomacy of the American Revolution*, 92–98.
87. Juan de Miralles to J. de Gálvez, December 16, 1777, Biblioteca Nacional, Madrid, Ms. 17616. Efforts to locate any correspondence bearing this signature have been unsuccessful.
88. Miralles to Navarro, January 21, 1778, no. 1, AGI, Cuba 1281.

smokers. He told his new American acquaintances that he had decided to stay in the United States and open a flour exporting business. He made quite an event of writing the captain general in Cuba that he was abandoning earlier efforts to secure the Asiento contract. The immense profits, he noted, that could come from trading with the "extended and rich provinces" of the United States had changed his mind. Miralles announced plans to petition the Continental Congress for permission to begin an export trade to Cuba. In that regard, he asked Navarro to send him letters of recommendation seeking the "protection of the Honorable Don George Washington and the *señores* of the Congress."[89]

Miralles continued to make friends after he had sent his letter to Havana by a vessel he chartered for the purpose. A devastating fire swept through the commercial center of Charleston shortly after his arrival, with over five hundred buildings and houses suffering heavy damage, and the loss of much personal and government property.[90] Miralles lent the state of South Carolina some twenty thousand Spanish milled dollars for public relief, food, and medicines.[91] His assistance considerably eased his efforts to ingratiate himself with Charlestonians and ended any difficulties he might have met from the Americans about his decision to remain in North America.

The *Nuestra Señora del Carmen* had been repaired by the end of January, 1778. It resumed its voyage to Spain, leaving Miralles behind.[92] He made ready to depart for the Continental Congress, which was meeting at York, Pennsylvania, because the British had captured Philadelphia. Shortly before setting out, he made a formal call on Rawlins Lowndes, the governor of South Carolina, to inquire about the course of the revolt and the political situation in the United States. The governor shared with him his assessments of the military situation in the South. He also complained to the Spaniard about Tory activity in the backcountry of the Carolinas and Georgia. The British in East and West Florida, the American remarked, provided these persons with safe haven and refuge, thereby complicating problems of

---

89. *Ibid.*

90. Edward McCrady, *The History of South Carolina in the Revolution, 1775–1780* (New York, 1901), 232.

91. Miralles to J. de Gálvez, February 13, 1778, Miralles to Navarro, January 21, 1778, both AGI, Cuba 1281. This loan was repaid by the Congress in the name of the state of South Carolina in the spring of 1779. See "Resolution of the Treasury Office, April 15, 1779" (Papers of the Continental Congress, item 136, III, 244, National Archives).

92. Miralles to J. de Gálvez, February 13, 1778, AGI, Cuba 1281.

defense for the Americans. Lowndes also asked Miralles to carry several letters northward, including a long report to the president of the Continental Congress detailing the military situation along the border between Georgia and Florida.[93]

The governor made arrangements for Miralles to travel with several Carolinians who were also departing for York by the post road. Miralles traveled north in the company of several returning delegates to Congress, including John Mathews, with whom Miralles developed a strong and genuine friendship. Miralles wrote the captain general to report his good fortune and note that his trip would probably take about thirty days.[94] By May, Miralles could write the captain general that he had formed friendships with six members of the Continental Congress and that they, he hoped, would introduce him to the rest of the membership in Pennsylvania.[95] The most fruitful and productive days of Miralles' sojourn in North America lay at the end of his journey north.

93. Rawlins Lowndes to Henry Laurens, April 13, 1778, in Papers of the Continental Congress, item 72, 445–48, National Archives.
94. Miralles to Navarro, March 16, 1778, no. 2, AGI, Cuba 1281. John Mathews had shortly before been elected to the Continental Congress from South Carolina. Only thirty-four years of age, he had already had a varied career. In 1760, he had been appointed an ensign in the Royal Navy. Four years later, he became a barrister by admission to the Middle Temple, in London. In 1772, he was elected to the South Carolina colonial assembly, and from 1776 to 1778, after the start of the Revolution, he had served as its speaker. *See Senate Documents,* 100th Cong., 2nd Sess., No. 34, *Biographical Directory of the United States Congress, 1774–1989,* 1436.
95. Miralles to Navarro, May 13, 1778, no. 7, AGI, Cuba 1281.

PART TWO

Spanish Belligerency

Spain remained officially neutral from the time of Lexington and Concord until the summer of 1779. It had numerous reasons for its neutrality, ranging from a latent distrust of the Americans—who, after all, were rebelling against the concept of monarchy—to a fear of angering Great Britain to the point of provoking a British attack against its Latin American colonies. Nevertheless, the Spanish government had accelerated the amount of material support sent to the Americans, and by 1779, Spain had become an unofficial, de facto ally with the United States in the cause against Great Britain. When Spain finally declared war against Great Britain in the summer of that year, it nonetheless refused to enter into formal alliance with, or recognize the independence of, the young republic. The Spanish king and his advisers feared to grant recognition because they felt confident that the United States would eventually replace Great Britain as Spain's territorial and commercial rival in North America.

In late August, 1779, Bernardo de Gálvez began a series of campaigns that would win for Spain most of the lower Mississippi Valley and all of the northern coast of the Gulf of Mexico. He captured control of the British settlements at Manchac, Baton Rouge, and Natchez, thus clearing Great Britain from the Mississippi. In 1780, he commanded a victorious army that took Mobile, and the year following, he conquered Pensacola. The Spanish war against England also involved campaigning in Central America, where British logwood cutters had long dominated the Mosquito Coast. Spanish armies commanded by Matias de Gálvez, father of the Louisiana governor, successfully drove the English occupiers from Belize and Roatán in 1779, although Spain was not able to clear the Mosquito Coast itself of British interlopers. The British soon afterward made a counterattack against Spain's holdings in the interior of present-day Nicaragua; they also captured the stronghold at Omoa. Nonetheless, by 1782 Matias de Gálvez had expelled his British adversaries from these locations.

Spain's military actions in the West Indies also achieved mixed results during 1779 and the early 1780s. Jamaica was an important war goal that Spain never realized. Bernardo de Gálvez, fresh from his victory at Pensacola, organized a major expedition against Kingston, but complications prevented his carrying it out. Field Marshal Juan María de Cagigal engineered a bloodless victory for Spain when his army invaded New Providence Island, in the Bahamas. In early May, 1782, Cagigal signed a capitulation by which the British turned over to Spain all the Bahama Islands.

Spain's participation in the wars of the Revolution as a belligerent officially not allied with the United States altered the way in which it had previously dealt with the American leadership. Since Spain had to coordinate its own war goals with the actions of the Continental Congress, Spanish observation of the Revolution centered increasingly on that body. Inasmuch as decisions by the American leaders had potentially a great impact on Spain's direct concerns as a belligerent, the activity of Spain's observer in Philadelphia took on a decidedly diplomatic cast after 1779. He became an unofficial point of contact between the governments of the United States and Spain. The observers the captain general employed elsewhere diminished in importance as Spanish interests focused on the Continental Congress. By 1780, almost all of them had been withdrawn by the captain general, because the quantity and quality of information from Philadelphia made their continued service increasingly unnecessary.

The success of Juan de Miralles as the first permanent Spanish observer in Philadelphia provided for opening structured, yet unofficial, relations between Spain and the Continental Congress. Even though he continued to provide an impressive amount of information about the revolt, he gradually assumed diplomatic and consular responsibilities as well. Francisco Rendon, Miralles' successor as the Spanish observer at the Congress, preserved much of the diplomatic role his predecessor had established there. What the two men did while serving as observers for the captain general of Cuba constituted the beginning of diplomatic and commercial relations between the United States and Spain.

5

Juan de Miralles, Observer in Philadelphia
1778–1779

Juan de Miralles found his trip northward from Charleston to be a highly convivial and agreeable journey. He traveled in style, with five mounts so that his horse would always be fresh. Upon arriving in Edenton, North Carolina, he was introduced by his companions to another member of the Continental Congress, Francis Lewis, who joined them.[1] Miralles, much to his satisfaction, learned that Lewis had authorization from Congress to secure foodstuffs for the Continental army. Sensing that the goodwill of such a figure might well become useful, the Spanish observer showed Lewis great courtesy and won his friendship.[2] Miralles soon enough found the relationship to his advantage. When he received word that his former vessel, the *Nuestra Señora del Carmen,* had been captured by an American privateer after departing from Charleston, Lewis interceded and got the ship released to its Cuban owners.[3]

Exciting news arrived in Edenton as Miralles and his party passed through: word of the French treaty recognizing the independence of the

---

1. Miralles to Navarro, May 13, 1778, no. 7, AGI, Cuba 1281. Lewis served as a delegate to the Continental Congress from New York from 1774 to 1779. A native of Wales, he came to North America in 1735, establishing merchant houses in New York and Philadelphia during the Seven Years' War. He secured a royal contract to supply clothes to the British army. He was taken prisoner at Oswego and interned in France. Upon his return to America, he became outspoken in opposition to the new imperial policy and later signed the Declaration of Independence. See *Senate Documents,* 100th Cong., 2nd Sess., No. 34, 1368–69.
2. Miralles to Navarro, May 13, 1778, no. 7, AGI, Cuba 1281.
3. Francis Lewis to John Lydon, June 12, 1778, in *Letters of Delegates to Congress,* ed. Smith, X, 82.

United States. In celebration, the town sponsored a large banquet that the officers and crew of a French vessel in port attended as guests of honor. Miralles, who received an invitation as an honored guest, sat at the head table to the right of his new friend Francis Lewis, the master of ceremonies. The assembled revelers celebrated with a succession of thirteen toasts, each accompanied by a cannonade fired outside the hall. Miralles offered the seventh toast in honor of King Charles of Spain. At the banquet, the Spanish observer secured a public copy of Franklin's letter to the president of the Congress outlining the treaty with the French. He transcribed it for the captain general and arranged for the copy he had made to be carried to Cap Français aboard the French ship when it departed.[4]

Miralles and his companions shortly thereafter resumed their trip. Arriving at Williamsburg, Miralles talked at length with the governor of Virginia, Patrick Henry, who entertained him with a formal dinner in the Governor's Palace.[5] The Virginia governor, hoping that Spain would declare war on England and join the alliance with France, proposed a daring plan to Miralles, which the observer passed on at once to the captain general: "The Governor intimated to me the facility of taking the Mississippi provinces (Mobile and Pensacola which France and Spain ceded to England). . . . The Americans might go down to Nichatoes [Natchez] and others be sent if necessary to join with the garrison at New Orleans (whose governor would command the expedition). In addition the province of Saint Augustine and Florida could be taken with some of the troops from Havana, and those from Georgia and South Carolina."[6] After Miralles' meeting with Henry, the House of Burgesses received the Spaniard in official session with a pomp and fanfare befitting an accredited envoy.

All the way to Yorktown and Baltimore, Miralles was the center of attention in the most fashionable homes, where he met the flower of rebel leadership. Miralles and his companions arrived at York on June 9, 1778. They found the town in an uproar, since news had just arrived of the British army's evacuation of Philadelphia. Everyone involved with Congress was making preparations for a return to Philadelphia, and Miralles went along.

4. Miralles to Navarro, May 16, 1778, Miralles to Monsieur Gautier, May 16, 1778, both AGI, Cuba 1281.
5. Herminio Portell Vilá, *Historia de Cuba en sus relaciones con los Estados Unidos y España* (4 vols.; Havana, 1938), I, 81; Miralles to J. de Gálvez, June 6, 1778, AGI, Cuba 1281.
6. "Extracto de noticias comunicadas por Don Juan de Miralles desde su salida de Charleston para York Town lugar del Congreso Americano done llego a 9 de junio de 1778," September 10, 1778, Havana, AGI, Cuba 1281.

Miralles' journey from Charleston had afforded him the leisurely opportunity to gauge the depth and popularity of colonial resistance against England while gaining familiarity with conditions in North America. Everywhere, the motives for his trip became a topic of discussion among the Americans he met. Some of them hoped his proposed residence in the colonies might be an unofficial sign of Spanish inclinations to enter the war. Miralles nonetheless continued publicly to insist upon his chance arrival at Charleston as the reason for being in the colonies.[7] He attempted, however, to maintain a delicate balance between his repeated protestations of being merely a merchant thrown by fate on the Atlantic Coast and his obvious appearance as a well-connected Spaniard with a pronounced interest in the military, political, and diplomatic events of the Revolution.[8] Whatever the public explanation for his presence in the colonies during 1778, many colonial leaders treated Miralles with a respect more appropriate an official diplomatic representative. The favorable receptions came no doubt as part of an American desire for a treaty of amity and commerce with Spain. During the spring of 1778, some members of Congress in fact suspected that such a treaty had already been signed in Europe, with the news of its negotiation retarded in arriving in America.[9]

Miralles had a clear grasp of his duties as an observer for the captain general of Cuba, whatever confusion existed about the nature of his mission among his hosts. He faithfully recorded information and sent it on in an effort to comply exactly with his instructions. One rather ambiguous clause in his instructions, however, eventually justified in his mind playing a more active diplomatic role with the American leadership. Floridablanca had suggested to the minister of the Indies that the observer going to Congress should do whatever he deemed necessary to persuade the Americans to seek the international protection of France and Spain. Congressional actions in

7. Herminio Portell Vilá, *Los "otros extranjeros" en la revolución norteamericana* (Miami, 1978), 58–61.

8. Most historians of the Revolution have concentrated on Miralles' diplomatic efforts, which became more intense in 1779. Several historians have highlighted his diplomacy to the point of ignoring his primary reason for being in Philadelphia, namely to provide strategic intelligence. Some have taken at face value the explanations he gave for his arrival in North America. See Richard B. Morris, *The Peacemakers: The Great Powers and American Independence* (New York, 1965), 220–21; Bemis, *The Diplomacy of the American Revolution*, 88; Helen M. McCadden, "Juan de Miralles and the American Revolution," *The Americas*, XXIX (1973), 63–64; and Smith, ed., *Letters of Delegates to Congress*, X, 82*n*.

9. Andrew Adams to Oliver Wolcott, August 28, 1778, in *Letters of the Members of the Continental Congress*, ed. Edmund Cody Burnett (8 vols.; Washington D.C., 1921–36), III, 390.

a contrary sense, the minister warned, would be risky to Spain and might produce grave consequences.[10] Subsequently reflected in the formal instructions from the captain general, this charge provided Miralles with some authorization to concern himself with diplomatic matters that had a bearing on relations between the United States and Spain.

Miralles arrived in Philadelphia during late June, as the American Congress returned to the city on the heels of the departing British army. He rented modest accommodations at 242 South Third Street and set about making the acquaintance of key people in the Congressional leadership.[11] Printers, members of Congress, businessmen, and social leaders in the Pennsylvania capital became particular objects of his efforts to build a circle of contacts. Robert Morris was Miralles' sponsor and chief promoter in Philadelphia society, since the two already knew each other. As the factor in Philadelphia for the Cuban Asiento firm of Aguirre, Aristegui, and Company, Morris had a long history of commercial ventures with Miralles dating back to the British occupation of Havana in 1762.[12] Their mercantile collaboration continued through the period of Miralles' residence in Philadelphia. For example, Morris and Miralles—along with Silas Deane and the lawyer James Wilson—soon became involved in a venture to supply ship masts to the French navy.[13] Morris also became Miralles' chief investment partner in building a lucrative trade between American ports and Havana.

The American financier's friendship with Miralles favored the observer with numerous opportunities to meet persons of rank in Philadelphia. The artist Charles Willson Peale became one of the Spaniard's companions and friends. Miralles provided the artist with money, enjoyed serving as a patron, and bought a number of his paintings. In particular, a portrait of George Washington captured the Spaniard's fancy and became a special favorite. Miralles commissioned Peale to make numerous copies of it for King Charles, members of the Spanish court, and various administrators in the

---

10. Miguel Gomez del Campillo, *Relaciones diplomáticas entre España y los Estados Unidos, segun documentos del Archivo Histórico Nacional* (2 vols.; Madrid, 1944), I, xi.

11. Portell Vilá, *Los "otros,"* 63–64.

12. Peggy Liss, *Atlantic Empires: The Network of Trade and Revolution, 1713–1826* (Baltimore, 1983), 113. At least initially, it is unlikely that Morris knew of Miralles' instruction to send intelligence to his superiors in Cuba and Spain. Although the American financier probably came to suspect surveillance, the primary relationship between the two merchants rested on mutual commercial interests.

13. Helen Augur, *The Secret War of Independence* (1955; rpr. Westport, Conn., 1967), 313.

Indies. During 1779 alone, Miralles sent at least one dozen copies of the Peale portrait to Havana and Madrid.[14] In return, Peale obviously enjoyed Miralles' company. The artist lived in a grand Philadelphia mansion, and Miralles was frequently among the company assembled there on social occasions. Indeed, Peale gave Miralles free reign of the house for his own personal entertaining, since the rented rooms on Third Street did not lend themselves to elegant functions.[15]

The Spaniard's popularity rested in large measure on his cordial manners and pleasing personality. Many of the Americans who met him remarked on his pleasant disposition, social grace, and ability to make friends. Henry Laurens called him a "worthy Old Castilian" and commented, "I have much of his company."[16] Hosts throughout Philadelphia welcomed him to their tables and into their salons. The sense of humor he displayed explained in part the feelings of fellowship shared by those who befriended him. One evening after dining in the company of several members of Congress and their wives, he engaged his male colleagues in a sporting bet. Once the ladies had retired to their sherry, he wagered Conrad Alexandre Gérard, the French ambassador, that Sarah Livingston, the wife of John Jay, had a naturally blushing complexion and did not wear cosmetics. Gérard took the gambit, claiming that she did. Once the stakes had been set, Jay agreeably settled the matter, with Miralles winning, much to the merriment of the assembly.[17]

Miralles also gained a reputation as a consummate host. He specialized in the intimate dinner party, drawing to his sideboard some of the best company of the town. George Washington and his staff officers, Robert Livingston, John Jay, John and Henry Laurens, Joseph Reed, and dozens of others among the American leadership were guests at his functions.[18] He also dispensed gifts and favors liberally, not so much to buy influence as to show affection for those who befriended him. After meeting Martha Wash-

14. Miralles to Navarro, March 29, 1779, no. 28, July 22, 1779, no. 8, October 1, 1779, no. 2, all AGI, Cuba 1281.

15. Portell Vilá, *Los "otros,"* 67–68. Miralles eventually leased more commodious quarters, which after his death became the Philadelphia residence of Benedict Arnold. See Douglas Southall Freeman, *George Washington: A Biography* (7 vols.; New York, 1948–57), V, 157*n*.

16. Laurens to John Laurens, July 26, 1778, in *Letters of Delegates to Congress,* ed. Smith, X, 356.

17. McCadden, "Juan de Miralles and the American Revolution," 362.

18. Diary of Samuel Holden, December 31, 1778, September 2, December 31, 1779, in *Letters,* ed. Burnett, III, 554, 550.

ington and Mrs. Nathanael Greene, he sent each a hamper of table delicacies including chocolate, sugar, guava jelly, and sweetmeats. He promised George Washington two fine Spanish mules for Mount Vernon, a gesture the general greatly appreciated.[19]

As Miralles settled into life at Philadelphia, he established a working relationship with Gérard, the French minister to the Congress. Gérard had evinced surprise at finding Miralles residing in the city; he wrote Vergennes shortly after arriving that the Spanish court might have someone functioning as an unofficial agent in the American capital. Upon discreet investigation, the French envoy learned that Miralles had become close to various members of Congress and seemed to be lobbying for Spanish interests. While awaiting instructions from Paris regarding the unexpected development, he decided to seek out Miralles at the first convenient opportunity in order to ascertain if the Spaniard represented the government of Spain and, if so, what his instructions might be. Meantime, the French envoy worried that he would have to be especially careful in dealing with the Americans on matters that might affect Spanish interests.[20]

Gérard's meeting with Miralles took place before a reply to the ambassador's report to Vergennes arrived from Paris. The French envoy dealt cautiously with the Spaniard and refrained from asking directly what he wanted to know. Miralles, for his part, was less than candid. He did not mention anything relating to his commission as an observer. Instead, he merely repeated the reasons he had already purveyed for being in Philadelphia, namely, to start a flour trading operation. He did intimate, however, that he had contact with important figures in Spain, and he professed Spain's goodwill and its desire to cooperate with France. Miralles clouded the ambassador's perception of his position in Philadelphia by launching into a discussion that went far beyond matters of commerce. He proposed to Gérard that France conquer Canada while Spain took from the British all of the territory along the Gulf of Mexico lost in the treaties of 1763. He also told the Frenchman that he favored a joint Spanish and American military expedition against Florida, although his efforts to promote this with Congress had until then been fruitless.[21]

---

19. McCadden, "Juan de Miralles and the American Revolution," 366.
20. Conrad Alexandre Gérard to Compte de Vergennes, July 16, 1778, in *Despatches and Instructions of Conrad Alexandre Gérard, 1778–1780,* ed. John J. Meng (Baltimore, 1939), 159.
21. Gérard to Vergennes, July 25, 1778, in *Despatches of Gérard,* ed. Meng, 185; Michael A. Otero, "The American Mission of Diego de Gardoqui, 1785–1789" (Ph.D. dissertation, Uni-

The French envoy learned from this conversation that Miralles harbored a rather hostile view of American territorial designs on the lands bordering Spanish Louisiana. Miralles feared that Spain would not be able to maintain control over the Gulf of Mexico and the northern Caribbean in the face of a growing United States influence in the region. He told Gérard that he had therefore made it his chief concern to urge Congress to grant the Floridas to Spain, to renounce the right of navigation on the Mississippi, and to cede the lands west of the Appalachian Mountains to the Spanish king. He confided in Gérard that he disagreed with the desires of some Americans to possess western lands along the Mississippi River; rather, he felt that the boundary of Louisiana should extend to the north and east of Natchez, so as to include much of the territory south of the Tennessee River.

Gérard's conference with Miralles did not clarify the French envoy's understanding of the capacity in which the Spaniard was serving in Philadelphia. The Frenchman therefore decided to treat Miralles with care and circumspection in case he had official standing. Gérard later reported to Vergennes that Miralles had a clear grasp of the Spanish court's major concerns about the Revolution and acted in concert with his king's interests.[22] The French envoy wrote Paris that in the absence of instructions to the contrary, he would cooperate with Miralles and work closely with him in coordinating matters of mutual interest.

The conference establishes that the Spanish observer had—at least in his own mind—diplomatic objectives and purposes far beyond his information-gathering duties. For the historian, that raises the question whether Miralles exceeded his instructions by taking stands on diplomatic matters when he clearly had no official designation as a Spanish envoy. It appears that, at least in his conversation with Gérard, Miralles saw the functions of being an observer and being an unofficial envoy as coequal responsibilities. There are three plausible explanations for his embarking upon a self-appointed career as diplomat in Philadelphia. First, as a member by marriage of the Elegio de la Puente family in Cuba, he strongly desired that

versity of California at Los Angeles, 1948), 19–20; William E. O'Donnell, *The Chevalier de La Luzerne, French Minister to the United States, 1779–1784* (Bruges, 1938), 34–36; Miralles to Navarro, August 13, 1778, AGI, Cuba 1281. For a published English-language translation of this letter, see Miralles to J. de Gálvez, December 28, 1778, in *Letters of Delegates to Congress,* ed. Smith, XI, 381*n*–383*n*.

22. Gérard to Vergennes, July 25, 1778, in *Despatches of Gérard,* ed. Meng, 185; Abernethy, *Western Lands and the American Revolution,* 203.

Spain regain control over Florida. He had long traded with Florida from his commercial base in Havana, and he played an active role in the circle of former Saint Augustine residents who lobbied for the reassertion of Spain's ownership of the area.[23] Second, it is likely that he and Navarro had informally discussed the possibility of his eventually playing a diplomatic role as the observer at Congress. Floridablanca and José de Gálvez had envisioned such a possibility from the very inception of their plan to send observers to North America. Indeed, when news of Miralles' diplomatic endeavors filtered back to Madrid through Gérard's dispatches, the Spanish foreign minister indicated to Vergennes that the activities met with unofficial approval at the Spanish court. Third, the Americans persisted in treating Miralles with the respect and consideration normally afforded a diplomatic representative. If Miralles seemed excessive and overzealous in pursuing diplomatic possibilities, he can be faulted seriously only because he began doing so prematurely according to the plans of the Madrid ministries.

The arrival in Philadelphia of Captain General Navarro's letters of recommendation concerning Miralles did not resolve the questions regarding the Spaniard's position. Navarro sent two letters, one to the Congress and the other to General Washington in his capacity as commander of the Continental army. The captain general perpetuated the fiction that Miralles had reached North America as a merchant en route to Spain. Since chance had caused the Spaniard's deposit in Charleston, Navarro explained, he hoped that the members of Congress and the officers of the army would offer Miralles their protection. Any assistance they tendered would be greatly appreciated in Havana. Navarro specifically refrained from offering any hint of official sanction for Miralles. Instead, he wrote with some flourish:

Disagreeable contrarities obliged Don Juan de Miralles to put into your Continent, where he informs me he was most graciously and in the most Polite manner received and treated by the Governor of Charlestown, Grateful for this favour and considering the criticalness of the times and how disagreeable his Passage had proved he has resolved to wait some time in that Country, then return to this Island from whence he may proceed with more security and convenience to Spain, in the mean time he desires I would recommend him to your Illustrious Body, to which I am induced, his being an Inhabitant of the City, distinguished by his personal qualification, hon-

---

23. See "Manifesto de descubrimiento, conquisto, y posesión de las provincias de Florida . . . ," May 4, 1778, AGI, Santo Domingo 1598-A. This document presents historical arguments aimed at persuading the court that the Floridas should be under Spanish control. See also Wright, *Florida in the American Revolution*, 68.

orable Proceedings, and Opulent circumstance, which has merited my particular affection, and I am certain he will gratefully acknowledge any favors that may be conferred upon him.[24]

Miralles personally presented the letter for Congress to its President, Henry Laurens, and engaged the public interpreter to make the certified translation of it into English. Laurens treated the letter as an official communication from the Spanish government, referring it to the committee dealing with foreign affairs for the framing of a formal reply.[25] In his response, Laurens noted that he had presented the captain general's letter to the Congress and thanked him for the affection professed for Miralles. The American leader reported that Miralles had exhibited excellent deportment during his stay in Philadelphia and appeared to be a person of great merit. He also referred to the need for close relations between the United States and Spain, expressing in fact a hope for a "friendly intercourse" between the two nations.[26]

Laurens thereafter dealt with the observer as if he had an official relationship to the Spanish government, although the American sometimes found humor in the ambiguity of Miralles' position. One evening during a formal dinner at Laurens' home, for example, the American engaged Miralles in conversation about the eventual disposition of East Florida in the event that the province was taken from the British. Laurens recounted: "A venerable Don who lately din'd with me let the Cat a little further out—speaking of the late abortive expedition against St. Augustine, a Gentleman observ'd in French that East Florida would be a great acquisition to South Carolina and Georgia, my good friend Don Juan, either unwarily or supposing I did not understand, replied with much gravity, 'and also for Spain.' I drank a glass of ale with the Don."[27] Washington treated Miralles with the same circumspection as Laurens did. The general's first opportunity to meet the Spaniard came soon after Miralles' arrival in Philadelphia, when, during a Christmas visit Washington made to the city, Miralles made a formal call on him for the purpose of presenting Navarro's letter of recommendation.

24. Navarro to the Congress, March 11, 1778, AGI, Cuba 1301. The American translation is in Papers of the Continental Congress, item 78, XIV, 47, National Archives.
25. Miralles to Navarro, July 24, 1778, AGI, Cuba 1281.
26. Henry Laurens to the captain general and governor of Havana, October 27, 1778, in *Letters of Delegates to Congress,* ed. Smith, XI, 132. See also Papers of the Continental Congress, item 13, II, 135, National Archives.
27. Laurens to William Livingston, August 21, 1778, in *Letters of Delegates to Congress,* ed. Smith, X, 486.

Washington received him courteously and responded by returning a visit to Miralles' lodgings the following day. The Spaniard then organized a New Year's Eve banquet in Washington's honor, inviting some seventy guests to fete the American commander and his wife. Since that affair conflicted with an already scheduled function of the General Society of Dames, a local ladies' organization, the Spanish merchant combined the two events into a gala evening that the gazettes reported favorably as a superior event of the holiday season.[28]

General Washington seemed pleased with the Spaniard's attentions and responded with gratitude. He wrote Captain General Navarro and complimented Miralles' behavior, expressing appreciation for the cordiality with which he had been treated. Proclaiming the "most respectful" sentiments for Spain and the Spanish people, Washington voiced the hope that he might someday be of service to the captain general.[29] Washington thereafter treated Miralles as if he had official standing before the government of the United States. When the general asked Gérard, the French ambassador, to visit the Continental army headquarters at Morristown soon after the holiday season, a similar invitation went to Miralles. The observer enjoyed this visit tremendously and felt that it symbolized the success his mission had met. He noted with some satisfaction that Washington's treatment of him seemed calculated to recognize a person of equal status with the French envoy and that the Americans lost no chance to impress him and Gérard during the visit. An escort of cavalry accompanied the two men as they departed Philadelphia. Upon crossing the Delaware River into New Jersey, they were met by a mounted troop from Washington's camp and formally convoyed to the outskirts of the bivouac area. There, a ceremonial platoon commanded by the Baron de Kalb and a company of dragoons brought them the final distance to their lodgings. The Americans staged a formal review with some three thousand men in muster, followed by a mock battle, as an entertainment to honor the visitors. After that spectacle, the guests adjourned for a banquet, with Martha Washington as hostess. Miralles found the most satisfactory touch of his three-day visit to be that the general had ordered the names of Spaniards—including himself, King Charles, Na-

---

28. Miralles to Navarro, February 15, 1779, AGI, Cuba 1281; Herminio Portell Vilá, *Juan de Miralles, un habanero amigo de Jorge Washington* (Havana, 1947), 17.

29. John C. Fitzpatrick, ed., *The Writings of George Washington, from the Original Manuscript Sources, 1745–1799* (39 vols.; Washington, D.C., 1931–44), XIV, 192.

varro, and Aranda—to be used as signs and countersigns by the sentries guarding the encampment.[30]

Miralles during his first months in Pennsylvania did not limit his activities to meeting prominent Americans and finding a place for himself in the shadow of the American Congress. He was busy as well meeting the primary goals of his mission, namely, providing news and information. He realized that secure lines of regular communication had to be arranged before he could dispatch reports to Cuba and Spain. It was also imperative that he have complete control over the lines of communication, since his letters might contain items of a candid and, at times, confidential nature. Miralles' long experience as a merchant trading with the Atlantic Coast placed him in a favorable position to create the communication network he needed. He spent much time and effort building a profitable and legitimate trade between Philadelphia and Cuba to serve as his cover and means of contact.

Miralles solicited various American merchants as partners in the commerce he was building, and all of them appear to have been unaware of his observation role. Miralles offered them something that had previously been hard, if not impossible, for American merchants to secure: entry permits for legal trade with Havana. George Abbot Hall, of Charleston, became the first of several merchants to go into partnership with Miralles. While still in Charleston, Miralles had promised Hall that he would be allowed to send foodstuffs into Cuba. As an inducement, Miralles underwrote part of the purchase price of a ship along with its first cargo of rice. Hall and Miralles engaged the services of a shipmaster, who took the job under the impression that the Spanish merchant had been sent to South Carolina expressly for the purpose of purchasing supplies for the Havana garrison. The purchased vessel, the *Saint Anthony,* arrived at Havana for the first time during early 1778 with a cargo of rice and a sealed packet of letters for the captain general. It returned loaded with sugar, tobacco, and tropical fruits, and its master carried a dispatch box for Miralles that included the letters of recommendation for Congress and General Washington.[31] Hall continued the trade

---

30. Miralles to Navarro, May 4, 1779, AGI, Cuba 1281; Miralles to J. de Gálvez, March 10, 1779, AGI, Indiferente General 1606; McCadden, "Juan de Miralles and the American Revolution," 365.

31. Miralles to Navarro, March 16, 1778, no. 2, March 24, 1778, no. 3, both AGI, Cuba 1281; "Conocimiento de Don Antonio Pueyo," *ibid.,* 1291; Miralles to J. de Gálvez, December 7, 1779, AGI, Santo Domingo 2598.

after Miralles' departure for Pennsylvania, and he served as a contact point in the Spaniard's line of communication until Charleston fell to the British in 1780.[32]

Miralles entered into a similar partnership with Robert Morris, whose merchant house had long been sending correspondents throughout Latin America in an effort to tap the Indies trade. Where possible, Morris' representatives had conducted legal trade within the confines of the Spanish commercial system. More often than not, however, his corresponding merchants engaged in contrabanding and illegal commerce when legitimate ways could not be found to outflank Spain's mercantile restrictions. So Morris eagerly consented to ventures with Miralles, and he purchased several boats especially for the new trade. The first of them, the *Greyhound,* represented a joint undertaking for the two men. Morris owned half the vessel while Miralles provided the remainder of the funds to make the ship ready for the Havana trade. They hired an American, Wolman Sutton, as captain and engaged the services of a Cuban, José Oller, as cargo master.[33] Morris also rented other boats owned by his firm to Miralles, including the *Buckskin,* the *Ranger,* and the *Swan.* The Spaniard remained in the background during the planning and execution of the voyages, although he made no secret of his partnership with Morris. The Philadelphia merchant, in fact, acknowledged Miralles' support by giving one ship the rather imaginative name of *Don Miralleson* in honor of his partner's son. Morris usually made all the arrangements for a voyage, prepared the ship, oversaw consignment of the cargo, and disposed of the goods carried on the return trip. Miralles handled the financial part of the transactions. He generally provided the money for outfitting the ship, hiring its crew, and purchasing the cargo.[34] The two merchants split the profits, though in Miralles' case the accounting became complicated because some of the funds he used came

---

32. After the British capture of the city, the English arrested Hall along with several dozen other American sympathizers and imprisoned them at Saint Augustine until the end of the war. See McCrady, *South Carolina in the Revolution,* 857.

33. Oller had been a pilot on the *Nuestra Señora del Carmen,* which had brought Miralles to Charleston. A British ship on blockade duty stopped this vessel and took it as a prize after it left South Carolina. Some of the crew eventually made their way to Philadelphia, where Miralles employed them in the Havana trade. See Miralles to Navarro, October 24, 1778, no. 16, AGI, Cuba 1281.

34. For examples of these arrangements, see Miralles to Navarro, October 24, 1778, no. 16, March 12, 1779, March 28, 1779, no. 27, November 11, 1779, no. 47, all AGI, Cuba 1281; and Miralles to J. de Gálvez, November 18, 1779, AGI, Santo Domingo 2598.

from his personal resources while others secretly belonged to the Spanish treasury in Havana.[35] The profits Miralles earned usually remained in Havana in the hands of his wife, María Elegio de la Puente, who claimed after the Revolution that the Philadelphia trade had produced a deficit and had occasioned a net loss for her family.[36]

Morris, on the other hand, made huge profits in his dealings with Miralles. He shipped large quantities of dried beef and pork, lard, soap, and fish to Havana, where royal officials either bought it for use by the local garrison or supervised its sale to the public. The American ships brought return cargoes of sugar, rum, honey, fruit, and tobacco. They imported military supplies as well when such items could be purchased on the Cuban market.[37] Miralles and Morris even dispatched ships directly to Spain. A congressional policy prohibiting the export of flour during much of 1778, however, hampered their efforts to build a substantial trade between Havana and Philadelphia, since Spain needed flour more than any other commodity for feeding the Cuban garrisons. In September, 1779, the Congress finally permitted the exportation of flour from the United States, since that year's crops provided more than enough for home consumption. Miralles and Morris thereafter dealt almost exclusively in flour shipments.[38]

Miralles realized the importance of building a diverse commercial network in order to provide him with multiple avenues of communication to his superiors. Consequently, he expanded his ventures to include partnerships with other American merchants, including George Mead, who also participated in the Philadelphia-Havana trade.[39] Many of the ships engaged in this commerce did not sail directly between Pennsylvania and Cuba. Instead, Miralles split their voyages, sending them to Puerto Rico, Martinique, New Orleans, and other ports to avoid the appearance of a direct and exclusive routing. Many of Miralles' partners found that acceptable, since the voyages with ports en route provided additional opportunities for

35. "Instancia de Maria Josefa de Miralles," November 3, 1785, AGI, Santo Domingo 2598.
36. See "Minuta número 4," n.d., AGI, Cuba 1291.
37. Miralles to J. de Gálvez, September 18, 1779, AGI, Santo Domingo 2598; J. de Gálvez to Miralles, October 24, 1779, royal order, AGI, Indiferente General 1606.
38. Miralles to J. de Gálvez, May 1, 1780, no. 110, Miralles to Navarro, September 29, 1779, both AGI, Cuba 1291.
39. Miralles to J. de Gálvez, November 9, 1779, Miralles to the governor of Puerto Rico, November 9, 1779, March 4, 1780, Miralles to J. de Gálvez, February 12, 1780, all AGI, Santo Domingo 2598.

trade. Two of Miralles' Asiento correspondents in Saint Eustatius, Bernard and Jacques Texier, routinely received sealed letters from the observer, with instructions to send them on to various Spanish officials. Moreover, Miralles sometimes sent packets of letters on regular merchantmen sailing from Philadelphia and Baltimore. That aroused little suspicion, since it was the common way for merchants to post their normal correspondence. It proved to be the easiest way for Miralles to send letters to Spain, since Iberian ports admitted American merchant vessels.[40]

Miralles clearly viewed the trade he supported not as a commercial venture but primarily as a means of carrying sealed dispatches to his superiors. His commercial partners undoubtedly knew that the Spaniard used the vessels to carry a large volume of correspondence. Upon occasion, the ships experienced troubles that made necessary either the destruction or the hiding of dispatches passing between Miralles and the captain general. In July, 1779, a ship returning to Philadelphia with letters from the captain general fell prey to a British privateer. Its captain and crew went as prisoners to Savannah, where the captured vessel and cargo became a prize. After some two months the captain made his escape and arrived in Charleston, where he told an incredulous George Abbot Hall that the sealed correspondence packet had been saved and kept secret from the British. Hall, supposedly without examining the contents, sent the letters on to Miralles, who could read them even though almost all of them had experienced bad water damage. It was unlikely, however, that any of the Spaniard's commercial partners realized that he was part of a structured information-gathering effort operated by the Spanish government. Some of them naturally wondered if Miralles wrote about what they told him.[41] Robert Morris realized that Miralles used the flour trade as a means of transmitting his numerous dispatches. The American approved to the extent that he also used the packets to write congressional agents in the Caribbean and the Gulf of Mexico. "As vessels are lately permitted," he told Oliver Pollock, "to pass & repass between this & the Havana for the conveniency of Don Juan de Miralles we think that this will be the best mode of conveyance for our future correspondence."[42]

40. Navarro to Miralles, November 23, 1779, Miralles to J. de Gálvez, December 7, 1779, both *ibid.*

41. Oliver Ellsworth Diary, in *Letters,* ed. Burnett, V, 131.

42. Morris to Pollock, July 19, 1779, in *Letters of Delegates to Congress,* ed. Smith, XIII, 257. See also Morris to Francisco Rendon, July 11, 1781, in *The Papers of Robert Morris, 1781–1784,* ed. E. James Ferguson (7 vols. to date; Pittsburgh, 1973–), I, 272–73.

The commercial operations Miralles implemented proved to be an efficient means of communication with the captain general, who also maintained great secrecy. The arrangements for handling the Havana end of the operation had, of course, been made before Miralles departed for North America. Diego Navarro superintended the receipt of Miralles' letters, made indexes to them, provided monthly extracts, and sent copies of all of this on to Spain. The commercial aspects of the mission remained the concern of the captain general's secretary, Valle. He acted as chief factor for the growing trade between Philadelphia and Havana, supervised the ships when they arrived, checked the manifests, paid the expenses of the captains and crew, and oversaw the warehousing and sale of the cargoes. He also directed the purchase and loading of the return shipments and secured the passports and tax licenses that permitted the American vessels to call at Spanish ports. Valle eventually sent blank customs forms to Miralles in Philadelphia so that the legalities could be executed in advance. The Cuban official also kept in the royal treasury the secret accounts regarding Miralles' expenses in Philadelphia. All official expenditures by Miralles had to be reimbursed from funds controlled by the secretary. In actual practice, Miralles usually spent personal funds for many of his housing, entertaining, and official expenses, with the understanding that the government would reimburse him.[43]

Miralles probably did that because he engaged in commerce for his own profit during the entire time he resided in Philadelphia. Not only did he underwrite personal cargoes to and from the United States on the vessels in the trade (the personal cargoes were handled by his wife in Havana and not by Valle) but he also made investments in North America and lent money to a number of borrowers. Although he made little profit from his ventures, they certainly complicated his accounts. In fact, his family later claimed that much of his personal fortune dissipated in Philadelphia because of expenses that the Spanish government later refused to compensate. Long after his death, Miralles' wife and his brother-in-law, Juan José Elegio de la Puente, devoted time and effort to settling financial disputes with the royal treasury stemming from the agent's outlay in Philadelphia.[44]

---

43. AGI, Cuba 1283, is composed largely of the correspondence between Miralles and Valle, along with the Spanish government's accounts of the trading operation. In this *legajo*, see Miralles to Valle, March 14, 1778, Valle to Miralles, June 9, 1778, Miralles to Antonio del Valle, October 24, 1778, "Recibo de Andrew Young," January 23, 1779, and Miralles to Valle, March 14, November 12, July 18, 1779.

44. Portell Vilá, *Los "otros,"* 76; Gardoqui to the Marqués de Sonora, June 18, 1786, no. 1, AGI, Santo Domingo 2598.

Miralles had begun sending reports back to Captain General Navarro soon after arriving in Charleston. By the time he settled in Philadelphia, each succeeding month saw an increase in the information the observer furnished his superiors. Much was news about public events, congressional happenings, the American leadership, and military operations. He employed five general methods for collecting and verifying his reportage: a cultivating of numerous personal contacts with Americans; a reading of gazettes and other periodicals; an amassing of documents, letters, and papers relating to the revolt; an interviewing of ship captains, travelers, and anyone coming to Philadelphia from other parts of the continent; and an attending to rumors, public discussions, and general talk among the populace. Some of the courses he took—such as simply paying attention to current events as they happened—were open to anybody on the scene. Others, however, required a much greater amount of work, planning, and expertise. Miralles maintained an extensive network of friends, acquaintances, and social contacts. Among them, the members of Congress and other people in Philadelphia usually proved to be Miralles' most fruitful and accurate sources of information. "It is impossible to exaggerate to Your Lordship," Miralles wrote to Navarro, "the general acceptance, courtesy and respect with which I am regarded by all these citizens and by persons who hold the highest offices, which they take pains to show to me and to make known to others."[45] Not only did his contacts have knowledge of congressional deliberations but they regularly received news of the revolt from throughout the continent. Miralles, for example, had a good working relationship with the Laurens family, and while Henry Laurens served as president of Congress, the Spaniard met with him weekly, sometimes daily, and learned much of value. Henry Laurens felt that Miralles was a person whose "worthy character merits regard from all the Citizens of these States."[46] The observer followed events in South Carolina through the Laurens family, especially in late 1779 and early 1780, as the British moved against Charleston.[47] Laurens

45. Miralles to the captain general of Cuba, February 17, 1779, in *Letters of Delegates to Congress,* ed. Smith, XI, 391*n*.
46. Martin I. J. Griffin, "Requiem for Don Juan Miralles," *American Catholic Historical Researches,* VI (1889), 61.
47. Miralles to Navarro, November 21, 1778, no. 20, AGI, Cuba 1281; Miralles to J. de Gálvez, October 24, November 3, November 10, 1779, Miralles to the governor of Puerto Rico, March 6, 1780, Miralles to J. de Gálvez, March 19, 1780, October 23, 1779, all AGI, Santo Domingo 2598.

also provided the Spaniard with copies of letters sent to Congress, including correspondence from General Washington reporting on military affairs in New York and dispatches from General Benjamin Lincoln in the southern theater.[48]

The French ambassador in Philadelphia, first Gérard and then his replacement, the Chevalier de La Luzerne, also proved to be important sources of information for Miralles. They kept the Spanish observer informed not only about diplomatic developments in Paris but about the French fleet as well. Following the operations of the French navy became one of Miralles' major preoccupations, especially after the Spanish declaration of war during the summer of 1779. Gérard and Luzerne regularly received dispatches from the French admirals and in many cases made them available to Miralles, who reported their contents directly to the captain general and the minister of the Indies.[49] Any number of acquaintances in Philadelphia—from the well-known, including John Jay, Silas Deane, and Robert Morris, to dozens of lesser-knowns—gave Miralles much of the information he sought. In January, 1780, for example, a Captain Robertson arrived in Philadelphia from Charleston, and Miralles in interviewing him learned much about events in South Carolina and British East Florida.[50] Talks with a Major Getty provided the Spaniard with information on events in Virginia. All of this went directly to the captain general and the Spanish court.[51]

Most people in Philadelphia knew that Miralles resided among them in a quasi-official capacity despite his protestations to the contrary. They also understood that he regularly sent news to his superiors in Cuba and Spain. Josiah Bartlett, who attended a dinner at which Miralles and a German visitor, the Baron von Knoblelauch, were present, remarked, "There is a Spaniard of Character here and a Prussian, Each of them sent as it is thought by their Respective Sovereigns, Tho at present they Do not appear in Public Characters as ambassadors, yet Keep up a Correspondence with their courts."[52] No evidence has been found, however, to indicate that Miralles' contacts and sources in Philadelphia attempted to manipulate his opin-

48. Miralles to J. de Gálvez, November 22, 1779, AGI, Santo Domingo 2598.
49. See, for example, Miralles to J. de Gálvez, November 18, 1779, *ibid.*
50. Miralles to J. Gálvez, January 29, 1780, *ibid.*
51. Miralles to J. de Gálvez, February 3, 1780, *ibid.*
52. Josiah Bartlett to Mary Bartlett, August 3, 1778, in *Letters of Delegates to Congress,* ed. Smith, X, 384.

ions by providing him specially tailored or misleading information for the ears of the Spanish court. Instead, most persons in Philadelphia adopted the cordial attitude toward him best expressed by Henry Laurens, who wrote that Miralles "is an Honorable Spaniard strongly recommended" and that he "wants nothing more but leave to spend his money and *look on.*"[53]

Miralles also regularly read a large number of gazettes and periodicals from throughout the region. He followed in their pages much of the propaganda of the revolt, which helped him assess the goals, aspirations, and climate of opinion in North America. He paid close attention to both rebel and loyalist publications, customarily sending on to Spain any items with a direct bearing on concerns of interest to his court. Reports in the Philadelphia gazette on deliberations in Congress regarding fishing rights off the Grand Banks, for instance, went intact to Spain.[54] In collecting copies of royalist publications, he commented that complete faith could not be given those from British-held New York since they never published anything contrary to the English viewpoint. Nevertheless, much of his news of events in that region, including that about the English capture of General Charles Lee, came from newspapers printed in New York.[55] Miralles also sought copies of gazettes from other parts of the world which found their way to Philadelphia. Since those from London circulated frequently in the Pennsylvania capital, they often found their way to Spain and Cuba as attachments to Miralles' dispatches.[56]

The observer also collected documents, papers, and broadsides available to the general public, sending many to Havana and Spain. Upon arriving in Charleston, he had obtained copies of the South Carolina State Constitution, translated it into Spanish, and sent it to the captain general.[57] In Philadelphia, he collected from the public record copies of letters sent to the Congress. Since he viewed General Washington as the most important military commander in North America, he especially sought copies of the general's correspondence with Congress, and he translated it and sent it to Spain and Cuba with his own commentaries. Copies of letters from lesser

---

53. Laurens to John Laurens, August 13, 1778, *ibid.*, 441; emphasis mine.
54. Miralles to J. de Gálvez, June 15, 1779, AGI, Indiferente General 1606.
55. Miralles to J. de Gálvez, August 25, 1779, AGI, Santo Domingo 2598.
56. See, for example, Miralles to J. de Gálvez, February 18, 1778, AGI, Cuba 1281.
57. Miralles to Navarro, April 2, 1778, *ibid.*

commanders to Congress, including Benjamin Lincoln, Nathanael Greene, Benedict Arnold, and others, landed in the hands of Miralles' superiors.[58] Miralles had a particular interest in the resolutions and acts of Congress, many of which he translated for dispatch along with his letters.[59]

He realized that ship captains, who brought news and reports from their travels, could serve as important sources for him. Information about distant events moved along maritime trade routes as a staple by-product of a vessel's itinerary. Since the majority of merchantmen calling at Philadelphia came from the French West Indies, much of the news Miralles collected from them reflected events in that region.[60] Reports on happenings at Martinique and Guadeloupe came to him by means of a ship that arrived in the fall of 1778. In December, 1779, a merchantman arriving from Saint Eustatius brought news on the status of the French fleet commanded by Admiral de Grasse. A vessel arriving from Bermuda carried information on recent developments in that quarter.[61]

Merchant vessels trading with Philadelphia were not the Spaniard's only source of maritime information. In November, 1779, a captured British vessel that was brought as a prize to Philadelphia provided Miralles the chance to interview its captain. This officer, whose ship carried dispatches from Saint Augustine to General Clinton, in New York, brought the observer up to date on events in East Florida, Pensacola, and Mobile. Miralles learned as well further details regarding the Spanish victories of Bernardo de Gálvez along the Mississippi River.[62] The captains of two French naval vessels enabled him to get copies of France's treaties of amity and commerce. He also sent along to the captain general a copy of a letter written by Benjamin Franklin to the Congress that had come to North America aboard the French vessels.[63]

Miralles in addition listened to common talk among the people of Philadelphia, although he relied on that source of information only after exercis-

58. Miralles to J. de Gálvez, April 7, 1780, AGI, Indiferente General 1606; Miralles to J. de Gálvez, December 31, 1779, AGI, Santo Domingo 2598; Miralles to J. de Gálvez, February 25, 1780, AGI, Cuba 1291.
59. Miralles to Navarro, November 9, 1778, March 15, 1779, both AGI, Cuba 1281.
60. Miralles to J. de Gálvez, October 14, 1779, AGI, Santo Domingo 2598.
61. Miralles to Navarro, September 30, 1778, no. 1, Miralles to J. de Gálvez, October 15, December 29, 1779, all *ibid.;* Miralles to Navarro, November 12, 1779, AGI, Cuba 1281; Miralles to J. de Gálvez, February 28, 1780, AGI, Santo Domingo 2598.
62. Miralles to J. de Gálvez, November 15, 1779, AGI, Santo Domingo 2598.
63. Miralles to Navarro, May 16, 1778, no. 8, AGI, Cuba 1281.

ing considerable care. He always made the effort to corroborate what he heard in that way with other information coming by more reliable avenues. Nevertheless, in some cases he used rumor and general reports to advantage. In October, 1779, people told him that the British had three ships at the entrance to New York harbor endeavoring to block a potential threat by the French admiral d'Estaing. Additional investigation produced a letter from Washington to the Congress that substantiated that story.[64] Several months later, Miralles reported to the minister of the Indies that rumors in the Pennsylvania capital spoke of heavy storm damage to the British fleet as it left New York. Indeed, from common talk in the city, the Spanish observer learned of the number and class of boats destroyed and damaged, along with the probable destination of the fleet.[65]

The variety and diversity of Miralles' sources provided him with an almost daily supply of news for the Spanish court. As a rule, he wrote voluminous dispatches, and he averaged over thirty a month throughout the period of his residence in Pennsylvania. They had a wide-ranging content that touched upon military, political, and economic affairs. A growing partisanship for the American cause became increasingly evident in his reports over time, but it did not seem to bother his superiors. On several occasions, the minister of the Indies departed from his usual practice of maintaining silence on the performance of subordinates and complimented Miralles for his diligence and devotion to duty.

The hundreds of letters the Spaniard wrote his superiors present a fairly complete account of the major events, concerns, and affairs in Philadelphia during his years there. Most reports of occurrences in his dispatches contained little error and relatively light distortion. The care the Spanish observer took in assembling his information only partly explains his accuracy. The nature of the information he was conveying also helps explain why his dispatches were a relatively exact reflection of the matters he was describing. For Miralles sought in the main information that could be obtained easily just by virtue of residence in an area. In some respects, his observation work seems similar to that of present-day journalists, since he often reported what could be verified locally by a wide range of sources. His informants in Philadelphia probably refrained from sanitizing or exaggerating the news they

64. Miralles to J. de Gálvez, October 14, 1779, AGI, Santo Domingo 2598.
65. Miralles to J. de Gálvez, January 9, 1780, *ibid.*

gave him, because they understood that he had available many ways to check and corroborate what they said.

Moreover, Miralles had precise instructions regarding the type of information he should gather. His reports covered a very broad spectrum of interests and occurrences. Problems with the Continental currency, monetary questions, diplomatic concerns touching on the navigation of the Mississippi and on western lands, relations with France, the personal character of various colonial leaders, the mood of the people, their gastronomic habits, styles of dress, and popular amusements, and countless other matters became the subject of his dispatches. Nevertheless, he used the instructions he had received for guidance, and for the most part the information he gathered fell into several well-defined areas: it had to do with an assessment of the goals of the two sides in the revolt, with a vigilance for possible British attacks against Spanish or French colonies, and with military or political events that might have a direct impact on Spanish interests. In the last category, Miralles focused above all on Florida, because of its proximity to Cuba and Louisiana; New York, because of its status as a major British garrison; and the Gulf of Mexico and the Caribbean.

The Spaniard made it his first order of business to assess the goals of both sides in the revolt. His arrival in Philadelphia coincided with attempts by the Carlisle Commission to negotiate an end to the war, and many of his dispatches during 1778 spoke of the progress of the commission as its members went about their business in New York. By late October, the observer was able to include in his correspondence to the captain general the major proposals of the commission and to detail for the Spanish court the "peace manifesto" published in New York. He remarked with some satisfaction that most Americans did not appear disposed to accept the offers of the British commission, and he noted that a group of citizens who assembled to hear a copy of it read in Philadelphia clamored for the document to be burned.[66] He later reported fully on Congress' rejection of the peace initiative and the failure of the commission. The activities of the Carlisle Commission during early 1778 provided confirmation, to Miralles' mind, that the British might move against Bourbon possessions in the Americas. He wrote the captain general that England wished to end its differences with the former colonies in order that the two sides might declare war in unison on

66. Miralles to J. de Gálvez, October 20, November 9, 1778, both AGI, Cuba 1281.

France and Spain. The observer feared that if Spain did not openly join the American cause by the end of the year, the rebels might well accept the British proposals for peace.[67] A meeting of the Council of State at Madrid echoed Miralles' concerns. The minister of state, Floridablanca, warned King Charles of the necessity of being vigilant for a possible British attack, and José de Gálvez, the minister of the Indies, aligned himself with the minister of state's sentiments.[68]

Miralles tried to elicit additional information about a possible English surprise attack against the Spanish possessions. Prior to Spain's entrance into the war, he worried that the British navy might threaten a Spanish colony as a diversion that could reunite the mother country with her colonies against a common foe. That had been a long-standing fear of the Spanish court, and Miralles had been instructed to be alert for such a turn of events. In fact, the French had learned in early 1777 that a proposal of the sort Spain dreaded had been advanced. In April, a British agent had approached William Carmichael, an employee of the American commissioners in Paris. The two men held clandestine meetings nightly near the statue in the Place Vendôme at which the Englishman discussed the possibility of an accommodation so that Britain and the colonies could jointly attack colonies belonging to France or Spain. The ambassador Gérard, while still in Paris, learned of the conversations and prepared a formal position paper on the possibility under discussion.[69] He carried his misgivings to North America and shared them with Miralles, who had already been primed to think along the same lines. However fanciful such a rapprochement might seem in retrospect, Miralles devoted much of his early intelligence gathering to signs of an attack by confederated British and American forces.

English troop and naval activities at New York during the summer of 1778 caused Miralles a great deal of concern, since he anticipated that if a strike against the Spanish Indies came, it would be launched from that major British garrison. The observer learned that the British commander Sir William Howe had relinquished his command to General Henry Clinton. The change of leadership, Miralles ventured, probably presaged a major British troop withdrawal from New York. Opinions differed in the American camp

67. Otero, "Gardoqui," 19.
68. "Dictamen de Floridablanca," January 22, 1778, in Yela Utrilla's *España*, II, 199; "Dictamen de Don J. de Gálvez," January 23, 1778, *ibid.*, 204.
69. Samuel G. Coe, *The Mission of William Carmichael to Spain* (Baltimore, 1928), 3.

regarding where the English land and naval forces that were removed, thought by some to number as many as ten thousand men, would go. Some members of Congress believed that they would attack Boston, others speculated that they would reinforce Halifax and the British possessions in the Caribbean, and some—including Miralles—felt that they would attack French or Spanish colonies in an effort to unite the colonies with the mother country against a common, traditional foe. Miralles decided in late 1778 to warn Bourbon military commanders in the Caribbean and the Gulf of Mexico of events at New York.[70]

Besides sending a flurry of letters to them, he dispatched communications to the French governors of islands in the West Indies. He explained to each that he resided in Philadelphia by royal order of King Charles of Spain and that in his capacity, he had recently learned that troops under the command of General Clinton were preparing to embark from New York. He mentioned that the Americans had differing opinions regarding the destination of the evacuating force but that opinion held that they might move against French or Spanish colonies.[71] The Spanish observer chartered an American merchant vessel to carry the letters directly to their recipients, who spread word of the British naval movement throughout the remainder of the region. Events in New York, however, soon showed that General Clinton did not plan an attack against the Indies. The troop movements that Miralles followed formed part of British preparations to attack Savannah. The expedition sailed from New York in November, eventually arriving off Georgia. It took Savannah from the American defenders in December.[72]

The respite for Spanish apprehensiveness was, however, short, since the campaigns of the following year renewed Miralles' fears of a British attack upon the Indies. Once again he worried that General Clinton planned an embarkation of troops from New York that might attack Spanish possessions. In September, 1779, he learned from dispatches sent to Philadelphia by General Washington that the British in New York appeared to be assem-

---

70. Miralles to Navarro, September 23, 1778, no. 13, AGI, Cuba 1281.

71. Miralles to the governor of Puerto Rico, September 21, 1778, Miralles to M. Dargout, September 21, 1778, Miralles to M. Bouville, September 21, 1778, Miralles to J. de Gálvez, September 26, 1778, all *ibid.* Miralles also persuaded the president of the Congress to send similar letters to the governors of Virginia and South Carolina. See Laurens to Patrick Henry, June 27, 1778, in Papers of the Continental Congress, item 13, II, 14–15, National Archives.

72. Kenneth Coleman, *The American Revolution in Georgia, 1763–1789* (Athens, Ga., 1958), 116–21.

bling a force of some five to eight thousand men. The Americans surmised that the troops might be deployed as reinforcements for the British garrison in Georgia or as part of an attack on Charleston. The Spaniard, on the other hand, wondered if the forces might join with the British fleet in the Caribbean for an attack on Puerto Rico or some other Spanish possession. Once again he decided to warn Spanish commanders in the region of the English troop movements.[73] He directed letters to the governors at Santo Domingo and Puerto Rico, and a complete report to the captain general.[74] For the remainder of the fall, Miralles monitored the mobilization in New York. In talking with a French subject who had gone there to negotiate for a prisoner exchange, he gained knowledge of the number and class of transports standing off Staten Island. He continued to receive copies of dispatches to the Congress from General Washington, and by November he had come to believe that the new expedition probably had either South Carolina or East Florida as its object.[75] He chartered the *Stephens,* belonging to Robert Morris, to carry his conclusion to Puerto Rico, Santo Domingo, and Cuba, and he continued his observations of the situation. Early in 1780, he sent Spanish commanders in the Caribbean updated news of the expedition as it moved against Charleston.[76]

The events in South Carolina and Georgia held strong interest for Miralles. He had a personal knowledge of the area because of his desire to see a joint Spanish and American attack upon East Florida. After the departure of Admiral d'Estaing's fleet for the Caribbean in 1778, he kept track of the expedition of British Lieutenant Colonel Archibald Campbell to Georgia and the fall of Savannah to that force. He was also aware of the arrival of General Augustine Prevost to command the English troops in Georgia and of the closely succeeding fall of Augusta. Although the Spanish observer placed faith in the ability of General Lincoln to rout the English, the increasing ineffectiveness of the rebel army caused him some uneasiness. He

73. Miralles to J. de Gálvez, September 10, 1779, AGI, Santo Domingo 2598.

74. Miralles to Navarro, September 29, 1779, AGI, Cuba 1281; Miralles to J. de Gálvez, September 29, 1779, AGI, Santo Domingo 2598.

75. This expedition left New York harbor on December 26, 1779, bound for what would be a successful British attack on Charleston. See George Smith McCowen, Jr., *The British Occupation of Charleston, 1780–82* (Columbia, S.C., 1972), 1–3.

76. Miralles to the governor of Puerto Rico, November 10, 1779, Miralles to J. de Gálvez, November 13, 1779, the governor of Puerto Rico to Miralles, December 31, 1779, all AGI, Santo Domingo 2598; Miralles to J. de Gálvez, February 12, February 18, 1780, both AGI, Indiferente General 1606.

thus joined in the chorus of voices at Philadelphia calling for a return of d'Estaing's fleet from the Caribbean to reinforce the army that Lincoln commanded. Cheered by the French admiral's arrival off Savannah in September, 1779, the Spaniard became increasingly anxious when the Americans struck no immediate blow against the British, although he took some satisfaction in the buildup of rebel troops for the attack on the Georgia port. The failure of the American attack when it came, in October, and d'Estaing's departure for Europe afterward dispirited him, but he still held to a hope for an eventual American victory in the region.[77] The British moves against Charleston in early 1780 and the victories of Bernardo de Gálvez, however, dashed his idea of a coordinated American and Spanish attack against East Florida.

By 1779, Miralles was generating a steady stream of information for Havana. The captain general regularly sent to his superior, the minister of the Indies, all the letters, reports, and data from Miralles. In addition, Miralles himself sent letters to Minister Gálvez.[78] In Spain, it was thus chiefly José de Gálvez who correlated intelligence on the American Revolution for the Spanish government. The material in his files came to a considerable quantity, with the dispatches of Miralles forming the major part after mid-1779. As a member of the Council of Ministers, Gálvez presented the reports he thought significant to his ministerial colleagues and King Charles. On occasion, he forwarded reports from Miralles to the minister of state Floridablanca for use in the formulation of foreign policy.[79] Miralles remained attached to the ministry of the Indies during his entire career in North America, and all concerned agreed that his mission was a success.

77. Navarro to J. de Gálvez, August 28, November 14, 1779, with enclosures, Miralles to J. de Gálvez, August 28, 1779, all AGI, Indiferente General 1606; Miralles to J. de Gálvez, September 1, 1779, AGI, Santo Domingo 2598.

78. For representative examples of the numerous extracts of Miralles' correspondence in José de Gálvez' office, see "Extracto de 18 cartas escritas por Don Juan de Miralles al Exmo. Señor Don Josef de Gálvez," December 12, 1779, AGI, Cuba 1281; Miralles to J. de Gálvez, April 26, July 7, 1779, both AGI, Indiferente General 1606; and Miralles to J. de Gálvez, September 6, 1779, March 28, 1780, both AGI, Santo Domingo 2598.

79. For examples of Miralles' correspondence in the files of the ministry of state, see "Correspondencia de D. Juan de Miralles, comisionado español en los Estados Unidos y de los franceses M. Gérard y el Caballero Cesar de la Luzerne, con noticias de la guerra de aquellos Estados," AHN, Estado 3884 bis, expendiente 6.

6

Juan de Miralles:
From Observer to Diplomat
1779—1780

Juan de Miralles' main reason for going to Philadelphia was to serve as an observer for the captain general, and information gathering remained his most important assignment. He also, however, in time discharged diplomatic responsibilities that went beyond the scope of his initial instructions. Increasingly, the diplomatic side of his work took on a prominence that made him more than a mere observer of events. Miralles became Spain's unofficial representative in the United States. His contemporaries in Philadelphia realized his standing and treated him accordingly. He assumed the expanded role for a variety of reasons: his interests, inclinations, and tact placed him at the center of the American leadership; the Americans who governed at the state and congressional levels viewed him as someone who represented the interests of neutral Spain in an unofficial manner; as a member of the *floridiano* circle in Cuba, he desired to return Florida to Spanish control and viewed his mission to Philadelphia as affording a chance to work toward that goal; and finally, he understood from the captain general that Floridablanca might eventually use the observer at the Congress to inaugurate formal relations with the United States.[1]

From the outset, Miralles therefore vigorously represented Spanish interests and functioned as a contact point for Americans who had dealings with

---

1. Miralles believed that he would be appointed Spain's first ambassador to the United States when and if formal relations between the two nations began. He construed several letters from José de Gálvez complimenting him on the performance of his duties in Philadelphia as a promise of the post.

Spain. His earliest involvement in that sort of thing had come soon after his landfall in Charleston. There he met Alexander Gillon, who desired a letter of recommendation to the captain general. Gillon styled himself the "admiral of the South Carolina navy" and had a naval commission from the state government. As commander of a small squadron, he planned to sail to France to arrange for the construction of warships, and he sought recommendations from Miralles in case his flotilla called at Havana. The Spanish observer obliged him with a letter that asked the captain general to extend the American every possible courtesy.[2]

Soon thereafter, Gillon arrived at the Cuban port, with a British squadron in pursuit of his small fleet. On the strength of Miralles' recommendation, Navarro allowed the American vessels to anchor in the royal roadstead and use its facilities to make repairs, and he waved away the British. He also permitted the Americans to purchase supplies in the city. Gillon, perhaps emboldened by the courtesy of the reception, asked Navarro for permission to sail for France under a Spanish flag in order to escape further harassment by the British navy. Understandably, Navarro refused the irregular request, but he did permit one of Gillon's ships to remain behind to undergo extensive repairs from damages suffered en route to Cuba.[3]

The assistance provided Gillon in Havana would have been but a happy testament to Miralles' gallantry had the affair ended there. But Gillon proved to be something of a rascal: the letters of credit he wrote on a Charleston merchant house in the amount of 14,424 pesos came under protest because of insufficient funds, and efforts to collect the debt in South Carolina, and later in Philadelphia, failed. Gillon's mission to France, in the meantime, came to nothing, and he fell into disfavor with some Americans, including Henry Laurens, who awaited the return of the South Carolina "admiral" in order to ask him some "hard questions."[4] In Philadelphia, Miralles joined the chorus and complained mightily about Gillon to all who would listen, for the captain general had made Miralles pay the protested bills from personal funds on deposit in Havana since the services extended

2. Miralles to Navarro, April 14, 1778, no. 6, AGI, Cuba 1281; Portell Vilá, *Los "otros,"* 60–61. Gillon also carried a letter of recommendation to the captain general from Rawlins Lowndes. See Lowndes to the governor of Havana, July 10, 1778, AGI, Cuba 1301. See as well Alexander Gillon, "Letters from Commodore Alexander Gillon in 1778 and 1779," *South Carolina Historical and Genealogical Magazine,* X (1909), 3–9, 75–82, 313–35.
3. Navarro to Miralles, September 9, 1778, no. 6., AGI, Cuba 1281.
4. Laurens to John Adams, October 4, 1779, in *The Works of John Adams: Second President of the United States,* ed. Charles Francis Adams (10 vols.; Boston, 1850–56), V, 498.

to Gillon had been made on the Spanish observer's recommendation.[5] The South Carolina State Assembly did not attempt to settle Gillon's debts until 1783, when it investigated the matter. But Miralles' investment was lost, because the government at Havana, already paid, did not press the observer's claim nor did his heirs know to do so.[6]

Nonetheless, Miralles continued to engage in activities of a consular nature, taking special pains in representing Spanish prisoners of war.[7] From time to time English or American naval vessels and privateers stopped Spanish ships on the high seas and took them as prizes. The crews of these vessels sometimes became prisoners, and on occasion Miralles became involved in securing their release. By late 1778, his residence in Philadelphia had become common knowledge all along the Atlantic Coast. It seems doubtful that Spanish ship captains had been told to turn to him if they were taken prisoner, but some of them learned about him and appealed for his assistance once they made North American ports in the custody of their captors.

The first such incident occurred in early 1779, when two Spanish merchant vessels fell prey to American privateers operating out of Massachusetts. In April, Miralles received letters from the two Spanish captains, whose ships had been taken to Boston, where admiralty proceedings had been instituted against them. One vessel, captained by Joaquín García de Luca, had been sailing from Cádiz for London with a cargo of wines, oils, cochineal, and fruits. An American privateer sailing under a Massachusetts patent stopped it in late December, 1778, seized its cargo, and imprisoned the crew. The other ship, the *Santos Martires,* captained by José de Llano, suffered a similar fate while returning from London to Spain. Both captains claimed the rights of neutrals, but their American captors ignored their pleas. By the time the seamen approached Miralles, Llano's vessel and its cargo had been declared a lawful prize by a Boston court and García de Luca feared that the same fate awaited his ship. In writing Miralles, both men requested that he negotiate with Congress to secure their release, the

5. Miralles to J. de Gálvez, April 25, 1779, AGI, Indiferente General 1606; Portell Vilá, *Los "otros,"* 77–78.
6. "Resolution of the House of Representatives of South Carolina, March 15, 1783" (Papers of the Continental Congress, item 95, II, 202–207, National Archives).
7. For example, in 1779 he certified the Spanish citizenship of serveral persons taken prisoner by a British naval vessel and arranged for their repatriation. See Miralles to Colonel Bradford, November 22, 1779, in Society Collection, Historical Society of Pennsylvania, Philadelphia.

freeing of their ships, and the return of their cargoes.[8] A third captured Spanish ship arrived in Boston shortly after Miralles received the requests for assistance from Llano and García de Luca.

The requests created a predicament for Miralles, since he knew that he could not formally engage in negotiations with Congress without diplomatic status. He therefore prevailed upon the French ambassador Gérard, writing a long memorial requesting that he intercede with Congress in behalf of the captured Spanish vessels. Miralles outlined for the French envoy the entire history of the affair, rehearsed arguments in favor of releasing the ships, and suggested points of international law that could be mustered in support of the Spaniards' case. After studying the matter, Gérard decided to act in the interest of the Spanish captains, although his instructions from Paris did not specifically charge him with doing so. He sent Miralles' memorial to the Congress, declaring that holding the Spanish ships in Boston deviated from commonly accepted practices of international law and constituted a threat to neutral security on the high seas. In particular, the Frenchman seemed solicitous that Spain not be nettled, since he deemed such an outcome unwise. Congress took notice of Gérard's letter in formal session and awaited further developments.[9]

Miralles himself labored strenuously for several weeks preparing a file of documents on the three captured vessels. He secured copies of the admiralty proceedings regarding the first two, which had by then been declared prizes. The Spanish observer learned as well that the Massachusetts Supreme Court had already agreed to hear the appeals lodged by Captains García de Luca and Llano. Because he was sure that this court would uphold the decision of the admiralty judges, he wanted the Congress to pass a resolution enjoining the supreme court in Massachusetts to suspend all proceedings against the Spanish vessels. Congress could then decide the fate of the ships and their cargoes. Miralles again enlisted the assistance of Gérard, and in late May the French ambassador submitted another memorial composed by Miralles to Congress petitioning for the release of the ships.[10]

8. Miralles to Gérard, April 21, 1779, in Papers of the Continental Congress, item 94, 174–77, National Archives; Jay to Gérard, August 24, 1779, in *Letters of Delegates to Congress,* ed. Smith, XII, 518–19.

9. Worthington C. Ford, ed., *Journals of the Continental Congress* (34 vols.; Washington, D.C., 1904–1937), XIV, 508–10.

10. Miralles to Gérard, May 18, 1779, in Papers of the Continental Congress, item 94, fol. 214, National Archives; Gérard to Congress, May 19, 1779, *ibid.,* 206; Jay to Gérard, April 25, 1779, in *Letters of Delegates to Congress,* ed. Smith, XII, 381–82.

Congress declined to accede to Miralles' requests, since it did not have authority over the state of Massachusetts in the matter. Instead, it appointed a committee of three to investigate the affair and make recommendations. Composed of Thomas Burke, James Duane, and James Lovell, the committee requested that Miralles furnish it with all the documents and information in his possession regarding the case. Both Gérard and Miralles received assurances from the Congress that it fully supported the laws of nations on the high seas and in particular wished to cultivate only the "most perfect harmony" with Spain. Miralles readily gave the committee the desired reports, although he doubted that any tangible result would come from its investigations.[11]

After considering all the materials presented to it by Miralles, along with the position taken by Ambassador Gérard in support of the Spanish claims,[12] the committee stated in its report to the Congress on May 18 that the Spanish ships had indeed been seized in violation of Spanish neutrality. Its report recommended that Congress notify the individual states that it had "by appeal in the last resort, overall jurisdiction for deciding the Legality of captures on the High Seas." Nevertheless, it decided that in the particular cases before it the state of Massachusetts could not be forced to return the prizes since Congress did not have the power to issue such an order. As the president of the Congress wrote Miralles, that body "cannot consistently with the Powers entrusted to them, and the Rights of the States and of Individuals, in any case suspend, or interrupt, the Ordinary course of Justice."[13]

As the summer of 1779 progressed, it became increasingly obvious that Congress would not intervene in what it felt to be a matter within the purview of the Massachusetts courts. The new owners of the privateers argued that the Spanish ships had been trading in war material with the British and had thus been captured as lawful prizes. From Philadelphia, Miralles watched the development of these cases in Boston and kept the ministry of the Indies informed.[14] By the fall, he had to report that all avenues toward

11. Ford, ed., *Journals of the Continental Congress,* XIV, 617.
12. *Ibid.,* 624.
13. "Resolves of Congress, 1778–1779," May 18, 1779, in Papers of the Continental Congress, item III, fols. 103–104, National Archives; Jay to the states, August 14, 1779, in *Letters of Delegates to Congress,* ed. Smith, XIII, 364–70.
14. Miralles to J. de Gálvez, June 1, July 14, August 9, September 8, 1779, all AGI, Indiferente General 1606.

securing the release of the ships and their cargoes had been exhausted. The three vessels had again been declared lawful prizes, and the division of the spoils among the interested parties had been made. In reporting to José de Gálvez, Miralles did not forgo pointing out that he had done all he could in the matter but that had he been given the powers of an accredited diplomat, he could perhaps have secured the speedier assistance of Congress.[15]

Another case arose in New York almost as soon as the Spanish observer had concluded his dealings over the prizes in Boston. This time, however, he had to negotiate with the British, who had taken two Spanish merchant vessels as prizes. The vessels had been seized by the Royal Navy while they were engaged in trade between Havana and rebel American ports. Since Spain and England had gone to war by the time the ships fell into the hands of the British navy, established procedures of international law for the treatment and exchange of prisoners took hold and there was less room for debate than in the cases at Boston earlier in the year. Miralles established himself as the Spanish representative responsible for negotiating with the British commissary of prisoners in the matter. He first proposed a prisoner exchange, with one captured Englishman being released for each Spaniard.[16]

When the British refused the offer, he took it upon himself to arrange food, lodging, and medical care for the two dozen or so Spaniards held in New York. When the masters of the captured ships wrote Miralles and told him that they lacked proper supplies, and when additional news coming from New York drove it home that the sailors indeed had very short rations, he arranged for money to be sent from Havana. The observer approached several contacts in Congress and prevailed upon them to have Washington's staff request that the British treat the Spanish prisoners on an equal footing with the Americans held in New York. The general's commissary of prisoners did that, to Miralles' satisfaction. The Spaniard also prevailed upon Gérard to include a supply of blankets and clothing for the prisoners as part of a shipment going to New York for French detainees.[17] Miralles' efforts proved more successful in New York than in Boston. In early 1780, the British released the Spanish crews, with the sailors returning directly to Spain

---

15. Miralles to J. de Gálvez, October 28, November 2, 1779, both AGI, Santo Domingo 2598.
16. Miralles to Admiral Arbothnot, October 25, 1779, *ibid.*
17. Don Pedro de Asaola to Miralles, October 28, 1779, Miralles to J. de Gálvez, October 25, November 8, November 16, November 17, 1779, all *ibid.*

on a truce vessel. The two Spanish captains crossed the American lines and made their way to Philadelphia, where they met with Miralles to thank him for his efforts in their behalf. He arranged for their return to Cuba on board an American merchantman sailing for Havana with a secret packet of his dispatches.[18]

Miralles took part in consular and diplomatic initiatives beyond representing the interests of Spanish prisoners. He played an active role in the affairs of the Roman Catholic church in the United States, thereby involving his nation in its concerns. As a Roman Catholic, he attended mass at the small congregation of Saint Mary's Church, in Philadelphia. Founded in 1763, it had combined with the older Saint Joseph's to provide a place of worship for the small number of Roman Catholics in the city.[19] Its priest, Father Ferdinand Farmer, became a particular friend of Miralles' and in early 1779 approached the Spaniard to propose that the bishop of Cuba assume responsibility for the small Philadelphia congregation. The Catholic parishes of the Atlantic Coast had traditionally fallen under the see of London, but because of wartime difficulties, Father Farmer found regular communication with the bishop there to be difficult. He asked Miralles' assistance in approaching the bishop of Cuba, and Miralles gave the idea his support.

The two men wrote the bishop of Cuba, requesting that religious supplies for the churches in Pennsylvania and Maryland be sent from Havana. Miralles in particular painted a fairly bleak picture of the Catholic parishes in North America, noting that they suffered from a lack of money, small congregations, no access to parochial education, and an infrequency of contact with England. Since it was difficult for them to hold regular mass, he asked that the bishop in Cuba ensure their welfare by taking them under his charge. Miralles sent the requests through the captain general, who discussed them with the bishop.[20]

A decision could come with relative speed because the bishop had already dealt with similar requests from the Minorcans living at the New Smyrna

18. General Kniphausen to Miralles, January 8, 1780, Miralles to General Kniphausen, January 20, 1780, Miralles to J. de Gálvez, January 20, March 8, 1780, all *ibid.*

19. Griffin, "Requiem for Don Juan Miralles," 60–72; Portell Vilá, *Juan de Miralles,* 13–17.

20. Miralles to the archbishop of Cuba, March 27, 1779, Ferdinandus Farmer to the archbishop of Cuba, February 15, 1779, Robertus Molineaux and Farmer to the archbishop of Cuba, February 21, 1780, all AGI, Santo Domingo 1526.

colony in East Florida. As soon as he decided to extend the North American parishes the same access to religious supplies that had been accorded Father Pedro Camps in Florida, the episcopal offices in Cuba wrote to the minister of the Indies requesting permission to send holy oils, candles, sacramental wines, and other supplies to Philadelphia. The request came to the personal attention of King Charles because of his involvement in the affairs of the church under the ancient rights of the *patronato real* granted by the pope to the Spanish monarchs. Since Spain maintained neutral status with England in the early summer of 1779, when Charles considered the matter, he decided on a more circumspect course of action than Miralles had sought. The bishop of Cuba would be allowed to send supplies to Philadelphia but could have no involvement apart from that assistance.[21]

The arrival of the supplies in Philadelphia nevertheless encouraged Father Farmer and Miralles greatly, especially since Spain had in the interim declared war against Great Britain, clearing the way for greater support from the bishop. The two requested a portable altar, a chalice, and a rosary from him, and Miralles outlined an ambitious plan for the Catholic authorities in Cuba to sponsor a parochial school in Philadelphia that would be associated with the parish. They asked the bishop to send two priests to the Pennsylvania capital in order to teach at the school. The Cuban prelate seemed impressed with the plans and went so far as to suggest to Minister Gálvez the names of two priests residing in Havana who could be dispatched for that service.[22] The changing fortunes of war and the costs of the Spanish expeditions in the Gulf of Mexico and the Caribbean, however, made the plan financially impossible. Still, Miralles' influence and his efforts in behalf of the Catholics of Philadelphia resulted in the forging of additional ties to Cuba.

Miralles' most significant diplomatic activity in Philadelphia, however, concerned more than consular duties. From the very start of his stay in North America, he had goals of his own that shaped his diplomacy: to reassert Spanish control over Florida, to ensure that Spain would have the sole right of navigation on the Mississippi, and to secure Spain's title to the fertile lands east of the Mississippi Valley. To a lesser extent, he had an interest in seeking a confirmation of Spanish fishing rights on the Grand

21. J. de Gálvez to Manuel Ventura Figuero, July 9, 1779, Figuero to J. de Gálvez, July 12, 1779, J. de Gálvez to the archbishop of Cuba, July 17, 1779, all *ibid*.
22. The archbishop of Cuba to J. de Gálvez, April 12, 1780, *ibid*.

Banks of the North Atlantic. Miralles' efforts to influence members of Congress toward accepting his objectives went hand in hand with his work as an observer.

He found his efforts hampered because he had no formal accreditation, even though it became increasingly obvious to his American hosts that he acted in an unofficial and ill-defined capacity on behalf of Spain. Several members of Congress paid him special deference during 1779, since they ardently desired closer relations with Spain as an ally against Great Britain. Richard Henry Lee hoped for such an alliance and looked forward to the time when he could report that Spain had formally joined the American cause. John Adams, John Hancock, Cyrus Griffin, and others echoed his desire.[23] Many American leaders, especially General Washington, consequently attached great importance to Miralles' presence in Philadelphia.[24] Miralles was alive to the difficulty of his situation, remarking to the minister of the Indies that although he had been authorized to collect intelligence for the captain general, there existed an important need for Spain to be represented formally before the Congress. He told his superiors that it would soon become indispensable for Spain to have an accredited envoy in Philadelphia who could speak for the Spanish government. "Although I have done what I could through the auspices of the French minister . . . to advance whatever influence he could, it would never be easy or favorable to treat with the Americans unless there could here be a king's minister," Miralles wrote Captain General Navarro. He proposed that he be given such status.[25]

The appointment Miralles wanted, however, never came for him. His status in Philadelphia continued to be ambivalent during his entire sojourn there. The ill-defined and vague nature of his position reflected the division at the Spanish court regarding fundamental policy questions concerning the Revolution. Two political factions represented in the Spanish Council of Ministers continued to have conflicting views about relations with an inde-

---

23. Richard Henry Lee to Arthur Lee, September 6, October 27, 1778, in *Letters*, ed. Burnett, III, 310, 402; John Hancock to Mrs. Hancock, July 1, 1778, *ibid.*, 310; Samuel Adams to Samuel Phillips Savage, July 3, 1778, *ibid.*; Cyrus Griffin to Thomas Jefferson, October 6, 1778, *ibid.*, 444.

24. McCadden, "Juan de Miralles and the American Revolution," 304. None of these people, however, apparently realized that Miralles had been dispatched by the Spanish court for the primary purpose of providing strategic intelligence information.

25. Gomez del Campillo, *Relaciones diplomáticas*, I, xviii.

pendent United States. The Conde de Aranda and the *aragoneses* advocated full-scale recognition of the United States by Spain and negotiating an alliance with Congress modeled along the lines of the Franco-American agreement of 1778.[26] As Spanish ambassador to France, Aranda often found that it served his purposes to give the French the impression that Miralles had much broader diplomatic powers than he did.[27] On the other hand, Foreign Minister Floridablanca rejected outright any alliance with the United States and advocated maintaining greater distance in Spain's relations with the Congress. He believed that Spain should not recognize the independence of the United States. Instead, he called for a Spanish-sponsored mediation between England and its colonies. If England refused the proffered mediation, Spain would have a good excuse to enter the conflict as an ally of France. But Spain, he warned, should take care that the United States, with its desire to expand into the Mississippi Valley, not replace England as a territorial adversary in North America.[28] In some respects, Miralles was the pawn of both factions in court circles, with his diplomatic efforts in Philadelphia alternately supported and disavowed by each group according to its needs of the moment.

Further compounding his problem, groups within the Council of Ministers differed regarding the goals Spain should pursue if it entered the war. Even though some differences lessened after the summer of 1779, when Spain declared war against England, competition continued among these groups as they debated national objectives. One faction, led first by Grimaldi, the minister of state, and then by Floridablanca, saw the major objective of the war to be the territorial gains Spain might make in Europe and the Mediterranean. The return of Gibraltar to Spanish control, a reduction of British influence on Portugal, and a greater independence for Spain in its Family Compact relationship with France emerged as the chief goals for this group in any war with England. Against that, Aranda and the *aragoneses* desired a closer relationship with France, along with a complete rout of England in the Americas wherever possible. Other groups with represen-

26. Samuel Flagg Bemis, *Pinckney's Treaty: A Study of America's Advantage from Europe's Distress, 1783–1800* (Baltimore, 1926), 12.
27. Miralles to J. de Gálvez, February 1, 1780, AGI, Santo Domingo 2598. Vergennes told the French ambassador Luzerne that, according to information furnished him in Paris by Aranda, Miralles had authorization from the Spanish court to represent its interests before the Congress.
28. See Yela Utrilla, *España*, I, 64–65.

tation at the Spanish court had other opinions about the geopolitical goals that Spain should pursue. The faction centered at Havana, led by the captain general and the Elegio de la Puente family—which included Miralles—advocated the restoration of Florida as the primary object of Spanish foreign policy. Their views ran counter to those of another group, headed by the powerful Gálvez family, which saw the war as an opportunity to end the British presence in the western Gulf of Mexico. Led by the minister of the Indies, José de Gálvez, they wanted to strengthen Louisiana as a buffer between the United States and New Spain, expel the British from Central America, and end English contraband in the region. The Gálvez family probably also saw a chance to increase its prestige should that area become the primary focus of the war with England. The minister of the Indies gave his nephew Bernardo advance notice of the Spanish declaration of war so that the younger Gálvez could attack English positions along the Mississippi.[29]

Miralles' unofficial diplomatic efforts in Philadelphia therefore shifted along with the changing fortunes and influence of the competing groups at court. On the whole, however, he reflected the views of the *aragoneses* as well as the desires of the *floridianos* for the return of East Florida to Spanish control. His attempts to influence Congress to conquer East Florida and return it to Spain were consistent with the desires of the Havana interests he identified with. He remained predominantly pro-American during his whole time in the United States, honestly presenting himself as a champion of the rebel cause. Many American leaders, including George Washington, took satisfaction from the zeal with which Miralles embraced their cause in matters not in conflict with Spanish interests.[30] Nonetheless, he disagreed with the congressional position in favor of free navigation of the Mississippi and that on the western boundary with Spanish Louisiana.

Miralles' diplomatic activities fell into three distinct periods, reflecting the concerns of the various groups at court. From his arrival in Charleston until late 1778, he operated completely on his own and independently of direction in diplomatic matters from Spain. That period saw his greatest efforts to influence events that might result in East Florida's return to Spanish control. Then, when the Spanish court began to formulate a policy of media-

29. Rumeu de Armas, *El testamento político de Floridablanca*, 113–16.
30. George Washington to Miralles, April 30, 1780, AHN, Estado 3884 bis.

tion and preparedness for war in early 1779, he began to receive closer direction from Madrid even though he never received any sort of accreditation. After the Spanish declaration of war against Great Britain in 1779, however, the Spanish court occasionally intimated to the French and the Americans that Miralles spoke for the interests of Spain. John Jay, for example, received assurances from Floridablanca that Miralles enjoyed the sanction of the court in discussing Spanish interests with the Congress. Yet, the minister of state could never bring himself to grant official plenipotentiary status to him.

In the absence of formal appointment, Miralles worked through the French ambassador in Philadelphia in presenting to the Congress Spanish concerns that required official communication and discussion. That placed France in a difficult position. Vergennes, the foreign minister, was uncomfortable that his envoys in Pennsylvania sometimes were the third party to discussions of Spanish interests with the Congress, since that exposed France to the risk of offending both Spain and the United States in connection with matters in which his nation had no direct interest.[31] He felt especially chary regarding navigation rights on the Mississippi and the boundary between the United States and Spanish Louisiana. Initially, Vergennes and Gérard favored the Spanish position and supported Miralles. Gérard at first supported Miralles even though he lacked specific instructions from Paris. When Vergennes learned in late 1778 of the Spaniard's endeavor to keep Americans off the Mississippi and to secure the lands east of the river for King Charles, he showed surprise that Spain appeared to be asking the Congress to give up so much. Both he and King Louis XVI believed that the Americans had a right to enjoy free navigation on the river and that Spain wanted too much in exchange for an alliance with the Congress.[32] Nevertheless, eventually Ambassador Gérard received instructions to support the positions taken by Miralles and to represent Spanish interests before Congress when such a course seemed warranted.

Cooperation of that nature continued between France and Spain when

31. O'Donnell, *The Chevalier de La Luzerne*, 89. This theme is developed by William C. Stinchcombe in "Americans Celebrate the Birth of the Dauphin," in *Diplomacy and Revolution: The Franco-American Alliance of 1778*, ed. Ronald Hoffman and Peter J. Albert (Charlottesville, Va., 1981). He notes, "France had a signal advantage in that none of its territorial aspirations conflicted with those of the United States, which could not be said of either the British or the Spanish" (pp. 67–68).

32. O'Donnell, *The Chevalier de La Luzerne*, 93–94.

Gérard's replacement, Anne César de La Luzerne, arrived in Philadelphia on September 21, 1779. The new French envoy had traveled to the United States on the vessel carrying John Adams home and he had visited General Washington at his headquarters en route to Pennsylvania.[33] Unlike Gérard, Luzerne had no written instructions covering his responsibilities in Philadelphia. He had engaged, however, in lengthy discussions with Vergennes before leaving France. The two men had apparently talked about Miralles and how the French envoy should deal with him. Vergennes had made clear that he wished Spain would join the alliance with the United States and had told Luzerne to do whatever was necessary to secure Spanish cooperation. On the voyage from Europe, Luzerne had long discussions of Spain's possible role in the Revolution with Adams. He affirmed to the American diplomat that France would exert its influence to bring the Spanish into an alliance of amity and commerce with the Congress. When visiting with General Washington, the Frenchman again pledged that he would do whatever was necessary to secure the cooperation and support of Spain. Washington agreed to support United States participation in efforts by Spain to reacquire Florida if that would bring the Spanish into the alliance.[34]

Luzerne received additional instructions from Vergennes regarding Miralles several months after taking up residence in Philadelphia. The French foreign minister directed Luzerne to support fully the positions taken by Miralles regarding Florida, navigation on the Mississippi, and the western boundary with Louisiana. The United States, Vergennes had decided, possessed no title to Florida. Spain had previously owned it and hence should get it back, especially since its location to the north of Cuba made it significant to Spanish commerce and defense. The French minister had also come to the conclusion that the United States did not have a valid claim to navigation rights on the Mississippi. That privilege had been granted to England under the terms of the 1763 treaty, not to its American colonies. Congress had no basis for asserting that the right had been transferred, since transfer was not the common practice of international law. Although the French minister favored Spain's receiving western lands along the eastern

33. *Ibid.*, 36, 96.
34. Richard W. Van Alystine, *Empire and Independence: The International History of the American Revolution* (New York, 1965), 169. For a concise biographical sketch of Luzerne, see James J. Walsh, "The Chevalier de La Luzerne," *Records of the American Catholic Historical Society*, XVI (1905), 162–86.

bank of the Mississippi, he realized that the point was a sensitive one with many congressmen, especially from the southern states. He therefore told Luzerne to use care in cooperating with Miralles and to ask that Congress define itself clearly on this point.[35]

In Luzerne's extensive discussions with Miralles about the matter, the Frenchman told the observer that the Spanish court had suggested to Vergennes that Miralles had powers to treat with Congress on the navigation of the Mississippi, the conquest of Florida, and the drawing of the western boundary. Vergennes had most likely heard that from the Conde de Aranda, whose pro-American sentiments would have been well served by intimating an official diplomatic sanction of Miralles' initiatives. It was all a surprise to Miralles, though, and he corrected Luzerne, explaining that neither José de Gálvez nor Floridablanca had sent formal instructions on the questions or given him official accreditation. The Spanish observer insisted that he had been dealing with the Congress only on an ad hoc basis.[36] Luzerne therefore pledged to continue the arrangements the Spaniard had enjoyed with Gérard, and Miralles for the remainder of his mission had the support of the French envoy. It was Luzerne who officially approached Congress, in the name of Miralles, on issues of concern to Spain.

Of these, the reassertion of Spanish control over Florida, particularly Saint Augustine, was central. Miralles had arrived in the colonies prepared to support a combined American and Spanish attack on British East Florida. He had discussed cooperation to that end with Patrick Henry, in Virginia, and with Rawlins Lowndes, the governor of South Carolina. He had been so positive in support of the venture that Lowndes sent John B. Hernant to Havana even before Miralles left Charleston, in order to serve as liaison for a joint attack.[37] Miralles had made a joint expedition against Saint Augustine one of the major themes in his discussions with members of Congress after he arrived in Philadelphia. He found allies in Henry Laurens, George Washington, and William Whipple, all of whom favored the kind

---

35. O'Donnell, *The Chevalier de La Luzerne*, 198. For an analysis of these issues in subsequent Spanish policy, see Elena Sánchez-Fabrés Mirat, *Situción histórica de las Floridas en la segunda mitad del siglo XVIII, 1783–1819: Los problemas de una región frontera* (Madrid, 1977), 46–60.

36. Miralles to J. de Gálvez, March 12, 1780, AGI, Santo Domingo 2598; Miralles to J. de Gálvez, February 2, 1780, AGI, Indiferente General 1606; Miralles to J. de Gálvez, February 1, 1780, AGI, Santo Domingo 2598.

37. Portell Vilá, *Los "otros,"* 59–60.

of campaign he proposed.[38] General Washington proved to be the most influential of the supporters. The general told Miralles that he would permit General Benjamin Lincoln's army to cooperate with a Spanish military expedition but only after British troops had withdrawn from Georgia and South Carolina.

Miralles also worked to secure formal congressional cooperation. At social events in his home for members of Congress during Christmastide of 1778, the joint conquest of East Florida was the chief topic of conversation. Miralles told his guests that Florida had been one of Spain's first colonies in the Americas and that the return of East Florida was consequently the chief condition for greater Spanish-American cooperation. By early January, the Spanish observer could report to José de Gálvez that the president of Congress, along with key members of that body, increasingly supported plans for the joint conquest. He did record, however, that negotiations had been made more difficult by Spanish claims to lands east of the Mississippi Valley and by Spain's insistence upon sole navigation rights on the river. Virginia and Georgia in particular, he reported, disagreed with the Spanish positions, because of their own desire for the lands.[39]

A basic divergence of viewpoint existed between the Continental Congress and Spain over who should possess the Floridas. Both sides agreed that Britain had to be expelled, but there was no meeting of minds on who should replace her. The French, especially Vergennes, contributed to the lack of consensus by vacillating, favoring at times the Americans and at other times Spain. At one point during 1779, Vergennes went so far as to suggest a joint Franco-Spanish expedition against East Florida and haggled with Floridablanca over the number of French troops such an effort might require. In connection with that plan, the French envoy in Philadelphia agreed that the Americans had no historical claim to the Floridas. Spain, to his mind, deserved them.[40]

All the while, Miralles continued his efforts to secure a joint Spanish–United States attack on East Florida. In April, 1779, he reported to Minister Gálvez that Congress appeared on the verge of renouncing any designs on

38. McCadden, "Juan de Miralles and the American Revolution," 367; Laurens to Livingston, August 21, 1778, in *Letters*, ed. Burnett, 380–81; William Whipple to Josiah Bartlett, February 7, 1779, *ibid.*, 60; McCrady, *South Carolina in the Revolution*, 434–35.

39. Gomez del Campillo, *Relaciones diplomáticas*, I, xiv.

40. This discussion of the Florida question in Spanish-American diplomacy is based on the analysis provided by Wright in *Florida in the American Revolution*, 111–24.

western territories east of the Mississippi, thereby clearing one obstacle to approval of the joint expedition. He felt as well that if Spain undertook to give the Americans the use of Saint Augustine and Pensacola as free ports once Spanish control became a reality, there would be a greater chance of approval of the cooperative venture.[41] But by the early fall, Miralles had been effectively thwarted, for on September 17, Congress agreed to guarantee the Floridas to Spain only if the Spanish joined formally the alliance with France and the United States. It noted that "His Catholic Majesty shall accede to the said treaties, and in concurrence with France and the United States of America, continue the present war with Great Britain." In addition, Congress required "that the United States shall enjoy the free navigation of the River Mississippi into and from the sea."[42] That resolution kept Miralles from negotiating further for the moment, since he could not consider agreeing to the American conditions.

Ever hopeful, however, he waited for an opportunity to reopen discussions. In late November, 1779, when he saw that military events had not favored the Americans in Savannah or Newport, he felt that the Congress might be willing to reconsider the conditions of its September resolution. He wrote to it that he had received a letter from Captain General Navarro giving him authority to negotiate a joint Spanish-American conquest of Saint Augustine. Spain's situation had changed since its consideration of the project at the end of the previous summer, he said, in that it had joined France as a full-scale belligerent in the war against England. Although the Spanish crown had not chosen to forge an alliance with the United States, Miralles professed the hope that eventually that might come to pass. In the meantime, Spain desired American cooperation in attacking East Florida. In addition, the captain general wished to buy foodstuffs and military supplies in the United States for the Spanish units that would participate in the operation.[43]

41. Gomez del Campillo, *Relaciones diplomáticas,* I, xv. Congress indeed considered these positions. See Thomas Burke's draft report [August 5, 1779?], in *Letters of Delegates to Congress,* ed. Smith, XIII, 327–28.

42. Ford, ed., *Journals of the Continental Congress,* 111–13. For a longer discussion of proposed boundary lines, see "Henry Laurens' Notes on a Treaty with Spain" [September 9–17, 1779?], in *Letters of Delegates to Congress,* ed. Smith, XIII, 488–89.

43. Miralles to the Congress, November 24, 1779, AGI, Santo Domingo 2598. The congressional copy, along with the French ambassador's letter of transmittal, is in Papers of the Continental Congress, item 95, I, 27–31, item 75, XV, 603–607, 611–13, National Archives.

Miralles' letter raised the question of a joint expedition in a manner that the Congress could not ignore. The Spaniard enlisted the help of Luzerne, disclosing to him that Spain hoped a combined attack on Saint Augustine would divert British attention from West Florida, where Spanish forces under Bernardo de Gálvez planned to reconquer Pensacola. Miralles asked Luzerne to arrange with the French admiral de Grasse for the convoying of troops from Havana to participate in the attack. He reaffirmed the Spanish desire to view England as the common enemy of the two Bourbon courts.[44] Luzerne agreed to support the Spanish observer's requests to Congress. Shortly after meeting with him, the Frenchman wrote to the president of Congress to voice his conviction that the Spaniard's letter warranted serious consideration. He mentioned that he had written de Grasse of the possible joint Spanish-American attack on Saint Augustine, soliciting his support.[45]

With the receipt by Congress of Miralles' letter, the Spanish observer began a period of intense activity to secure congressional approval for the joint attack. Congress appointed a three-member committee to meet personally with him and draft a recommendation on the matter. In visiting with him, the members expressed their desire to cooperate in any reasonable manner. Miralles thus reached a very positive opinion about the probable success of his bid for American cooperation and decided to seek General Washington's support for the combined expedition. The Spanish observer and the committee agreed that a messenger should go to the general in order to hear his ideas about the number and kind of troops needed for the attack. At the same meeting, Miralles learned the price of American participation in the joint attack: a cash loan to Congress to defray the costs of sending an army southward to join with the Spanish. Because Miralles did not have the power to commit Spain to such a loan, he forwarded the request to the Spanish court.[46]

General Philip Schuyler, a member of the delegation that met with Miralles, decided that it should be he who visited General Washington to learn the American commander's opinions about an East Florida campaign. Schuyler hoped he might be named the American commander of the expe-

44. Miralles to Chevalier de La Luzerne, November 25, 1779, in Papers of the Continental Congress, item 95, I, 21, National Archives.

45. Luzerne to the president of the Congress, November 26, 1779, *ibid.*, 13.

46. Miralles to J. de Gálvez, November 25, November 27, 1779, both AGI, Santo Domingo 2598.

dition and had discussed that possibility with Miralles, apparently winning the Spaniard's support.[47] Schuyler carried a letter from Miralles to the American general, pressing for the cooperation of the Continental army. Miralles sent along copies of the Spanish declaration of war and of the captain general's letter to the observer requesting the joint expedition. General Washington read the documents, listened to Schuyler, and tactfully agreed with Miralles' proposals—but only in a general fashion and without giving specific information about the troops he would commit to the venture.[48] Washington had powerful reasons for offering only vague and lukewarm support: he felt the troops could not be spared. Furthermore, since Savannah remained in British hands, it seemed to him unwise to bypass Georgia for an attack against Saint Augustine.[49] Although Miralles took immediate encouragement from Washington's vague support, little of benefit ever came from it toward gaining congressional approval for the expedition he desired.

The Spaniard therefore decided to take a bold step greatly exceeding both the letter and spirit of his instructions. General Lincoln, the American commander at Charleston, badly needed materials and supplies to bolster the defense of the city he was protecting. Miralles, acting entirely on his own, permitted General Lincoln to draw a bill of exchange on him personally at Philadelphia in the amount of some $140,000.[50] Executed as a ten-day sight draft, the funds permitted Lincoln to finance the purchase of supplies. Nevertheless, the support had little impact on American policy regarding East Florida. Indeed, when Congress decided on its course, the resolution it passed in December, 1779, fell far short of anything Miralles had envisioned. Congress still insisted upon a loan and an alliance, but since the proposed expedition might prove more expensive than Congress could afford and more demanding of manpower than the Continental army could endure,

---

47. Schuyler had been relieved of his military command in 1777 because of controversy surrounding his role in the American loss of Ticonderoga. Although in 1778 he was acquitted in a court martial, he resigned his commission. He went to Congress in 1779 as a delegate from New York. With Miralles he discussed his desire to redeem his military career by participating in a Spanish-American attack on East Florida. See Miralles to J. de Gálvez, November 27, 1779, *ibid.*

48. Miralles to Washington, November 29, 1779, Washington to Miralles, December 7, 1779, both *ibid.*

49. Portell Vilá, *Los "otros,"* 70–71.

50. Benjamin Lincoln to Samuel Huntington, February 22, 1780, in Papers of the Continental Congress, item 158, fols. 331–32, National Archives; "List of Bills of Exchange Drawn by Major General Lincoln," *ibid.,* 329–30.

Samuel Huntington, the president of the Congress, sent a carefully crafted but uncompliant reply to Luzerne. It professed the strongest desires for Spanish-American cooperation in general and the attack on Saint Augustine in particular. In fact, Congress would like to participate in such a venture, the letter said, but could not do so fully because of other demands on its army. Huntington informed Luzerne that as an alternative Congress had directed additional troops to the American force in South Carolina. That, he noted, would bring garrison levels in Charleston to approximately four thousand men. In addition, Congress had ordered three frigates to the South Carolina capital. The augmented military force would constitute a powerful diversion of the British which would benefit the Spanish army coming from Havana to attack East Florida. But apart from that troop reassignment, no support for an attack on Saint Augustine would be available.[51]

Miralles reported the congressional decisions to the captain general as optimistically as he could, expressing the view that a Spanish attack against Saint Augustine should come as quickly as possible, before the British could reinforce the city.[52] But in fact the attack never came to pass, and not entirely because of the congressional refusal to cooperate. In Spain, the Gálvez interests who had lobbied at court for concentrating on the Spanish conquest of West Florida, which included Pensacola and the Mississippi River, won against those who supported the *floridianos* and their plan to attack East Florida. In early 1780, the captain general learned that the Council of Ministers had decided not to mount a Spanish expedition to retake East Florida and to focus instead on the English holdings to the west.[53] The decision effectively ended for Miralles any realistic hope that Spain would participate in a joint attack with the United States. The fall of Charleston to the British in 1780 put an end to discussion, in both Philadelphia and Madrid, regarding plans to attack Saint Augustine.

In addition to the efforts Miralles made in promoting an attack on East Florida, he also became involved in discussions about Spain's claims to lands along the eastern side of the Mississippi and its desire to reserve navigation of the river to itself. It did not solidify its position on those issues until 1778,

---

51. Huntington to Luzerne, December 17, 1779, in *Letters of Delegates to Congress*, ed. Smith, XIV, 274–75; Miralles to J. de Gálvez, December 16, 1779, AGI, Santo Domingo 2598; "Traducción de lo resulto por el congreso en 10 de diciembre de 1779," AGI, Santo Domingo 2598; McCadden, "Juan de Miralles and the American Revolution," 369.
52. Miralles to J. de Gálvez, December 17, 1779, AGI, Santo Domingo 2598.
53. Navarro to J. de Gálvez, January 11, 1780, AGI, Cuba 1291.

the year that Miralles took up residence in the United States. Early in the year, when the French ambassador in Madrid asked Floridablanca about Spain's view concerning navigation rights on the Mississippi, the Spanish foreign minister had replied that his court had no quarrel with the Congress on the point since the Mississippi obviously served as the western boundary of English, and now United States, territory. By November, however, Floridablanca had reversed his opinion, with his new outlook becoming Spain's formal position. He told the French ambassador that neither the English nor the Americans had right to territory on either side of the Mississippi in a region the exact boundary of which apparently remained undefined in his mind. In particular, the Americans had no right to free navigation on the river, he said, because that privilege had been extended only to the British by virtue of the Treaty of 1763 and could not be transferred to the American Congress.[54]

By 1780, navigation rights on the Mississippi had become the major Spanish concern in diplomatic discussions with the United States. William Carmichael wrote the Congress from Spain that "the navigation of the Mississippi appears to be the great, and if we can credit the assertions of men in power, the sole obstacle" to better relations between the two powers.[55] When John Jay began discussions in Spain as the American ambassador later that year, it became obvious that information furnished by Miralles to the Spanish court had shaped its policy regarding navigation on the Mississippi. The Conde de Floridablanca, meeting with Jay in May, flatly told the congressional envoy that Miralles' information had directly influenced Spain's decision not to enter into a treaty with the United States. As Jay noted,

[Floridablanca] proceeded to observe that there was but one obstacle, from which he apprehended any great difficulty in forming a Treaty with America, and plainly

54. O'Donnell, *The Chevalier de La Luzerne*, 91–92. O'Donnell feels that Miralles, through his dispatches, influenced Floridablanca's change of heart. Miralles did adopt this view much earlier, but no evidence can be found to prove his influence. Instead, Floridablanca's change of opinion probably represents the evolving of Spanish policy during 1778 as the Council of Ministers debated and refined the goals and objects of Spain's possible participation in the war. Robert R. Rea, in considering Spanish interests in resecuring West Florida, shows that some ministers in Madrid, including Floridablanca, always considered the return of the province to Spain a chief end of Spanish diplomacy. See his "British West Florida, Stepchild of Diplomacy," in *Eighteenth Century Florida and Its Borderlands*, ed. Samuel Proctor (Gainesville, Fla., 1975), 72–73.

55. Carmichael served as private secretary to John Jay. See William Carmichael to committee on foreign affairs, April 22, 1780, in Papers of the Continental Congress, item 88, fol. 80, National Archives.

intimated that this arose from the Pretensions of America to the Navigation of the Mississippi. He repeated the information which he had received from Monsieur Miralles, that Congress had at one Time relinquished that Object. That he also knew from the same Source that afterwards they had made it an essential Point of the Treaty. He expressed his uneasiness on this Subject, and entered largely into the views of Spain and Respect to the Boundaries.[56]

Miralles had from his arrival in North America consistently opposed American rights to navigation on the Mississippi. Nevertheless, on occasions in late 1778 and early 1779 he admitted to Gérard and certain members of Congress that he had no formal instructions on the point from the Spanish court. He assured them, however, that his views on the matter were also those of the Spanish king and Council of Ministers, although he of course did not imply that he was the author of this position.[57] Miralles' efforts to secure a Spanish claim to lands along the eastern bank of the Mississippi proved no more effective than his attempts to get the Americans to renounce free navigation of the river. Just as some of the southern states had strong feelings about navigation rights, they made powerful arguments in favor of annexing the lands that Spain claimed along the eastern bank of the Mississippi on the grounds that they were once part of Spanish Florida or French Louisiana. On August 14, 1779, acting largely under the influence of those states, Congress passed a resolution designating lands on the eastern bank of the Mississippi north of the thirty-first parallel as belonging to the United States. Later in the year, another resolution charged the American minister who was eventually to be sent to Spain to seek additional territory below that line, preferably a port on either the Mississippi or the Gulf.[58]

Further negotiations became moot when word arrived in Philadelphia of the victories of Bernardo de Gálvez along the Mississippi. Soon after Spain entered the war in 1779, the young governor of Louisiana had taken the British posts at Manchac, Baton Rouge, and Natchez. Miralles heard of these conquests from the captain general and immediately made the details known to Congress. He had a formal notice of Gálvez' victories placed in the Philadelphia gazettes and wrote a letter to General Washington giv-

56. "Recital of Notes of a Conference with Conde D. F. Blanca," May 11, 1780 (Papers of the Continental Congress, item 110, I, 138, National Archives).
57. Miralles to Navarro, February 14, 1779, AGI, Cuba 1281; Gomez del Campillo, *Relaciones diplomáticas*, I, xvi.
58. O'Donnell, *The Chevalier de La Luzerne*, 95.

ing the American commander a full recounting of the news then available.[59] The victories by Gálvez—including the subsequent capture of Mobile and Pensacola—closed, at least until the peace treaties of 1783, any meaningful discussion on the disposition of western lands between the United States and Spain, although the congressional envoy to Spain, John Jay, unsuccessfully attempted to negotiate with Floridablanca about the two powers' common boundary.

By early 1780, Miralles was firmly established in Philadelphia, readily accepted in the society of that city, and acknowledged by all as an unofficial spokesperson and observer for Spain. He clearly enjoyed the status of an accredited diplomatic envoy in the treatment the Americans accorded him, though he was careful in matters of an official diplomatic nature to address the Congress formally through the French ambassador. Miralles counted among his friends and acquaintances the leaders of the American Congress and military, chief among them George Washington.[60] As a gesture of goodwill, the general invited Miralles and Luzerne to visit his headquarters at Morristown, New Jersey, as soon as the arrival of spring weather in 1780 made the trip feasible. Miralles had looked forward to the visit for much of the winter and embarked with keen anticipation on April 17 in the company of the French ambassador.[61] The two men arrived at Washington's camp two days later, where they witnessed an impressive military review staged in their honor. En route, however, Miralles contracted "pulmonic fever," and soon after his arrival he took to bed at Washington's headquarters. The Spaniard's condition did not improve, much to Washington's distress. By April 25, when Luzerne returned to Philadelphia, Miralles could not travel

59. James Lowell to Adams, February 8, 1780, in *Letters of Delegates to Congress*, ed. Smith, XIV, 396–97; Miralles to J. de Gálvez, February 27, 1780, AGI, Santo Domingo 2598; McCadden, "Juan de Miralles and the American Revolution," 369; O'Donnell, *The Chevalier de La Luzerne*, 101–102. For a concise overview of these Spanish victories, see Albert W. Haarman, "The Spanish Conquest of British West Florida, 1779–1781," *Florida Historical Quarterly*, XXXIX (1960), 107–34; and Light Townsend Cummins, "Spanish Historians and the Gulf Coast Campaigns," in *Anglo-Spanish Confrontation on the Gulf Coast During the American Revolution*, ed. William Coker and Robert R. Rea (Pensacola, Fla., 1982), 194–205.

60. Some historians have perhaps overstated the depth of friendship that existed between Miralles and Washington. See, for example, Portell Vilá, *Juan de Miralles*, 9–12. Still, although Washington's reactions are less well documented, a reading of Miralles' correspondence makes clear that he felt a genuine respect and affection for Washington as a person.

61. Miralles to J. de Gálvez, March 14, 1780, AGI, Santo Domingo 2598; Gomez del Campillo, *Relaciones diplomáticas*, I, xviii. Miralles, in addition to making a social visit to the general, wished to discuss prospects for the joint Spanish-American attack on East Florida. See McCadden, "Juan de Miralles and the American Revolution," 369–70.

and remained behind under the care of Washington's physician. The general visited him daily, noting that the Spaniard had an elevated fever and high pulse. His condition continued to worsen. Juan de Miralles died at three in the afternoon on April 28, 1780, in a bedroom of Ford House, the general's official residence.[62]

Miralles' passing saddened General Washington, who wrote a letter of condolence to Captain General Navarro that praised the Spaniard in eloquent terms. Washington sponsored a memorial service for Miralles at the Continental army headquarters. The general and members of his staff walked as mourners to the service, followed by a caisson that carried the coffin to the local church, where a Catholic priest said mass. Afterward, a solemn procession accompanied the remains to the local burial ground at Morristown. In May, Miralles' friends and acquaintances remembered him with a requiem mass in Philadelphia. Many of the delegates to Congress attended, along with the military figures in the city and the leaders of Philadelphia society.[63]

At the time of his death, some Americans realized that they had lost an advocate for closer relations between their country and Spain. Oliver Ellsworth wrote, "This gentleman during his residence here appeared zealously attentive to the political interests and views of this country, as well as his own, and waited with impatience to see the ties between the two countries indissolubly formed by a ratification of treaties of amity and commerce, which he expected would take place on the arrival of our Minister at the court of Spain."[64] John Jay, the minister of whom Ellsworth spoke, felt too that Miralles represented the best hope for a firm alliance with the Spanish. When the new American envoy arrived at his post in Europe, he sought out Miralles' son, who then resided in Spain. They discussed the admiration the elder Miralles had for the American cause, and the son expressed his own

62. "Extracto de la infermidad que padecio Don Juan de Miralles Hecho por el Medico Mayor del Ejercito de estos estados que lo asistio todo el tiempo que estuvo enfermo," April 30, 1780, AHN, Estado 3882 bis; "Materials Relating to the Maneuvers of the Four Continental Battalions Before the French Minister in April, 1780, and Subsequent Maneuvers" (Typescript in Chevalier de La Luzerne Files, Morristown National Historical Park Library, Morristown, New Jersey).
63. Alexander Scammel to General Edward Hand, April 29, 1780, in Smith Collection, Morristown National Historical Park Library; "Death and Burial of Don Juan de Miralles" (Typescript in Juan de Miralles Files, Morristown National Historical Park Library); Andrew M. Sherman, *Historic Morristown: The Story of Its First Century* (Morristown, N.J., 1905), 359–61.
64. Oliver Ellsworth to the governor of Connecticut, May 9, 1780, in *Letters*, ed. Burnett, V, 131.

desire to visit the United States.[65] Jay was soon to learn that the information Miralles provided the Spanish court had influence at the highest levels. William Carmichael also, soon after arriving at Madrid in order to prepare the way for Jay, had heard from clerks in the Ministry of State that dispatches from Miralles regularly had arrived there about affairs in North America.[66]

Miralles' death left a considerable void in the captain general's observation network, since the observer in Philadelphia had become its major source of information. In addition, his passing silenced in Spanish councils a powerful voice that favored American interests. The following months saw the Spanish court and the captain general cast about for a way to replace the deceased Spanish observer. For the time, his secretary, Francisco Rendon, served in his stead. Rendon went through Miralles' papers, set aside sensitive material, worked to settle his estate, and continued to send reports to Havana.[67]

In those months, Rendon awaited word from Havana about a replacement. Desiring the appointment for himself and not wishing to lose the opportunity for it, he wrote to the captain general to tell of his availability. Navarro eventually decided to keep Rendon temporarily in charge.[68] In a technical sense, however, the captain general did not formally appoint him to Miralles' position. Navarro merely issued orders for him to take charge of the deceased's correspondence and to continue sending news.[69] Rendon's residence in Philadelphia was clearly intended to be a temporary assignment, lasting only until a regular replacement could be named. The captain general wrote to José de Gálvez seeking advice on how to fill the vacancy but assuring him that since Rendon had been a trustworthy employee and loyal subject, he could remain in place for a while. Still, the Cuban commander gave the young Spaniard in Philadelphia more circumscribed and closely defined duties than he had Miralles. Rendon was to continue collecting news about the Revolution and to pay particular attention to information furnished by the French minister. Rendon was also to go through

65. Richard B. Morris, ed., *John Jay: The Making of a Revolutionary, Unpublished Papers* (New York, 1975), 755, Vol. I of *The Papers of John Jay*, ed. Morris, 2 vols.; Jay to Mrs. Margaret Cadwalader, May 12, 1780, *ibid.*, 755; Sarah Livingston to Catherine W. Livingston, May 14, 1780, *ibid.*, 697.

66. Carmichael to Jay, May 25, 1780, *ibid.*, 759–76.

67. Rendon to Navarro, August 20, 1780, no. 112, AGI, Cuba 1283. Rendon had gone to Philadelphia from Havana in early 1779 to serve as Miralles' assistant and clerk.

68. *Ibid.*

69. Navarro to J. de Gálvez, July 14, 1780, reserved, no. 116, *ibid.*

Miralles' files and send to Havana any records pertaining to the commercial activities of the deceased. The captain general also directed Rendon to handle all matters in the United States relating to Miralles' personal estate.[70]

Part of this assignment Rendon had undertaken before receiving instructions from Havana. He, along with Robert Morris, had been named an executor of Miralles' estate by the Pennsylvania courts, and for much of the remainder of 1780, he administered what must have seemed a complicated probate proceeding. Miralles had intermingled his own funds with those of the Spanish court in the exercise of his commission.[71] He had purchased cargoes with his own money, acquired personal possessions including furnishings and a coach with horses, and even bought real estate in Philadelphia. In addition, he had leases on buildings and had lent money to both private individuals and public officials.[72] It fell to Rendon to sort all this out and somehow to close Miralles' affairs in a manner acceptable to both his widow and the captain general.

Rendon began by taking a complete inventory of Miralles' possessions. He reconciled financial accounts the observer had kept, in an effort to ascertain their current status. He found that Miralles had been operating with a deficit, advancing his own money toward the objectives of his mission and waiting for reimbursement from the royal treasury in Havana. Rendon prepared a list of debts the Cuban government owed the estate and sent it to Antonio Ramón del Valle. Valle approved a partial payment to Miralles' heirs, but held that some of the money supposedly due the observer resulted from private transactions unrelated to his commission. Miralles' wife and children had to wait over a decade for complete repayment, the last portion of which came only after they submitted a direct appeal to the king in the early 1790s.[73]

70. Rendon and Robert Morris served as joint executors of Miralles' estate, which was probated in Philadelphia according to Pennsylvania law. See Will Book M, 1682–1900, Probate Proceeding 1780, no. 294, Probate Court Records, Municipal Archives, City Hall, Philadelphia.

71. Robert Morris attempted to salvage some funds from Miralles' dealings in Philadelphia for the immediate benefit of the widow and her children. Morris apparently liquidated some of his own assets so that money could be sent on to the family in Havana. See Morris to Jonathan Hudson, June 8, 1780, in Gratz Collection, Historical Society of Pennsylvania.

72. "Quenta Relación jurada de los Gastos por mi Don Juan de Miralles," December 3, 1780, AGI, Cuba 1291; "Quenta jurada que por orden del Exmo. Sor. Don Diego Josef Navarro," August 4, 1780, *ibid.;* Rendon to Valle, August 20, 1780, no. 63, *ibid.* 1283.

73. Navarro to J. de Gálvez, April 20, 1781, no. 140, *ibid.* 1291.

Besides settling Miralles' estate, Rendon continued the observation activities his predecessor had conducted. The deceased observer had been careful to maintain secret archives of papers and letters relating to his mission, with Rendon perhaps the only person in Philadelphia knowing about them. Navarro and Rendon discussed by mail what should be done with the potentially incriminating papers. Some of them might be so sensitive that they could not be permitted to fall into American or French hands. On the other hand, whoever took Miralles' place should have access to the correspondence for reference. The two men agreed that Rendon should prepare and forward to Havana an index of all Miralles' documents. From that inventory, a decision would be made regarding what should be destroyed. Rendon and Navarro created three classes of documents: one group to be burned, another to be shipped to Havana, and a third to remain in Philadelphia. The sanitizing of Miralles' files was completed by the late summer of 1780.[74]

By then, the decision had been made in Spain and Cuba about Miralles' official successor, deliberations about which had been going on at court since word of the observer's death arrived in late spring of 1780. The court's preoccupation with that, however, united with several others regarding Spain's American policy. By the middle of 1780, the minister of state, Floridablanca, had to address three significant matters in connection with the American Revolution: differences between Spain and the Congress regarding the navigation of the Mississippi; the arrival of John Jay as an official envoy to the Spanish court; and a tentative, covert effort on the part of King Charles and his ministers to negotiate a separate peace with England that would ensure attainment of their war goals.[75] Each of the three matters had a direct bearing on the discussions about the person to succeed Miralles in Philadelphia.

Although when Floridablanca took office, he did not have strong views on Spain's claim to the sole right of navigation on the Mississippi, he increasingly came to hold well-defined opinions about it. In particular, he came adamantly to reject the idea of granting the United States any access to the river. He saw the opening of the Mississippi to free navigation by citizens of the United States as the replacement of one enemy with another.

74. Navarro to J. de Gálvez, July 14, 1780, *ibid.*
75. Morris, *The Peacemakers*, 218–47.

Indeed, for the rest of his diplomatic career, into the 1790s, he persisted in his opposition.[76] He wished to avoid any situation that would expose Spain to requests to negotiate further on the question. The vacancy in Miralles' post came at exactly the time that Spanish military victories on the Gulf Coast created an opportunity for maintaining the status quo regarding the river in favor of Spain.

The arrival of John Jay as a congressional envoy during the summer of 1780, however, shattered any hope for a temporary end of discussions with Congress on the Mississippi question. Jay came specifically empowered to entreat for the "free navigation of the Mississippi into and from the Sea." He sought, as well, a free port for the United States on the river below the thirty-first parallel. Through Jay, Congress hoped also to secure loans from Spain to support the expenses of the war. Although Jay hoped for both an alliance and financial aid, Floridablanca seemed reluctant to grant either, since the Mississippi question served as a deterrent against each.[77] The Spanish minister therefore adopted a policy of obstruction and delay in dealing with the American envoy.

Jay's arrival coincided with secret efforts by Floridablanca to negotiate a separate peace with England through a Spanish-educated Irish priest, Thomas Hussey, and a British observer, Richard Cumberland. Hussey had been living in London since before the outbreak of the Revolution, and as chaplain to the Spanish embassy, he had played an important role in the collection of information for the Principe de Masserano, Spain's ambassador to England. During June, 1780, when he returned to Spain in the company of Cumberland, the two men became involved with Floridablanca in negotiations for a separate peace that would guarantee the return of Gibraltar to Spain. The discussions continued for months, with the minister of state hoping that he might remove Spain from the war and, at the same time, acquire major concessions from the British.[78]

Those secret negotiations, coupled with the arrival of Jay in Madrid, resulted in a shift of Spanish diplomatic initiatives away from Congress. With the reorientation, events in Philadelphia became less important for the Spanish ministries. Spain's entry into the war and its military campaigns

76. *Ibid.*, 222; Rumeu de Armas, *El testamento político Floridablanca*, 113–14.
77. Morris, *The Peacemakers*, 222–23.
78. Pedro Voltes Bou, "Thomas Hussey y sus servicios a la política de Floridablanca," *Hispania*, XIX (1959), 92–141; Bemis, *The Diplomacy of the American Revolution*, 106–107. These negotiations came to nothing, because George III refused to consider the cession of Gibraltar. For the complete story, see Bemis, *The Hussey-Cumberland Mission, passim.*

as a full-scale belligerent contributed to that result. The court's interest in the day-to-day activities of the Congress abated and its concern with the affairs of Bernardo de Gálvez along the Gulf Coast and with the Spanish fleet in the Caribbean intensified. Consequently, Floridablanca had less need of an observer in Philadelphia. Indeed, he foresaw that someone as active as Miralles might cause problems. By the summer of 1780, it had become fairly obvious to Floridablanca, besides, that congressional policy affecting Spain remained firm and clearly articulated, especially regarding the western boundaries of the United States and the navigation of the Mississippi. Maintaining a dynamic and personable Spanish presence in Philadelphia therefore did not seem as crucial to him as when Miralles had been sent in 1778, and a career Spanish bureaucrat who would concentrate on the observation of events in the United States seemed to him ideal.

Although there is some evidence that the Spanish court toyed with appointing a person of stature—most likely Diego de Gardoqui—to replace Miralles, its decision was to offer Rendon formal appointment to the post.[79] He was not, however, to be given the freedom of diplomatic action and initiative that Miralles had enjoyed. Instead, his assignment was to be strictly limited to collecting news; in all other matters, he was to act only on specific instructions from his superiors. In early October, José de Gálvez drafted the orders appointing him. Rendon could unofficially represent Spanish interests in the United States but only after coordination with the French ambassador and specific permission from the ministry of the Indies. Beyond that, he had no duties except for intelligence.[80] Captain General Navarro formally notified the American leadership that Rendon would be the Spanish observer in Philadelphia, stressing, however, that the appointee did not have diplomatic powers.[81] Unlike Miralles, Rendon was not a participant in the larger diplomatic issues of the Revolution. His role in Philadelphia was a passive one in comparison with that of Miralles.

---

79. Jay to the president of the Congress, July 1780, in Papers of the Continental Congress, item 110, I, 251, National Archives. See also Carmichael to committee on foreign affairs, July 17, 1780, *ibid.*, item 88, fol. 68. Carmichael noted in a later communication that "the gentleman expected by the Minister has arrived, & proves to be Don Diego de Gardoqui, who is already known by his former correspondence with America" (Carmichael to committee on foreign affairs, August 22, 1780, *ibid.*, item 88, fols. 84–85).

80. J. de Gálvez to Rendon, October 20, 1780, AGI, Indiferente General 1606; Rendon to Navarro, August 20, 1780, no. 112, AGI, Cuba 1282.

81. Navarro to Huntington, May 4, 1781, in Papers of the Continental Congress, item 987, fol. 426, National Archives.

7

Francisco Rendon, Spanish Observer
1780–1786

The death of Juan de Miralles occurred less than a year after Spain's formal entry into the war. As a nation at war, Spain had a more pressing need for detailed, combat-related intelligence. Its armies along the Gulf Coast, the Spanish fleet in the North Atlantic and Caribbean, the forces commanded by Matias de Gálvez in Central America, and the besiegers of Gibraltar all needed reports and assessments of enemy troops contiguous to their positions. In large measure, the field commanders of these theaters themselves collected what information they required, using resources routinely available from military and combat intelligence sources under their commands.[1] The captain general's observation system had relatively little to offer Spain's military commanders, because it was oriented toward gathering general information in North America.

Largely for that reason, Francisco Rendon was by 1781 the only observer left who made reports to the captain general. The Spanish court no longer needed a flow of information about the nature of the Revolution and the goals, intentions, and objectives of the warring parties. The reports on such matters that it had received for years from its observers had already helped shape its decisions both to support the Americans and to enter the war. From 1775 until 1779, agents of the observation network—most prominently Miralles and Herrera—had provided the Spanish court with ample political

1. Gold, "Governor Bernardo Gálvez and Spanish Espionage," 91.

168

and economic information about the rebels for policy making in Madrid. After that, Spanish diplomatic policy regarding the United States remained constant for most of the remainder of the century.[2] Moreover, the intentions of the various nations involved in the war had become fairly settled by early 1780, especially as they related to the views of American congressmen on the issues of navigation on the Mississippi River, the western lands, and the Floridas. Hence, the revision of Spanish war goals in the light of information from Philadelphia seemed a remote possibility to the Spanish king and his ministers after their nation declared war against Great Britain.

Another factor in reducing the significance of the captain general's observation network after 1780 had little to do with Spain's status as a belligerent. The early years of the Revolution marked the start of a regular commerce with the rebellious colonies, some of it the by-product of the activities of the observers, especially Eduardo and Miralles. Because of Miralles, hundreds of Americans went to Havana in a growing commerce that provided significant contact between the Spanish colony and important North Atlantic ports.[3] Although Spain made an attempt to restrain this trade in the mid-1780s, it never fully succeeded. As a result, the captain general no longer found himself short of knowledge about events in the United States. Spanish Louisiana also became an area of regular and close contact with Americans during the Revolution. The westward movement during the revolutionary years had begun to push Americans into the Mississippi Valley by the early 1780s. For Don Esteban Miró, the Spanish officer who succeeded Bernardo de Gálvez as governor of Louisiana, dealing with the new settlers was a major responsibility.[4] But whatever problems that demographic phenomenon created for the Spanish in the Mississippi Valley, there was certainly no lack of news in the region about the United States. The abundance of information available lessened Spain's reliance on special observers.

The early 1780s also saw the venue of unofficial Spanish diplomatic contact with the United States shift from Philadelphia to Madrid. The new decade brought a congressional restructuring of the American diplomatic corps in Europe, with the appointment of John Jay as minister to Spain. In Madrid, Jay began regular discussion with the Conde de Floridablanca, al-

2. Rumeu de Armas, *El testamento político de Floridablanca*, 113–16.
3. Casa Mena, *Españoles en Nueva Orleans*, 44–51; Caroline Burson, *The Stewardship of Don Esteban Miró* (New Orleans, 1940).
4. Liss, *Atlantic Empires*, 80–82, 132–34.

though he was never officially accredited at the court. Meetings between the two diplomats constituted a forum for the free exchange of opinions between the two nations. Since ministers at the court could thereafter speak with an American representative on their own soil, the importance of the Spanish observer at Philadelphia was greatly diminished for Spanish policy makers. The discussions in Madrid became the Spanish ministries' most important point of diplomatic contact with the Americans.

Floridablanca looked toward a peace settlement that maintained at least a limited Spanish hegemony in Europe if not a substantial increase in power and prestige. The victories of Bernardo and Matias de Gálvez had ensured the attainment of Spanish war goals in the Americas. The major policy considerations faced by Floridablanca after 1780 had relations with England and France in view, along with the eventual disposition of Gibraltar. Negotiations on those matters were determined by the chanceries in Madrid, London, and Paris, often with the involvement of the congressional representatives in France and Spain.[5] Demanding central coordination at court, the negotiations could not be conducted by an observer in Philadelphia. Anyway, in many cases the position of Congress as it bore on them had already been clearly and frequently stated.

It was under these conditions that Rendon began his tenure in Philadelphia. A native of Jerez de la Frontera in Spain, he came from relatively humble circumstances and as a career civil servant in the Spanish colonies had held minor positions in Cuba before going to Philadelphia in early 1779 to serve as Miralles' personal secretary.[6] He did not have the ease of manner, however, that had permitted Miralles to be received as an equal by the leaders of the American cause. He also had no background in commercial activities. And unlike Miralles, he did not appear to be a particular partisan of the American cause. He lacked, it is said, the "magic ingredient" for full-scale acceptance at the Congress—"enthusiasm for the American cause."[7]

Nevertheless, Rendon did have a large measure of enthusiasm for serving the needs of King Charles. He vigorously undertook his observation duties during 1780, collecting news for the captain general, upon whom he relied for closer direction than Miralles had done. The Chevalier de La Luzerne also had a greater day-to-day influence over Rendon than he had had

5. Morris, *The Peacemakers*, 218–47.
6. Portell Vilá, *Los "otros,"* 92–93.
7. McCadden, "Juan de Miralles and the American Revolution," 372.

over Miralles. Rendon regularly sought counsel from the Frenchman, with whom he met soon after Miralles' death in order to request assistance in collecting information. For much of Rendon's residence in Philadelphia, the French ambassador proved to be an important source about the Revolution.[8]

Since the captain general sought to limit Rendon's diplomatic activities, it is ironic that the observer's first major assignment during 1780 was consular in character. Since the armies of Bernardo and Matias de Gálvez depended upon the captain general for logistical support, he needed foodstuffs for the increasing number of Spanish troops in the Gulf of Mexico and Caribbean regions. During the spring of 1780, he therefore conferred with the intendant of Cuba, the official charged with financial matters in the colony, regarding the cheapest and most efficient way by which Spanish army and navy garrisons in the Americas could be supplied with what they needed. The two men agreed that the United States was perhaps the best source, and with the approval of the Spanish court, they laid plans for a trade between Philadelphia and Havana that would furnish Spanish troops in the region with needed foods, especially flour. The Spanish king decided that the observer in Philadelphia should negotiate for large-scale shipments from the United States to Cuba.[9]

The captain general wrote to Miralles about this, unaware that his observer had died and that Rendon had had to take charge. Navarro explained that the needs of war had brought a large number of troops to his command region and that he expected the arrival of a large naval squadron from Spain that contained twelve ships of the line and some eight thousand men. The Havana squadron had also been expanded by an additional four vessels, and the regular army garrison stationed at Havana had increased by two regiments since the declaration of war the previous summer. All of that, he acknowledged, had created such a great strain on the traditional supply channels from New Spain that the court was permitting him to seek new suppliers. Navarro had therefore authorized the free and unlimited importation of flour, beef, pork, lard, and almost every other class of foodstuff from the United States into Cuba and had issued orders to port commanders throughout the island permitting any ship arriving with those goods

8. Rendon to Valle, August 27, 1780, no. 65, AGI, Cuba 1283; Rendon to Navarro, August 23, 1780, no. 113, *ibid.* 1282.
9. "Minuta" May 29, 1780, *ibid.* 1282; Navarro to Miralles, May 30, 1780, *ibid.*

from North America to sell them without prejudice. No special licenses would be needed. In addition, the delivery vessels would be allowed to return to North America with sugar, tobacco, fruits, honey, brandy, and any other of the island's products potentially salable in northern markets. Trade would be unrestricted. Moreover, in a radical departure from Spanish commercial laws, Navarro announced that he would sanction the export of bullion from Cuba as payment to North American merchants for the imports. He instructed Miralles to make all the arrangements necessary to begin this trade.[10]

Navarro's letter crossed in transit with the notification going to him of Miralles' death. When Rendon promised to make all the arrangements himself,[11] Navarro consented but cautioned him not to approach the Congress directly but to work through the French ambassador. That Rendon did, conferring with Luzerne on the best way to export the needed supplies, especially since the export of flour required a congressional license because of the product's importance to the American war effort. Luzerne cautioned the Spaniard not to expect the full-scale cooperation of the United States, since food supplies, particularly flour, were scarce and many in Congress felt that it was difficult enough to provision American troops without having to attend to those of Spain. Nevertheless, Luzerne laid the Spanish case before the Congress, personally meeting with several members of Congress in lobbying for the proposed Cuban trade.[12] The French minister received assurances regarding the congressional desire for friendship with Spain but also protestations that Congress was experiencing severe difficulties in finding adequate rations and supplies for just the Continental army. In addition, the members of Congress reminded the French ambassador of the expected arrival of the French fleet in American waters, which would only increase the demand for provisions. Luzerne saw that there was little chance the Americans would permit the exportation of food supplies in the quantities the captain general desired. A disappointed Rendon urged that they press ahead on the matter nonetheless. He took some encouragement from Luzerne's securing an agreement with leaders in the Congress to enable the

---

10. Navarro to Miralles, August 30, 1780, *ibid.;* Rendon to J. de Gálvez, June 19, 1780, AGI, Santo Domingo 2598; Navarro to J. de Gálvez, June 6, 1780, no. 155, AGI, Cuba 1291.

11. Rendon to J. de Gálvez, June 19, 1780, AGI, Santo Domingo 2598.

12. Rendon to Navarro, August 20, 1780, no. 112, AGI, Cuba 1232; Rendon to Navarro, June 19, 1780, AGI, Santo Domingo 2598.

sale of some three to four thousand barrels of flour to the Spanish army provided that it could be certified as nonessential for the American forces.[13]

In late June, Luzerne formally requested that the Congress authorize the sale of three thousand barrels of flour to the captain general in Havana. He also asked for beef, pork, lard, vegetables, and suet. The merchants of Philadelphia, Luzerne stressed, could make the sales and would be freely admitted to Havana under a special suspension of Spanish colonial trade laws.[14]

Much to Rendon's satisfaction, Congress passed a resolution on July 11 authorizing officials in the state of Maryland to sell three thousand barrels of flour in Cuba. Rendon saw the prudence in looking to Maryland, since flour was more easily available in Baltimore than in Philadelphia. Some of the other products, Congress noted, could be secured more cheaply outside the United States, and it recommended an attempt along that line to Luzerne. Congress professed a greater desire to assist Spain than it could fulfill with this transaction. The fall of Charleston to the British, the increased need for provisions by the French fleet, and the short harvests of 1779 limited the amount of flour that could be spared for Cuba.[15]

Rendon, however, did not rest with this relatively meager congressional response. Robert Dorsey and Robert Morris, two of the several merchants he had been working with confidentially in Baltimore and Philadelphia about undertaking the trade once Congress granted approval, told him that besides furnishing any flour Congress officially authorized for export, they could through a subterfuge arrange for the other requested supplies and flour to reach the Havana market. Apparently led by a desire for profits which made them willing to defy congressional policy, they offered to effect the transactions through the Dutch trading houses in Saint Eustatius with which many American merchants had regular contact. The warehouses there often contained large amounts of flour stockpiled by American commercial houses. Although the Congress would permit the export of only some three thousand barrels of flour, Morris assured Rendon that it would be easy to send the rest of the supplies from the Dutch colony, since no prohibitions controlled the shipment of flour from that island. Morris affirmed that he could send three of his vessels to Saint Eustatius to begin the

13. Rendon to Luzerne, June 19, 1780, AGI, Santo Domingo 2598.
14. Rendon to Navarro, July 6, 1780, nos. 94, 95, AGI, Cuba 1282.
15. "Verdadera traducción de lo resuelto por el congreso de los Trece Estados Unidos de America en 7 de julio de 1780, como sigue . . . ," July 7, 1780, *ibid*.

trade. Rendon, after negotiating a contract with Morris, wrote to the captain general about the arrangement; each of Morris' vessels carried his letter in triplicate so that the boats would be admitted to the port of Havana in the same way as those coming directly from North America.[16]

The first consignments from Saint Eustatius arrived in Havana during late 1780 and many more followed from the United States.[17] Unlike the flour trade underwritten by Juan de Miralles to carry his intelligence reports, this commercial operation became a major source of food for Cuba, especially flour. Most of the ships involved did not carry secret dispatches from Rendon but sailed solely for trade. From 1777 to 1779, approximately 50 North American vessels called legally at Havana from ports in the United States. Once the flour trade initiated by Rendon had begun, the numbers of colonial vessels making the run to Havana from Philadelphia increased dramatically. For example, in 1780 alone some 32 ships engaging in that trade called at Havana. The number rose to 126 in 1781 and 211 the following year. Although not all of the vessels had flour as their major cargo, it is probable that most of them did.[18] So lucrative did the North Americans find the trade that the Congress appointed Robert Smith to serve as the official representative in Havana for superintending it. Smith oversaw commercial matters in Cuba for the United States until his premature death in 1782, whereupon the New Orleans merchant Oliver Pollock moved to Havana and assumed the duties on behalf of the Congress.[19] The flour traffic begun by Rendon had by 1783 become a major trade between ports in the United States and Havana, with a significant impact on the island's economy.[20]

Rendon was involved in the Philadelphia end of the flour trade for the remainder of the Revolution. He contracted with merchants for the continuing export of provisions, underwrote shipping costs, and kept records

16. Rendon to J. de Gálvez, July 12, 1780, AGI, Santo Domingo 2598; Rendon to Navarro, no. 97, July 12, 1780, AGI, Cuba 1282.

17. For a detailed discussion of this trade, see James A. Lewis, "Anglo-American Entrepreneurs in Havana: The Background and Significance of the Expulsion, 1784–1785," in *The North American Role in the Spanish Imperial Economy, 1760–1819,* ed. Jacques A. Barbier and Allan J. Kuethe (Manchester, Eng., 1984), 112–26.

18. *Ibid.,* 117.

19. Clarence L. Ver Steeg, *Robert Morris: Revolutionary Financier* (Philadelphia, 1954), 69; James, *Oliver Pollock,* 283–89.

20. See Lewis, "Anglo-American Entrepreneurs in Havana," tables, 116–17; See also Linda K. Salvucci, "Anglo-American Merchants and Stratagems for Success in Spanish Imperial Markets, 1783–1807," in *The North American Role in the Spanish Imperial Economy,* ed. Barbier and Kuethe, 127–33.

for the captain general of the vessels engaged in the Havana commerce. He monitored the dealings of Robert Morris and John Dorsey, each of whom regularly shipped large cargoes of flour and other comestibles into Havana.[21] He regularly made overtures to other prominent merchants along the eastern seaboard to add to the growing volume of food supplies going to the Spanish military. He made an agreement with the Philadelphia firm of Mathews, Irwin, and Company, for their vessel *Minerva* to make the regular flour run to Havana.[22] In all, he entered into contracts with over a dozen American merchants, favoring them with huge profits. There was a pattern to the contracts he offered: he underwrote the costs of sending the merchants' ships to Havana by paying the basic expenses, along with the salary of the master and crew; furnished the vessels with letters of recommendation to the captain general that spelled out their right to sell their cargoes at a guaranteed profit; and granted the merchants the privilege of exporting major Cuban crops such as sugar, tobacco, and fruits for sale in North America. Robert Morris, John Dorsey, George Mead, the Wilcox family, the Smith family, the firm of Lacaze and Millet, John Pringle, and others all made lucrative deals with Rendon under the conditions he bestowed. Some of the merchants prospered to the extent that they purchased new ships especially for the Cuban trade, naming some of them in honor of prominent figures on the island, including Captain General Navarro and Miralles' widow Doña María Elegio de la Puente, and in honor of the city itself in the case of the brigantine *La Havana*.[23] Although the large numbers of North American merchants who came to Havana because of the flour trade eventually raised apprehensions among the Cuban authorities, with the result that they attempted to end the traffic after the Revolution, the part Rendon played in creating the commerce during the early 1780s was undoubtedly successful.

The same may be said of his role during 1780 and 1781 in connection with Spanish prisoners of war. The court had instructed Miralles to act as Spain's

21. Rendon to Navarro, July 12, 1780, no. 97, July 25, 1780, no. 101, both AGI, Cuba 1282.
22. Rendon to Navarro, December 4, 1780, no. 134, Navarro to Rendon, September 10, 1780, no. 96, both AGI, Cuba 1282.
23. These contracts made with American merchants served as a significant subject of correspondence between Rendon and the captain general for most of late 1780. For representative individual transactions, see Rendon to Navarro July 15, 1780, no. 118, August 10, 1780, no. 102, August 12, 1780, no. 103, November 12, 1780, no. 131, and November 14, 1780, no. 129, all AGI, Cuba 1282. Replies from the captain general may be found in the same *legajo*.

de facto agent in Philadelphia in such matters. When Rendon inherited the responsibility, he had as much difficulty as Miralles did before him. Like his predecessor, he was constrained by the limited diplomatic standing he possessed, and he had to work closely with the French ambassador in matters touching on the prisoners. Luzerne had already dealt successfully with the British at New York in securing guarantees of the humane treatment of the Spaniards held there. When Miralles died, it fell to Rendon to see that Spain did what depended upon it for the prisoners at New York. In particular, Luzerne wished the Spanish court to pay its share of the costs associated with sending supplies to French and Spanish prisoners in British custody. In addition, the French diplomat requested that Rendon seek some sort of official instruction from the ministry of the Indies that would empower the Spaniard to speak for his country regarding prisoner exchanges in North America.[24]

Rendon requested such authority and, in the meantime, continued to monitor the prisoner problem. In July, 1780, he arranged for some of the prisoners released by the British in New York to come to Philadelphia and book passage to Havana aboard the ships of the flour trade. The Spanish seamen arrived in Pennsylvania with a letter to Rendon from Captain Ambrosio de Jardines, who described conditions at New York and disclosed that some eighty-five Spaniards remained in British custody. Many of them, he related, would probably be released in exchange for an equal number of Englishmen. Shortly thereafter, Rendon was told that British authorities intended to repatriate the prisoners through London rather than Havana.[25] That was a relief to him, since providing for the return of that large a number of Spaniards from Philadelphia would have taxed his resources.

In most other matters of a consular nature, Rendon worked through Luzerne rather than approaching Congress directly. During 1781, he represented Spanish interests in the case of a brigantine that had been seized on the high seas by an American corsair. Bernardo de Gálvez had permitted British soldiers and subjects to sail for New York to be repatriated, as part of the terms of surrender at the Battle of Pensacola. A merchant captain, Jahleel Smith, master of the brig *Sally* and a Spanish subject, provided pas-

---

24. Rendon to J. de Gálvez, July 1, 1780, AGI, Santo Domingo 2598.
25. Rendon to Navarro, July 4, 1780, no. 92, Rendon to J. de Gálvez, July 10, 1780, both *ibid.*

sage for one group of British subjects leaving West Florida for New York. When the captain of the American sloop *Betsy,* which sailed under a commission from the state of Pennsylvania, observed the brig, his ship overtook it and seized it. Admiralty proceedings in Philadelphia later declared Smith's vessel a legitimate prize, and the captain applied to Rendon to intercede in his behalf before the Congress.[26] The captain gave Rendon a certified copy of the safe-passage permit that had been provided the *Sally* by Arturo O'Neil, the Spanish commander at Pensacola. Rendon went to Luzerne, who presented the case to the Congress. The commerce committee of Congress, noting that the *Sally* may well have been a lawful prize under the laws of Pennsylvania, asked Luzerne to have Rendon provide a copy of the formal surrender instrument signed by General Gálvez at Pensacola so that the status of the captured brigantine could be clarified.[27] That Rendon did, also furnishing correspondence between Bernardo de Gálvez and other officials about the matter.[28] Little came from his effort, however, since the Congress—as it had done in earlier incidents of a similar nature—denied that it had the power to intervene in matters before the state courts.[29]

Rendon became involved the following year in the case of Antonio Argote, a New Orleans merchant whose trading vessel had been seized during November, 1782, by an American privateer, the *Patty.* His ship, the *San Antonio,* had been sailing under a truce flag in order to exchange prisoners when the American privateer stopped it en route from London to New Orleans and took possession of it and its cargo, apparently because it had embarked from England. When Argote enlisted the assistance of the Louisiana governor Esteban Miró in an attempt to be compensated by the Americans for his loss, the governor referred him to Rendon in Philadelphia. Argote provided the Spanish observer with a packet of documents, depositions, and manifests that indicated that the *Patty* had not been trading with the enemy but had been exchanging Spanish prisoners of war for English troops captured by Bernardo de Gálvez at the Battle of Pensacola. Rendon again laid the matter before Luzerne, who agreed to act on his behalf and presented all the materials on the case to the Congress. The

26. Petition of Jahleel Smith to Rendon, September 7, 1781 (Papers of the Continental Congress, item 95, II, 11–13, National Archives).

27. Rendon to Luzerne, September 20, 1781, *ibid.,* 5–7; Luzerne to the Continental Congress, September 24, 1781, *ibid.,* 1; secretary of the Congress to Luzerne, *ibid.,* 19.

28. Rendon to president of the Congress, *ibid.,* item 78, IXX, 394–401.

29. "Report of Committee, September 28, 1781" (*Ibid.,* item 112, 200).

special committee that investigated the affair recommended that Argote be paid one thousand dollars in damages, at the cost of the owners of the privateer.[30]

Still, Rendon's lack of diplomatic powers placed him on the sidelines in other matters. By the early 1780s, many Americans saw free navigation on the Mississippi as a right. Rendon, clearly less influential in congressional leadership circles than Miralles had been, nevertheless attempted to keep viable Spain's position that citizens of the United States did not have unfettered navigation of the river. During the summer of 1780, Rendon held a series of informal conferences with Luzerne in order to make clear once again Spain's position. The Spaniard assembled for the captain general a portfolio of letters written by Luzerne to the French foreign minister on the question.[31]

In addition, Rendon was anxious about the western boundary of the United States with Spanish Louisiana. Like Miralles, he wanted Spain to gain control over as much land east of the river as possible. When the Spanish Council of Ministers decided to register formally its dissatisfaction with congressional action taken on this matter, the minister of the Indies Gálvez sent Rendon a delineation of the Spanish position regarding both American navigation rights on the Mississippi and the western boundary. Rendon prepared a letter of transmittal to the Congress for the minister's communication. The Spanish observer, however, did not directly communicate with the Americans in any formal diplomatic capacity. Instead, he presented the letter from Gálvez to François de Barbé-Marbois, the French consul in Philadelphia, who delivered it officially to the Congress.[32] To Rendon's credit, he was dissatisfied with having to work through France's representative in Philadelphia. He felt that the French legation played a conciliatory

30. Antonio Argote to Rendon, March 25, 1783, *ibid.*, item 79, III, 145; "Report of Mr. Duane, Mr. Lee, and Mr. Carroll on August 11, 1783," September 10, 1783 (*Ibid.*, item 19, V, 267–70).

31. "Extracto de despachos de Luzerne a Vergennes relativos a limites entre Espana y los Estados Unidos," June 11, August 3, August 25, 1780, AHN, Estado 3884 bis, expediente 6, no. 31; Rendon to Navarro, August 20, 1780, no. 107, AGI, Cuba 1282. Rendon's role in these discussions has often been ignored by historians. See, for example, James A. Padgett, ed., "Discussion in the Continental Congress Relative to Surrendering the Right to Navigate the Mississippi River," *Louisiana Historical Quarterly*, XXVI (1943), 12–36.

32. Marqués de Barbe-Marbois to Congress, November 19, 1784, in Papers of the Continental Congress, item 96, 286, National Archives; Francisco Rendon to the president of the Congress, November 26, 1784, *ibid.*, 294–96; J. de Gálvez to Rendon, June 26, 1784, *ibid.*, 290–91.

game, attempting to keep both Spain and the United States placated. Like Miralles before him, he argued unsuccessfully with his superiors for formal diplomatic accreditation.

Rendon's efforts to speak in favor of Spain's exclusive right to navigation on the Mississippi were thus compromised from the start. Congressmen favoring joint rights of navigation maintained that he could not represent Spain on the issue. Even though he claimed to have authority from the Spanish court to voice an opinion on the matter, he always had to work through Barbé-Marbois. The relevant congressional committee wryly noted in its minutes that it had read the "letter from Mr. De Marbois who ushered in a kind of remonstrance on that subject from a Mr. Rendon, who is said to be invested with some public appointment from the court at Madrid, but who has yet produced no credentials."[33]

Rendon's only effective course lay in monitoring for Spain the penetration of Americans into the Mississippi Valley. During the remainder of his stay in Philadelphia, he gathered and forwarded to Spain news about American expansion into the Ohio and Mississippi valleys.[34] The information did not encourage optimism on the part of either Rendon or the minister of the Indies about Spain's ability to control American access to the Mississippi. By early 1783, Rendon noted that a growing illegal trade in flour and other foodstuffs operated between western Pennsylvania and New Orleans by way of the inland river system. Americans living in the Ohio Valley found it profitable to ship their flour down the rivers to the Gulf of Mexico, where it could be sold at a handsome profit. Although the trade contravened Spanish law, Rendon noted that the need for flour in New Orleans made it undesirable for Spain to try to stop the commerce. Even though the Americans realized substantial profits from the sale of their flour, the price they charged represented a net saving for New Orleans over other sources.[35] During 1784, Rendon provided the Spanish court with details of settlements

33. Samuel Hardy to the governor of Virginia, December 5, 1784, in *Letters*, ed. Burnett, VII, 620. François de Barbé-Marbois served as first secretary, or consul, to the French legation in Philadelphia. He arrived with Luzerne in 1779 and worked closely with the French ambassador as his chief assistant. Barbé-Marbois was charged with cooperating with Rendon on the question of navigation rights on the Mississippi, but his efforts to mediate between the Spanish agent and Congress failed. See E. Wilson Lyon, *The Man Who Sold Louisiana: The Career of François Barbé-Marbois* (Norman, Okla., 1942), 18, 24–25.
34. Arthur Preston Whitaker, *The Spanish American Frontier, 1783–1795: The Westward Movement and the Spanish Retreat in the Mississippi Valley* (1927; rpr. Gloucester, Mass., 1962), 34.
35. Rendon to Gálvez, February 28, 1783, no. 72, AGI, Santo Domingo 2597.

in Kentucky and showed on a map he provided the major populated areas in the region.

Although he did not have a significant impact on the official deliberations of Congress regarding the Mississippi Valley, he did serve as a minor conduit of information to the Americans. In late 1784, when Spain decided to restrict American traffic on the river, Rendon served notice in Philadelphia of its action. Charles Thomson wrote to Thomas Jefferson: "I find that Spain is still bent on obtaining the exclusive navigation of the Mississippi. Rendon shewed me this morning a letter from Galvez the Minister of the American department wherein he desires him to inform the Congress that the intercourse with New Orleans and with Havannah is shut until the boundaries between the U.S. and S. are settled."[36] It would fall to Rendon's successor in Philadelphia, Diego de Gardoqui, to continue negotiation on the question.

Rendon did not, however, have a complete lack of influence in Philadelphia. In reality, he played an active part in the social whirl of Philadelphia even if he never matched Miralles' level of bravado and charm. He attended most of the functions, dinners, and gatherings that brought together the American congressional leadership, and as a result he became increasingly identified with the group who supported the financial operations of Robert Morris. Rendon inherited his close personal and economic tie to Morris from Miralles. Both Morris and Rendon gained from the expanded flour trade with Cuba that began in late 1780. The American merchant reaped great profits while the Spanish observer fulfilled his assignment to supply the Cuban military garrisons. By March, 1781, Rendon estimated that the two men had been responsible for shipping over forty thousand quintals of flour and meat to Havana. Pleased, the captain general instructed Rendon to continue his arrangement with Morris, since the shipments more than adequately met the supply needs of Spain's military forces in the region.[37] The commercial cooperation of the two men apparently engendered a friendship as Rendon supported with increasing vigor various of Morris' political and economic ideas.

Rendon looked with approval upon Morris' appointment as superintend-

---

36. Charles Thomson to Thomas Jefferson, October 1, 1784, in *The Papers of Thomas Jefferson*, ed. Julian P. Boyd *et al.* (22 vols. to date; Princeton, 1950–), VII, 213.

37. Rendon to J. de Gálvez, March 10, 1781, no. 3, AGI, Santo Domingo 2598; Rendon to Valle, December 4, 1780, no. 75, AGI, Cuba 1283.

ent of finance. Upon taking office, Morris proposed a far-reaching set of economic measures that he hoped would cure many of the financial problems plaguing the young nation.[38] Rendon endorsed his proposals and worked with him by attempting to secure Spanish support for them. The American's hope was to obtain a special loan from the Spanish government in order to generate badly needed capital. He hoped that Jay, the American envoy in Spain, could persuade King Charles and his ministers to expedite the needed money. Rendon's support of this scheme lay in forwarding to his superiors a long letter that Morris had written to him detailing the plan. The communication argued that the Congress would be put on a sound financial footing once it enacted Morris' program.[39] Rendon supported Morris' appeal for a Spanish loan and attempted to influence the captain general and the minister of the Indies in favor of the plan. The observer applauded Morris' plan for a central national bank and sent to Madrid and Havana a detailed prospectus for such an institution which he had received from the American.[40]

Rendon tried to convince the captain general and the minister of the Indies that Congress had a realistic chance of bettering its financial outlook by adopting Morris' plan. He mentioned that many in the Congress supported the creation of the central bank and that it should help solve the problem of inflation. Because of the depreciated American currency, he reported, the Congress had difficulty gathering adequate supplies for the army and navy. Without the Spanish loan, Congress would be unable to break the vicious spiral of inflation, he said, and it would therefore be robbed of the potential for fiscal reform promised by Morris.[41]

Rendon's endorsements notwithstanding, the Spanish court decided against action favorable to Morris. Earlier requests by the Americans for loans had been made with similar reassurances, all of which seemed to the court unrealistic.[42]

38. Ver Steeg, *Robert Morris,* 66–67, 84–87, 90–94, 109–10, 115.

39. "Copia de carta escrita por el Honorable Robert Morris a Dn Francisco Rendon fha en Philadelphia a 11 de julio de 1781," July 11, 1781, AGI, Santo Domingo 2597.

40. "Plan para establecer una Banca Nacional en los Estados Unidos de America," July 11, 1780, *ibid.* The proposed bank was to be opened with some $400,000. It was to be administered by a board of a dozen directors. Morris furnished Rendon with, besides this information, eighteen rules and regulations that were to govern the bank's operation. See Ver Steeg, *Robert Morris,* 66–67.

41. Rendon to the captain general of Cuba, July 11, 1781, AGI, Santo Domingo 2597.

42. Ver Steeg, *Robert Morris,* 114.

In spite of Rendon's quasi-consular duties, both he and his superiors continued to see his primary task as the collection of information. That was so
even though the Council of Ministers had a decreasing need for intelligence
as the 1780s progressed. Although Rendon sought to emulate Miralles' mas-
terly reporting, he lacked his predecessor's meticulousness and attention to
detail. In addition, he did not seem to be as well organized or as prompt in
his communications with the captain general and the minister of the Indies.
He did not send reports to Havana and Madrid as frequently as Miralles
had done. Instead, he preferred to gather his information, collect it over a
period of weeks, and then forward a packet of letters that might cover as
much as three months. During early 1781, he failed to communicate with
his superiors from January until March, and during the following year his
dispatches averaged only one packet of information every two to three
months.[43] Neither the captain general nor the minister of the Indies seemed
to mind the sporadic arrival of news from Philadelphia, since the increasing
Spanish military activity around the globe made information from North
America less urgent for Spanish policy makers.

From the very outset, Rendon suffered from a paucity of confidants and
sources of information, compared with the many Miralles had developed.
He had to rely to a greater extent on public newspapers and gazettes. He
collected journals published not only in rebel areas of North America but
also in British-held zones and foreign parts. During 1780, he depended
heavily on the gazette printed in New York for news of British actions.[44]
From ships calling at Philadelphia, he regularly received copies of journals
published in the Caribbean.[45] The captains and crews of the ships also pro-

43. For the frequency with which Rendon sent his reports to Havana and Madrid, see
"Indize de los oficios que en esta ocasión y con los Números desde 71 hasta 99, ambos inclusivos, dirje Don Francisco Rendon al Exmo Don Josef de Gálvez," October 20, 1780, AGI,
Cuba 1291; "Indice de los oficios que en esta ocasión y con los números 100 hasta 115, ambos
inclusivos, remite Don Francisco Rendon al Exmo Señor Don Josef de Galvez," November 12,
1780, *ibid.;* Rendon to J. de Gálvez, March 5, 1781, November 20, 1782, Rendon to the captain
general of Cuba, November 20, 1782, all AGI, Santo Domingo 2598; Rendon to J. de Gálvez,
November 15, 1783, AGI, Santo Domingo 2597. It is likely that the captain general and the
minister of the Indies permitted this relatively infrequent contact because Spain's need for
strategic intelligence had diminished as the war continued after 1780. Spain's major military
interest shifted to the Caribbean and Europe. And, as noted, diplomatic initiatives shifted to
the European capitals.

44. Rendon to Diego Navarro, September 23, 1780, no. 119, AGI, Cuba 1282. The correspondence Rendon directed to Cuba and Spain contains many copies of gazettes that the agent
sent intact to his superiors, sometimes without translating their contents into Spanish.

45. Rendon to J. de Gálvez, March 20, 1781, no. 10, AGI, Santo Domingo, 1598-A.

vided Rendon with information. The observer cultivated their company and learned what he could from them. He often relied upon a Captain Taylor, master of the *Miralleson*, the flour vessel owned by Morris, for accounts of events from abroad. In addition, many of the vessels that called at Saint Eustatius routinely provided the Spanish observer with notices of events from that quarter.[46] In time, Rendon also drew upon the French ambassador in Philadelphia for reports about the war. Not only was Luzerne much better connected in Philadelphia society but he also received regular information from the French military commanders in North America.[47]

On the whole, Rendon had less success than his predecessor in cultivating important members of the Congress as sources. He realized that and deliberately tried to engage several officers of the Congress in regular written communication. Trading on the common knowledge that he had semi-official status as an observer for the Spanish king, he regularly talked with committee heads in an effort to learn about official policies and public activities. In 1782, he sent Robert Livingston a lengthy set of questions relating to the foreign-policy, military, and financial problems facing the Americans. Livingston responded with a long formal letter that enlarged on many of the critical diplomatic concerns confronting the United States. He laid out for Rendon the amounts of money appropriated by the Congress to maintain the army and navy, the source of the body's funds, and what might happen in the event of a deficit. In particular, he recommended that commercial relations between Spain and the United States be increased.[48] But formal contacts with American leaders, although affording congressional officials the opportunity to voice platitudes about Spanish-American relations, in reality brought Rendon little significant information. Frequently he received nothing but the enunciation of official government policies already known in Spain.

Nevertheless, Rendon did deliver some reports of significance during the early 1780s. The captain general and the minister of the Indies had instructed him to pay special attention to three geographic areas that they believed to be of continuing moment to Spanish planning: British-held New York, the

46. Rendon to Navarro, July 4, 1780, no. 91, AGI, Cuba 1282; Rendon to J. de Gálvez, July 11, 1780, March 10, 1781, no. 1, both AGI, Santo Domingo 2598.
47. Rendon to J. de Gálvez, June 22, 1781, no. 24, AGI, Santo Domingo 2597; Rendon to J. de Gálvez, June 29, 1780, *ibid.* 2598.
48. Rendon to Robert Livingston, January 30, 1782, in Papers of the Continental Congress, XIX, 407–11, National Archives.

southern theater of North America, especially the Carolinas, and the Caribbean. Each of the areas had importance for Spanish military interests since any one of them might be the springboard for a British attack on the Spanish Indies.

Rendon therefore followed specifically the events in New York—especially the movements of the Royal Navy—that could prefigure an attack against Spanish colonies to the south. He maintained secret contact by mail with several merchants in New York City who sent him reports. During June, 1780, he learned of the arrival of General Sir Henry Clinton with a large convoy coming from South Carolina. He continued reporting on Clinton's movements for the rest of the summer, as he attempted to learn if they threatened Spain.[49] The Council of Ministers found Rendon's reports useful and instructed him to continue sending what he could find out about events at New York. Rendon turned to the Chevalier de La Luzerne for additional intelligence about the British at New York, especially about Clinton.[50] The spring of 1781 became a relatively hectic time for the Spaniard because of the rumored departure from New York of a major expedition under Clinton's command. The general's household effects had apparently been loaded on a transport. In late April, Washington wrote the Congress that the British seemed to be preparing a major embarkation of troops from New York. Although the exact destination of the force could not be determined, some members of Congress felt that it could be en route to either the Chesapeake Bay or the West Indies.[51] Rendon reported everything he had heard to Spain.

Rendon realized the potential gravity of the situation, but his concern was soon dispelled, for in May he learned that the troops from New York had been dispatched to the southern theater of the continent. News also came that Cornwallis' army appeared to be moving to the Chesapeake region, while the Americans under Lafayette and the Baron von Steuben had some three thousand troops in the environs of Richmond.[52] Rendon decided that the British troop movements did not pose a threat for Spain, and in late May he predicted that the American forces commanded by Generals

49. Rendon to J. de Gálvez, June 27, 1780, AGI, Santo Domingo 2598; Rendon to Diego Navarro, August 27, 1780, no. 115, AGI, Cuba 1282.
50. Rendon to J. de Gálvez, March 10, 1781, AGI, Santo Domingo 2598; Diego Navarro to Rendon, April 19, 1781, AGI, Cuba 1282.
51. Rendon to J. de Gálvez, April 27, 1781, no. 15, AGI, Santo Domingo 2597.
52. Rendon to J. de Gálvez, May 8, 1781, no. 17, *ibid.*

Greene, Lafayette, and von Steuben would combine later in the year to move against the British in the South.[53] Consequently, the southern theater of North America became the main focus of his dispatches. The fall of Charleston in 1780 coincided with his appointment as Miralles' successor, and one of his first acts as the designated observer involved sending confirmation of that English victory to his superiors in Havana and Madrid.[54] Rendon conscientiously attempted to stay abreast of events in the region for the remainder of the year, although he felt that developments in New York held the potential for a greater impact on Spanish concerns.[55]

The spring campaigns in 1781 especially captured the agent's attention, and his reports focused increasingly on the American and British operations commanded by Generals Greene and Cornwallis. Rendon's ability to keep the captain general and minister of the Indies informed about events in the southern theater was largely the consequence of the close touch that General Greene maintained with the Congress. Much of the information the Spanish observer sent on to Cuba and Spain came from letters Greene wrote to Philadelphia that sympathetic members of the Congress passed on to him. The observer often prepared translations that found their way to the Spanish court, as, for example, in late March, when he sent his superiors a lengthy translated extract from Greene's report to Congress on the Battle of Guilford Courthouse. From such reports, Rendon and his superiors got the impression that American military operations had forced Cornwallis into a full retreat.[56]

The observer's interest in Greene's southern campaigns continued through the remainder of the year. For the most part, Rendon's dispatches adequately reflected the broad outline of Greene's pursuit of Cornwallis, although they had a tendency to mirror the American viewpoint because of their reliance on Greene's letters. In any case, account after account of events in the southern theater arrived for the captain general and the minister of the Indies. From Rendon's messages emerged the picture of an eventual American victory in the region, a prospect that encouraged the Spanish

53. Rendon to J. de Gálvez, May 21, 1781, no. 19, July 4, 1781, no. 26., both *ibid.*
54. Rendon to J. de Gálvez, June 17, 1780, *ibid.* 2598; Rendon to Diego Navarro, July 13, 1780, no. 98, AGI, Cuba 1282.
55. Rendon to J. de Gálvez, March 17, 1781, no. 8, AGI, Santo Domingo 2598.
56. "Extracto de carta escrita por el General Greene al Presidente del Congreso, su fha en el campo de Saunders Creek en la Carolina del Sur, 27 de April de 1781," *ibid.* See also Rendon to J. de Gálvez, April 8, April 23, 1781, both *ibid.* 2597.

ministers.[57] To Rendon, Greene's campaigns clearly meant that the power of the British had been broken in the South. Except in Virginia, it appeared to Rendon that the Americans were victorious in the region.[58]

His attention therefore turned to Virginia as the summer of 1781 wore on and his sources yielded reports of increasing activity there on the part of both armies. Rendon concluded that American forces in Virginia had been placed in danger because of the British squadrons in the Chesapeake region. The flow of information to him allowed him to follow the American evacuation of Richmond and the disembarkation of additional British troops at Portsmouth.[59] Convinced that a major confrontation could well occur in Virginia, he increased the frequency of his reports to Havana and Madrid, continuing them throughout the remainder of the summer and fall. For the most part, his dispatches accurately described the complicated troop movements that ended in the encounter at Yorktown. The siege there did not come as a surprise to Spanish officials, since dozens of Rendon's letters during the previous months had prepared them for it.[60]

His dispatches for the remainder of 1781 kept the Spanish court apprised of the demobilization of the defeated British army after the surrender at Yorktown. The observer chronicled Cornwallis' departure from North America and events associated with it. During December, he learned the names and numbers of the British troops that had been killed or wounded at Yorktown, and he furnished lists of them to his superiors. He dispatched copies of congressional resolutions regarding the victory at Yorktown, along with transcriptions of letters that Cornwallis had written to General Clinton describing the English surrender. Although he did not recognize Yorktown as the end of the military conflict, it was clear to him from his sources that the British surrender there was the turning point in the struggle.[61]

In the months following Yorktown, the character and nature of the data

57. "Carta que el General Greene escrive al President del Congreso fha en el Campo de Maobords Ferry 14 de mayo de 1781," *ibid.* 2597; "Extracto de carta escrita por el Mayor General Green al Presidente del Congreso, fha en el campo de Little River, serca de Ninety Six, en la Carolina del Sur, a 20 de junio 1781," *ibid.*
58. Rendon to J. de Gálvez, June 19, 1781, no. 23, *ibid.*
59. Rendon to J. de Gálvez, March 27, 1781, no. 11, April 2, 1781, no. 12, both *ibid.* 2598; Rendon to J. de Gálvez, May 15, 1781, no. 18, May 28, 1781, no. 20, both *ibid.* 2597.
60. Rendon to J. de Gálvez, June 6, June 26, July 8, July 10, November 27, 1781, all *ibid.* 2597.
61. Rendon to J. de Gálvez, December 15, 1781, no. 45, December 20, 1781, no. 46, both *ibid.*

Rendon sent to Cuba and Spain changed. Although he was still concerned with naval events in the Caribbean and continued to supply news of events there, his attention began to reorient itself subtly toward political and economic developments in the United States.[62] On his own initiative, he started to place an emphasis on the various factions and groups in the Congress, and on the formation of American policy. Behind the change in his focus lay the decrease in military activity in North America after Yorktown. Early in 1782, Rendon related to the minister of the Indies that little of military consequence appeared to be happening anywhere in North America. Most of the congressional leaders, he added, had gone home to their families for visits in the wake of the English surrender.[63]

The observer also struck up a strong working relationship with George Washington. During 1782, the two men became much closer, largely because of overtures of friendship on the part of the Spaniard. Rendon offered the general lodging in his home during the Washingtons' Christmas visit to Philadelphia in 1781. He interpreted their acceptance of his hospitality as a gesture of respect for the Spanish king.[64] It was with obvious satisfaction that he explained to his superiors that although the president of the Congress, a number of its members, and other leading figures in the city had offered accommodation to the Washingtons, the general had decided to lodge with him. When the Washington family arrived with their own food, housewares, and a cook, Rendon graciously insisted to his guests that the king of Spain meant to meet their every domestic need. The Spaniard later offered a gala banquet in honor of General and Mrs. Washington, and it attracted most of the important members of Philadelphia society.[65]

Washington reciprocated by entertaining Rendon in grand fashion at West Point in the new year. Much as the general had done for Miralles in 1780, he gratified Rendon with a visit that had the pomp and formality normally reserved for an accredited diplomatic envoy. Arriving at Washington's headquarters in early July for a five-day visit, Rendon found that the general had organized a banquet in his honor that was attended by most of the staff officers. The following afternoon, Baron von Steuben directed two

62. For examples of correspondence about the Caribbean, see Rendon to J. de Gálvez, December 31, 1781, February 14, 1782, no. 80, February 22, 1782, no. 51, all *ibid.* 2598.
63. Rendon to J. de Gálvez, March 8, 1782, no. 52, *ibid.;* Rendon to Mr. Matlack, November 9, 1782, in Gratz Collection, Historical Society of Pennsylvania, Philadelphia.
64. Otero, "Gardoqui," 23.
65. Rendon to J. de Gálvez, December 10, 1781, no. 44, AGI, Santo Domingo 2598.

hours' worth of maneuvers that impressed Rendon with the high state of training and military discipline that had been instilled into the Continental line. After that display, General Washington and the Spaniard visited on horseback all the posts and redoubts in the neighborhood, where the general pointed out improvements that had been made in the defenses. Washington used the opportunity of the leisurely ride to impress upon Rendon his desire for close and harmonious relations with Spain. Looking ahead to peace negotiations, he expressed to Rendon his hope that the Spanish king could be counted on to support the independence of the United States.[66]

Rendon also began to cultivate other influential members of the American government after 1781. Many of them were among the political allies and supporters of Robert Morris. It was natural for Rendon to seek harmony with them, since he had been heavily involved with the superintendent of finance in a number of business dealings. Rendon actively worked for the friendship of Robert Livingston. He made it a practice to solicit Livingston's opinions on the financial and foreign-policy questions affecting the young nation. By 1783, the two men had taken to meeting together informally, with Rendon asking numerous questions about the nation's possible policies on currency reform, payment of the congressional debt, and the support of the army and navy, and discussing the general opinions Livingston had formed about the peace settlement and the commercial role for the United States in postwar trade. Although Rendon certainly used his acquaintance with Livingston to serve his own ends, the New Yorker had much to gain in return. Livingston's brother had shipyard interests along the Atlantic Coast, and the two men approached Rendon to inquire if Spain had an interest in underwriting the costs of shipbuilding in their family's yards. They prepared elaborate proposals for the construction of vessels for the Spanish navy in their facilities and convinced Rendon of the soundness of their ideas. Firmly in their camp, the Spanish observer sent the minister of the Indies a strong endorsement of the Livingstons' scheme, though nothing ever came of it.[67]

Rendon learned from his influential sources that the United States expected a peace settlement within the coming year. He explained to his superiors that in that case, since there would be little of urgent significance in

66. Rendon to J. de Gálvez, July 30, 1782, no. 61, *ibid.*
67. Rendon to J. de Gálvez, April 20, 1782, no. 56, *ibid.*

his dispatches, he could prepare for the Spanish court a series of memorandums by which the king and his ministers might become better informed about the nature and character of the government of the new nation. He thus began researching and compiling a detailed portrayal of the financial condition of the Congress, along with a more general depiction of the commercial potential of the country. Out of his labors came two long reports that gave Spanish policy makers their first insights into many of the economic and foreign-policy problems faced by the United States in the early 1780s.[68]

Much in Rendon's extensive report on congressional finances undoubtedly came from Robert Morris. Still, the Spaniard attempted to present an impartial analysis. For that reason, his memorial had a basically negative tone, reflecting the financial strain the Congress was suffering. According to his report, the exiguity of gold and silver specie, a devalued paper currency, poor credit, rapid inflation, and poor fiscal planning were the major economic problems besetting the American government.[69] He reviewed the development of financial policies in the Congress, providing a short history of the fiscal measures enacted by that body during the Revolution. He also provided a survey of the currency, banking, and taxation practices common in state governments.[70] He concluded his assessment of financial planning in the Congress by reviewing the debates surrounding Robert Morris' appointment as superintendent of finance and the program Morris had proposed once in office. As might be expected, the Spaniard had little but praise for Morris' actions and affirmed that should the ideas of the Pennsylvania merchant prevail, the operations of Congress would surely have acquired a sound fiscal basis. Rendon reiterated his conviction that in the meantime Congress vitally needed foreign financial assistance in the form of loans.[71]

He wrote his second memorial during late 1782 and early 1783. Dealing with the potential of an independent United States for commerce and

68. It took Rendon almost a year to assemble and write these two reports. The first arrived at court in the spring of 1782; the second came over a year later, during the fall of 1783. The first is "Memoria sobre las finanzas de los Treze Estados Unidos de America Seteptrional," April 20, 1782, *ibid.;* the second is "Primera y Segunda parte de la memoria sobre las produciones exportaciones e Ymportaciones y modo de hacer el comercio con los Estados Unidos: Que Don Francisco Rendon remite al Exmo Senor Don J. de Gálvez," September 8, 1783, *ibid.* 2597.
69. See "Memoria sobre las finanzas," 533.
70. *Ibid.*, 640–70.
71. *Ibid.*, 576.

trade, it was perhaps Rendon's greatest accomplishment in Philadelphia. Although Spanish policy makers did not fully take its recommendations to heart, it provided what may have been the most complete assessment of American commerce up to that time. Rendon divided it into two parts. The first was designed to show the condition of American commerce by analyzing the trade of each of the states, and it included an impressive array of statistical information about agricultural production, trade levels, and export data for each. The second part, more interpretive in nature, speculated on the commercial potential of the nation. Reflecting what must have been the opinion of Robert Morris, Rendon predicted that an independent United States would become a serious commercial rival to the nations of Europe within a generation.[72]

The transmittal of this commercial memorial to Spain marked a milestone for Rendon: he no longer saw a purpose to remaining in the United States. He therefore wrote the minister of the Indies, requesting a transfer to another post in the Spanish Indies. Rendon felt that the original objectives of his sojourn in Pennsylvania had long been fulfilled. The other observers superintended by the captain general of Cuba had been retired from the field years before, he pointed out, and he asked the same for himself. In particular, he hoped to be appointed the new intendant in Spanish Louisiana. In a long letter setting forth his achievements after arriving in North America to serve as secretary to Miralles in January, 1779, he underlined the successes of his mission. To his view, he had adroitly completed all the assignments given him as part of the captain general's observation network. He had skillfully discharged as well the other responsibilities he had been given from time to time, most important the opening of Cuba to the North American flour trade. Rendon repeated his belief that Spain no longer required an observer in Philadelphia, especially if the court decided to open diplomatic relations and establish a formal mission. The time had come, he wrote Havana and Madrid, to recall him and appoint an accredited ambassador.[73]

For the time being, however, the minister of the Indies decided to keep Rendon in Philadelphia without a change in status. He felt that the Spanish court still needed the observer on the scene in order to report on the British

72. A discussion of the full content and detail of these memorials, which present a great deal of specific data, falls well beyond the scope of this study.
73. Rendon to J. de Gálvez, September 8, 1783, no. 86, AGI, Santo Domingo 2597.

army in the South. Although military activities had come to an end in North America by 1782, the war between England and its enemies in Europe continued. The siege of Gibraltar in 1782 was to be one of the largest single campaigns of the war. Moreover, naval confrontations between England and the fleets of France and Spain demanded that the court at Madrid remain well informed about British troop movements in the Western Hemisphere. King Charles and his ministers had already decided sometime during late 1782 that Spain would eventually send an accredited diplomatic envoy to the United States who would assume many of the diplomatic functions Miralles and Rendon had been performing on a de facto basis since 1778.[74] But the Spanish court needed Rendon in Philadelphia until the envoy arrived. Anyway, the policy makers in Madrid had use for Rendon's reports on the progress of peace negotiations as the Congress understood them. The members of the Council of Ministers understood that knowledge about American aspirations and desires regarding the peace treaties would be essential to Spain.

Rendon consequently remained in Philadelphia, giving special emphasis to the British forces in North America. He sent on to Madrid, for example, copies of the London papers that had arrived in the city. They contained the news that Sir Guy Carleton, the British commander in chief in North America, had been empowered to undertake separate peace negotiations with the Congress. Rendon suggested several reasons to his superiors why that might be a reasonable objective for the British. For one thing, they did not have a sufficient number of troops in North America for a new offensive campaign. Their numbers permitted them the possibility of holding present positions and little else. Rendon surmised that British failures in the southern theater had forced a reconsolidation of military power in the Caribbean, especially at Jamaica, as a defensive measure. He also conjectured that the sheer incidence of casualties suffered by Britain in North America might be disposing it to end the fighting. He predicted confidently, however, that Congress would refuse to engage in separate peace negotiations with Carleton but would insist on going to the peace table in the company of Spanish and French representatives.[75]

The information Rendon provided seemed of decreasing importance to

---

74. Morris, *The Peacemakers*, 231.
75. Rendon to J. de Gálvez, May 16, 1782, no. 57, AGI, Santo Domingo 2598.

the Spanish ministries. With the congressional envoys in Europe in regular contact with the French and Spanish ministers, much of the general information Rendon could furnish proved little more than corroboration of what was first known in Europe. The observer in Philadelphia dutifully passed back to his superiors news they had had long before. From time to time, however, he was able to report on deliberations in Congress that they were unaware of. He wrote about factions in the Congress that disagreed on certain provisions of the peace treaties. He observed, for example, that the Louisiana boundary question had been a topic of discussion among some representatives, "malcontents," as he called them. They wished to see unlimited rights of navigation on the Mississippi given to the United States, and they desired the cession to the new nation of territories in the West that Rendon felt properly belonged to Spain. The Spanish observer cautioned that this faction might eventually prove troublesome for Spain.[76] On other matters, however, he furnished scant information, and occasionally he seemed unconcerned about important diplomatic problems touching upon Spanish interests. He reported nothing of substance on the secret Anglo-American Treaty of 1782 or on Britain's attempts to increase the number of loyalists moving to Florida and the West Indies. Lord Dunmore's efforts to create a loyalist asylum in East Florida seemed to make little impression on him.

With few demands upon him, Rendon partook of an increasingly active social life. He met a young Philadelphia woman, Margarite Marshall, the daughter of one of the city's mercantile families. The two began to spend a great deal of time together, and by 1783 their close relationship had become well known, if not notorious. Rendon bought a house that they used as a rendezvous.[77] The couple soon became the object of a great deal of gossip, since to proper Philadelphians their open and illicit relationship was scandalous. The Marshall family apparently accepted the situation; although active in the business community of the city, they had never been among the socially prominent. Margarite's father had a fairly undistinguished career, which included several financial failures, so that he could not provide a dowry for his daughter.[78] Although by 1784 the couple had decided to

76. Rendon to J. de Gálvez, April 12, 1783, no. 75, *ibid.* 2597.
77. This house was located on Union Street. Rendon sold the property to Miss Marshall in 1786, after he returned to Spain. See Rendon to Marshall, Chancery Records, Book No. 12, p. 194, Municipal Archives of Philadelphia.
78. Gomez del Campillo, *Relaciones diplomáticas*, I, xxii.

marry, a number of obstacles stood in their way. Spanish law required officers of the crown serving in colonial appointments to secure royal permission before marrying local women. The marriage in addition had to meet
the requirements of the Roman Catholic church. Winning church approval
for a mixed marriage involved a long, time-consuming process that, at a
minimum, took many months. In addition, Rendon was seeking a new
posting in the Indies that would take his bride into an alien culture, and
this could be expected to cause the crown misgivings. Nevertheless, Rendon
and Miss Marshall announced their engagement in early 1784, and Rendon
initiated the paperwork for obtaining royal permission to marry.

The observer's decision to marry Margarite Marshall coincided with the
formal abolition of his position in Philadelphia. With the end of the revolt
and the Peace of 1783, the Conde de Floridablanca decided to recognize the
independence of the United States and to send an accredited representative
to Philadelphia. The Council of Ministers agreed that the envoy should be
Diego de Gardoqui, who had a long and successful record of working with
the Americans. Gardoqui had the reputation of dealing very effectively with
Englishmen and Anglo-Americans in a wide variety of business, social, and
diplomatic contexts. He had, for example, served as head of Spain's consular
service in London in addition to having had contacts with American envoys
during the Revolution.[79] In September, 1784, a royal order appointed him
chargé d'affaires in the United States and instructed him to take up residence in Philadelphia. The same directive designated Rendon secretary to
the legation. It was reasoned that Rendon, having already resided in North
America for over five years, could acquaint Gardoqui with the history of
Spanish concerns at the Congress while delivering to him all the agency's
correspondence. In making this appointment and formally creating a Spanish diplomatic legation in the United States, King Charles took special notice of Rendon's contribution as Spanish observer in Philadelphia and complimented him on his services to the crown.[80]

Gardoqui's appointment led Rendon to ask again for immediate reassignment. Wanting a more prestigious appointment, he was not pleased to serve
as secretary to the legation. But the court denied his request for a new
posting, since the king wanted him to remain in Philadelphia to help
smooth Gardoqui's assumption of office. The new chargé d'affaires arrived

79. Otero, "Gardoqui," 53.
80. Gomez del Campillo, *Relaciones diplomáticas*, I, xix.

in May, 1785, and almost from the beginning the two Spaniards had difficulty working together. Rendon's desire to marry Miss Marshall exacer-
bated the relations between the two men. Spanish law required Gardoqui,
as Rendon's supervisor, to act on his application for marriage, but the new
envoy refused to approve it, citing reasons that to Rendon seemed inappro-
priate if not groundless. Gardoqui questioned Miss Marshall's sincerity in
professing a willingness to become a Roman Catholic. In addition, the
chargé d'affaires intimated that the Marshall family desired the marriage in
order to elevate their social standing in Philadelphia society. The Spanish
minister of state Floridablanca decided to recall Rendon to Spain to learn
more about the marriage application, at the same time removing the former
observer from a deteriorating situation that had the potential for embarrassing Spanish interests in the United States.[81] Rendon left for Madrid in late
November, 1786, never to return to the United States. Indeed, he left Pennsylvania so suddenly that some in Philadelphia wondered about the nature
of his business.[82] Miss Marshall remained behind, expecting to join him
once he received royal permission for the marriage and arranged a new assignment in the Spanish Indies.

At court, Rendon devoted his full efforts to the twofold goal of winning
permission to marry and receiving an assignment of prestige in the Spanish
colonial service. He personally laid his arguments in support of the marriage application before officers at the ministry of state, including Miguel
de Otamendi, the official responsible for ruling on such approvals. Miss
Marshall wrote several letters to Otamendi, as well, reiterating her commitment to becoming a practicing Roman Catholic. Eventually, however, Rendon realized that his career in the colonial service depended heavily on the
very people who were reluctant to approve his marriage request. Word of
his immodest relationship with the young lady had apparently prejudiced
his case. Faced with a choice between the hand of Miss Marshall and his
career, he selected the latter. In the spring of 1787, he assured Otamendi that
he would abide by whatever decision the ministry of state made. By August,
he received formal notification that permission to marry had been denied.[83]
The Spanish ministry apparently acted at the recommendation of Gardoqui,
who felt that there might be a scandal in Philadelphia should the two marry.

81. *Ibid.*, xxii.
82. William Grayson to James Monroe, in *Letters,* ed. Burnett, VII, 511.
83. Gomez del Campillo, *Relaciones diplomáticas,* I, xxii.

The chargé d'affaires feared that the marriage could jeopardize his dealings with the Americans on the wide-ranging and complicated set of issues he had to negotiate. Although heartbroken, Rendon remained true to his word. Soon thereafter he received the appointment he had long desired, as intendant of Louisiana. He held that position during the 1790s.[84] His departure from Philadelphia marked the end of the observation activities overseen by the captain general of Cuba.

84. "Relación de los meritos y servicios de Don Francisco Rendon," AGI, Mexico 3189.

8

Observers and Strategic Intelligence

Two centuries of heated and at times bloody Anglo-Spanish rivalry had planted in the Spanish of the late eighteenth century a desire to witness the demise of the British Empire. Their embarrassing losses in the Seven Years' War, coupled with the terms of the Peace of Paris in 1763, made urgent Spain's desire to weaken the British. The American Revolution gave Charles and his ministers the chance they sought. Spain, as a major colonial power in the Western Hemisphere and a traditional rival of the British, had to reckon with the beginning of open warfare in North America during 1775. Events at Lexington and Concord signaled the start of a conflict from which there would be few chances for it to escape and, once it became a belligerent, little opportunity for it to retreat. Early on, the fighting forced King Charles and his ministers to make two important decisions: they had to formulate Spanish policy for a diplomatic response to the revolt, and they had to take steps to receive timely information about events in North America.

King Charles and his ministers saw that failure to secure intelligence about the insurrection could doom any policy made by them. Such failure, they felt, would be inexcusable. They realized from the outset of fighting in Massachusetts that the English colonial revolt could work to Spain's international advantage. The American Revolution might well provide them with a ready-made weapon, almost too good to have hoped for, to humble the British Empire at the same time that it presented them with the chance to assert themselves in the development of a strong and independent foreign policy.[1]

A deliberate and considered response to the Revolution had to be based on sound information from trusted sources. Creating an intelligence network seemed to the ministers at the Spanish court the best way to get the information they needed. The Spanish government therefore directed the captain general of Cuba to provide news, reports, and notices about events of the American Revolution. Although King Charles and his advisers sometimes failed to make full use of the information they received, it unquestionably influenced Spanish diplomatic policy regarding the revolt.

During the period of Spain's declared neutrality, however, its ability to profit from the revolt was limited.[2] For one thing, the conflict raised vexing questions of ideology and perspective for the Spanish court. King Charles understandably viewed any rebellion like that in North America as little more than a felony against the authority of monarchy.[3] In addition, the court saw the rebellious Americans as Englishmen, with strong political and cultural ties to their British homeland. Charles and his ministers worried about a settlement between England and its rebellious provinces after which both the European and the American English might unite forces to attack Spanish possessions. Fears of a reconciliation gave pause to the Spanish ministers during the early years of the rebellion, especially after Great Britain began to augment its forces in North America.[4]

Spain's other foreign commitments in the late 1770s also dictated a cautious initial response to the revolt. As the fighting began in Massachusetts, the Spanish general Alejandro O'Reilly was mounting a major assault in

1. This theme informs the basic interpretation in most works dealing with Spain and the American Revolution. For early examples, see Joseph H. Burke, *Spain's Attitude Toward the War for American Independence* (Ph.D. dissertation, Catholic University of America, 1909), and José Pérez Herváas, *España y los Estados Unidos: Nuestra participación en la independencia de aquel país* (Barcelona, 1918).

2. For a discussion of these concerns, see J. Leitch Wright, Jr., *Anglo-Spanish Rivalry in North America* (Athens, Ga., 1971), 121–23.

3. W. N. Hargreaves-Mawdsley, ed., *Spain Under the Bourbons, 1700–1813: A Collection of Documents* (London, 1973), xxix; José Antonio Armillas Vicente, "Europa y la revolución americana: Un nuevo mito," *Estudios del departamento de historia moderna, 1976* (Saragossa, 1976), 64–66.

4. This seems a justifiable fear, considering the historical traditions of over two centuries of Anglo-Spanish rivalry. During 1775 and 1776, much of the official correspondence between the minister of the Indies and his New World subordinates spoke of the "European" and the "American" English. See Wright, *Anglo-Spanish Rivalry,* 123.

North Africa as part of Spain's Moroccan policy. That venture consumed a great deal of attention in the Spanish ministries, as much of Spain's military plant was monopolized by a projected attack in Algeria. O'Reilly suffered a completely unanticipated defeat in July, 1775, and his forces met heavy losses at the hands of the North Africans.[5] His defeat temporarily cooled much of the ardor in Madrid for an aggressive foreign policy and military adventures. Charles and his ministers were also constrained by a possible confrontation with Portugal. Some members of the king's council, including the minister of state, felt that the summer or early fall of 1775 would bring war with Portugal over territorial disputes along the Río de la Plata, in South America.[6]

The greatest check on Spain's response to the Revolution during 1775 sprang from its relations with France, however, for a powerful faction in the Spanish Council of Ministers had been advocating greater independence from France in the formulation and implementation of Spanish foreign policy. The traditionally close ties between the two Bourbon monarchs had been substantially weakened after the Seven Years' War, and France had failed to support the Spanish position during the diplomatic confrontation with Great Britain in 1770 over the Malvinas, or Falkland, Islands, off the coast of South America. Key ministers in Madrid smarted from what they perceived as a Gallic desertion and did not wish to follow French diplomatic initiatives regarding the American Revolution until there was a patent advantage for Spain. Those ministers advised Charles to consider the English colonial revolt within the context of relations with France.[7]

All these circumstances counseled delay and caution for Spain in responding to the nascent revolt in British America during 1775. Yet, Charles and his ministers certainly understood the importance and necessity of being as fully informed as possible about events in North America. The Spanish court required what twentieth-century diplomats call strategic intelligence.

5. Rodríguez Casado, *La política marroquí de Carlos III*, 235–43.
6. A review of Grimaldi's correspondence with the Spanish ambassador in London during the summer months of 1775 shows that the minister of state appeared more concerned about possible English reactions to Spain's policy regarding Portugal than the unfolding revolt in North America. See AGS, Estado 7016. Grimaldi's preoccupation with Portuguese problems continued well into the following year. See Van Alstyne, *Empire and Independence*, 92–94.
7. Víctor Morales Lezcano, "Diplomática y política financiera de España durante la sublevación de las colonias ingleses en América, 1775–1783," *Anuario de estudios americanos*, XXVI (1969), 507–65.

That is the sort of intelligence that assists in the fashioning of national policy in the broadest sense. It is much more encompassing than the limited operational or combat intelligence that addresses primarily wartime enemy military tactics. Strategic intelligence involves the coordinated assessment of the military, political, economic, and psychological power of a foreign government for the purpose of forming national policy. It provides a constant flow of information to policy makers during both peacetime and wartime about every manner of occurrence in the relevant geographical areas.[8] That kind of information cannot be acquired quickly but requires the relatively slow assembling of reports from a wide variety of sources. It also involves an attempt to evaluate all factors that might influence the foreign power's potential international activity. Strategic espionage operations therefore demand evaluation of the other government's capabilities, vulnerabilities, and tendencies.[9] That was the job of Spain's observers during the American Revolution. Harking back to the biblical story of Moses' spies sent into Canaan, it may be said that the captain general's agents were dispatched "to spy out the land."

The captain general's observation network evolved from contacts developed in the Caribbean and Gulf of Mexico during the period after the Seven Years' War. For some fifteen years prior to the American Revolution, he had been developing a local observation network in order to monitor activities

8. For the modern definition of the term *strategic intelligence*, see U.S. Department of the Army, *Military Intelligence, Operational*, ST30-6-2 (1954), 3. Strategic intelligence, according to present application, may be defined as the "product resulting from the collecting, evaluation, analysis, interpolation, and interpretation of all available information which concerns one or more aspects of foreign nations or areas of operations and which is immediately or potentially significant to planning" (U.S. Department of Defense, Office of the Joint Chiefs of Staff, *Dictionary of United States Military Terms for Joint Usage*, quoted by Charles H. Andregg, in *Management of Defense Intelligence* [Washington, D.C., 1968], 3). For modern uses of strategic intelligence, see William M. McGovern, *Strategic Intelligence and the Shape of Tomorrow* (Chicago, 1961). Listing the extensive literature of a theoretical, historical, and foreign-policy nature regarding strategic and other types of intelligence falls well beyond the scope of this study. See instead William R. Harris, *Intelligence and National Security: A Bibliography with Selected Annotations* (Cambridge, Mass., 1968). The Spanish government, as part of its normal diplomatic activities in London, collected intelligence—as did all nations—by using the resident legation at the embassy. In addition, the minister of state from time to time employed espionage agents in England, especially after 1779, when Spain entered the war. Those agents, however, had little success in reporting on events in North America even though they provided a wealth of information about Great Britain. For the story of Spain's espionage system in England, see Voltes Bou, "Thomas Hussey y sus servicios a la política de Floridablanca," 92–141.

9. Light Townsend Cummins, "Spanish Espionage in the South During the American Revolution," *Southern Studies*, XIX (1980), 39–49.

in the English colonies bordering on his command. Its efforts furnished regular and extensive intelligence about occurrences in the British Floridas, on Jamaica, along the south Atlantic Coast, and on the various English islands of the northern Caribbean. Since the network served the captain general in his capacity as the regional army commander, it closely followed the lines of Spanish military organization.

The governor of Spanish Louisiana assisted in many of the efforts because of his location at New Orleans. The two Spanish commanders relied on sources such as the Minorcan colony in British East Florida, Luciano de Herrera in Saint Augustine, and several traders along the Mississippi who had English commercial connections, the most important of whom was Juan de Surriret. Spanish officials in the captaincy general of Cuba also collected news from ship captains and crews calling at ports in the area. By the start of the American Revolution, the captain general at Havana operated as the chief of an intelligence-gathering system that covered Louisiana, the British Floridas, and various islands of the Gulf of Mexico and the Caribbean. It became a relatively simple task for the ministers in Spain to expand and reorient the network into a system designed to provide regular reports about the American Revolution.

José de Gálvez and the Marqués de Grimaldi, as ministers at the Spanish court, took a special interest in what the observers presented, since their departments dealt with colonial and foreign-policy matters respectively. José de Gálvez served in Spain as the cabinet-level supervisor of the observer network, and Grimaldi's department applied the acquired information in formulating policy. Gálvez and Grimaldi took steps during late 1776 to reorient the captain general's observation system into an organization that could provide a steady stream of news about the American Revolution.

As captain general, the Marqués de la Torre developed a network of observers that included merchants employed by the Asiento de Negros, Floridian Spaniards living in Cuba as exiles, and various figures—Miguel Antonio Eduardo and Luciano de Herrera most notably—who made personal contact with British and rebel American leaders. The governor of Louisiana, Luis de Unzaga, vigorously supported the observation effort by supervising similar undertakings along the lower Mississippi, the reports from which went to the captain general. Bartolomé Beauregard, a New Orleanian, visited Philadelphia at Unzaga's behest to gauge the caliber of the American leadership. The governor also learned much about the revolt from travelers, shipmasters, and crewmen passing along the Mississippi. Thanks to the support of the New Orleans merchant Oliver Pollock, the American emissary George Gibson had several audiences with Governor Unzaga that resulted in Spain's shipping supplies to the rebels by the Mississippi and Ohio river systems.

The information arriving in Madrid from the captain general's office indicated the sincerity of purpose and the firm conviction of the American rebels about achieving their goals. It became clear that the American Revolution would continue for some time. In large measure because of the reports, Charles and his ministers came to view the American rebels as a group that could not be ignored and that Spain would eventually have to deal with. This conclusion prompted a movement away from the court's official policy of neutrality to one in favor of the Americans. By the time of the Willing raid on the Mississippi, during 1778, Spain had for all practical purposes abandoned its neutral stance, though it still professed to British diplomats in Europe that the neutral policy continued in force.

Having decided on a benevolent neutrality tilted in favor of the United States, Spain began to use its observers as conduits for aid and material assistance to the Americans. Spanish policy makers had the luxury of covertly deviating from their proclaimed neutrality, surreptitiously aiding the Americans, and monitoring the results of their secret assistance all within the services provided by the captain general's observer system. In addition, the Spanish decision to send secret aid to the Americans demanded that the activities of the observers be enlarged to track the expanded role for Spain in the conflict. For that reason, the captain general posted Miguel Antonio Eduardo to Philadelphia and increased the number of observations by Asiento merchants in the Caribbean. While these operations were in progress, the captaincy general of Cuba passed from the Marqués de la Torre to Diego Joseph Navarro, who continued to direct Spanish observation of the revolt.

Even with the new, bolder policy of limited support for the Americans, debates within the Council of Ministers clearly showed conflicting schools of thought. The aggressive views of the anti-British *aragoneses* contrasted with the more conservative positions of the ministers of state Grimaldi and Floridablanca. In addition, the desire of the Gálvez family for vigorous military action in the Mississippi Valley and Central America pulled against the lobbying at court by the *floridianos*, who made the return of British East

Florida the highest international priority for Spain. All of the viewpoints found their way into the management of the observation network. The aims of its intelligence gathering and the focus of the information acquired vacillated according to the temporary ascendancy of one group over another at court.

The Franco-American Alliance of 1778 placed new pressures on the Spanish observers. The Council of Ministers decided in the wake of France's entry into the war that the time had not yet arrived for Spain to become involved in the conflict. The feeling was that the Spanish colonies in the Indies needed to have their defenses strengthened first. A Spanish declaration of war in the spring of 1778, some ministers worried, would give the British navy an excuse to attack the Spanish treasure fleet en route to Europe. Those ministers also cautioned that the United States would likely simply replace Great Britain as a New World rival.

Spain therefore decided not to follow its Bourbon cousins into open warfare against Great Britain. Its independence from France in foreign policy required the Spanish court, for its own self-assurance, to establish closer links with the Americans, for King Charles and his ministers no longer had the option of coordinating a neutral policy with their counterparts in Paris. The Franco-American alliance at the same time encouraged the Americans to seek stronger ties with the Spanish in the hope of establishing an alliance similar to the one forged with France. Concurrently, the Mississippi Valley became the scene of increased rebel military action against the British in the Illinois country and West Florida. The expeditions of James Willing and George Rogers Clark both depended upon support and material assistance furnished from the Spanish territory by partisans of the American cause. Governor Unzaga's successor, Bernardo de Gálvez, found himself caught during 1778 between the two warring sides as he maintained a formal neutrality. Gálvez adopted a cautious policy that obliquely supported the Americans while trying to placate British officials in West Florida. The military ferment in the Mississippi Valley, however, diverted the attention of the governor from the captain general's observation network. Young Gálvez increasingly focused his efforts on increasing the military defenses in Louisiana and on developing offensive plans against West Florida in case Spain entered the war.

Given all this, the ministers at the Spanish court decided to send an observer to the meeting place of the Continental Congress to establish direct, ongoing contact with the American leadership. As the minister of the Indies put it, the observer was to establish permanent residence in Philadelphia so that he could report promptly on any "prejudicial designs" affecting Spain and Spanish interests. Juan de Miralles was sent to North America during 1778 charged with the responsibility of reporting news about the revolt.

Miralles proved to be a uniquely gregarious person who was able to form friendships with a wide range of people holding significant positions. Within a year of his arrival in Philadelphia, the volume of timely information he was regularly furnishing the captain general made the dispatches from most of the other observers superfluous. The Spanish court came to rely exclusively on the observer in Philadelphia for reports about the American side of the Revolution. The pro-American character of Miralles' reports had a direct impact on the formulation of Spanish policy. By early 1779, the ministers at court were moving cautiously toward a declaration of war against Great Britain. As they did, Miralles' residence in Philadelphia let them follow the American discussion on the gamut of matters affecting Spain.

Once Spain entered the conflict, the observer in Philadelphia began to play a more open role as a diplomat. Although laking the status of a *chargé*, Miralles was certainly more in the eyes of his American hosts than the private merchant he had seemed on arrival. He took an active role in discussing points of diplomatic concern between the United States and Spain, including joint navigation of the Mississippi River, the American boundary with Spanish Louisiana, and trade relations. He was the first person to articulate the Spanish position on these matters at the Congress. Miralles' reports about the growing American population in the Ohio Valley also confirmed the fears of some Spanish ministers, especially the Conde de Floridablanca, that the United States would replace Great Britain as a rival. A steady stream of similar information, first from Miralles and then from his replacement, Francisco Rendon, certainly contributed to Spain's decision not to recognize the independence of the United States until after the Revolution.

The Spanish observers created the first opportunity for North American merchants to engage in legal commerce with Spain's colonies. The restrictive trade laws that kept Spain's colonial empire a closed mercantilistic system had hampered open contact between ports in English and Hispanic America. The observers employed by the captain general conducted over a dozen missions posing as merchants. Their commercial example, especially

Miralles' and Rendon's, helped awaken American merchants to the profits of legal trade with Hispanic parts of the hemisphere, where previously only contraband had been possible, and constituted the foundation for trade relations between the United States, Spain, and the Spanish Indies. In addition, Miralles and Rendon became Spain's unofficial consuls and ministers in the United States. The progression from Miralles as a completely unaccredited representative to Diego de Gardoqui as the head of a formal Spanish mission seems in retrospect natural and unavoidable.

The American Revolution marked the beginning of a new epoch for Spain as well as for Great Britain. Within a generation of 1776, a fire storm of rebellion and independence would consume Spain's New World colonies, since the forces set in motion at Lexington and Concord could be stopped by no man or empire. The American Revolution was the occasion of Spain's final flash of glory in the Americas. The military victories of Bernardo de Gálvez in the Gulf of Mexico and the Caribbean, the establishment of diplomatic foundations in Philadelphia by Miralles and Rendon, and the attainment of Spanish war goals at the peace table—with the important exception of Gibraltar—left Spain feeling justified for participating in the Revolution. By 1783, King Charles had seen the British Empire humbled, the flag of Spain flying over the entire Gulf of Mexico, and a temporary restoration of Spanish international prestige which let his ministers contemplate an increased independence from France in foreign policy. Although some of the ministers in Madrid, including Floridablanca, fretted that a newly independent United States would supersede Great Britain as an irksome New World rival, their concern did not seem compelling in the years immediately following Yorktown. Instead, Spanish policy makers could take satisfaction in having steered their nation through difficult and treacherous times. The Spanish observers had helped make that possible.

Glossary

ARAGONESES. Members of a faction at the Spanish court who generally followed the policies and opinions of the Conde de Aranda.

ASIENTO. A government trade monopoly. The Asiento de Negros constituted a concession from the Spanish court to a private merchant house for the importation of blacks into Cuba.

AUDIENCIA. A tribunal or council that provided judicial functions of government for a Spanish colony. From 1526 on, the island of Cuba and its dependencies fell under the jurisdiction of the audiencia located at Santo Domingo.

CABILDO. A town council.

CAPTAINCY GENERAL OF CUBA. A command unit that served as the basic structure of military governance for the Spanish colonies contiguous to English America.

CONTADOR. The chief accountant in a Spanish colonial government.

COUNCIL OF MINISTERS. A body comprising the heads of the Spanish government departments and serving to advise the king of Spain.

FLORIDIANO. A resident of Spanish Florida. After 1763, many lived as exiles in Cuba.

INDIES. In Spanish usage, the Western Hemisphere.

LEGAJO. A bundle of documents, and the basic filing unit of Spanish archives.

MINISTER OF STATE. The member of the COUNCIL OF MINISTERS who directed Spain's foreign policy. This official functioned as chief minister, though he did not enjoy official designation as such.

MINISTER OF THE INDIES. The member of the COUNCIL OF MINISTERS who directed all Spain's colonial matters and had direct command of all Spanish officials in the INDIES.

NEW SPAIN. The northern viceregency of the Spanish Indies, including the territory of present-day Mexico, the Central American states, and most of the Caribbean holdings of Spain.

PESO FUERTE. A monetary unit. It had a value of eight *reales* and served as the basis for the dollar created by Congress. For most of the revolutionary period, a *peso fuerte* and a United States dollar may be considered equivalent units of currency.

QUINTAL. A dry unit of weight, often used for gunpowder and flour. It roughly equaled one hundred pounds avoirdupois during the revolutionary period but is pegged today to the metric system.

VICEROY OF NEW SPAIN. Spain's chief colonial officer in NEW SPAIN. This official had command of all Spanish regions north of the Isthmus of Panama. Although the captain general technically fell under the command of the viceroy, in practice he operated independently.

Key to Spanish Surnames

Given here are the full names of persons of Spanish heritage who play a significant role in the narrative. The list is alphabetical by the forms used in the text.

ARANDA. Don Pedro Pablo Abarca de Bolea, Conde de Aranda (b. 1718, d. 1799), Spanish ambassador to France during the American Revolution. In 1792, Aranda returned from Paris to become president of the Council of Ministers.

ARRIAGA. Fray Balío Julián de Arriaga (d. 1776), minister of the marine and minister of the Indies from 1754 until his death.

BUCARELI. Don Antonio María de Bucareli y Ursúa Hinostrosa Lasso de la Vega (b. 1717, d. 1779), captain general of Cuba, 1766–1771, and viceroy of New Spain, 1771–1779.

EDUARDO. Miguel Antonio Eduardo, public interpreter of Havana, 1769–1776. Eduardo served as an observer in the network of the captain general of Cuba during most of the American Revolution.

ENRILE. Don Geronimo de Enrile, Marqués de Casa Enrile, director of the Asiento de Negros in Cuba.

FLORIDABLANCA. Don José de Moñino, Conde de Floridablanca (b. 1728, d. 1808), minister of state, 1777–1792.

GÁLVEZ. Don Bernardo Vicente Pólinarde de Gálvez y Gallardo (b. 1746, d. 1786), governor of Louisiana, 1777–1785, captain general of Cuba, 1785, and viceroy of New Spain, 1785–1786. Bernardo de Gálvez was the son of Matías de Gálvez.

GÁLVEZ. Don José de Gálvez y Gallardo, Marqués de Sonora (b. 1720, d. 1786), minister of the Indies, 1776–1786. José de Gálvez was the brother of Matías de Gálvez and the patriarch of the Gálvez family.

GARDOQUI. Don Diego de Gardoqui de Jaraveita, an adviser on English matters to the Spanish court and Spanish consul in London, 1783–1785. Gardoqui was appointed Spanish minister to the United States in 1785.

Key to Spanish Surnames

HERRERA. Luciano de Herrera, a *floridiano* who lived in British Saint Augustine from 1763 until after the American Revolution.

MIRALLES. Don Juan de Miralles y Trajan (d. 1780), a Cuban merchant. Miralles was the Spanish observer in Philadelphia from 1778 to 1780.

MIRÓ. Don Esteban Rodríguez Miró y Sabatier, governor of Louisiana, 1785–1791.

NAVARRO. Don Diego Joseph Navarro Garcia de Valladares, captain general of Cuba, 1777–1780.

O'REILLY. Don Alejandro O'Reilly y McDowell Sillon, Conde de O'Reilly (b. 1725, d. 1794). O'Reilly established a permanent Spanish government in New Orleans in 1769 and later served as a military adviser to the Council of Ministers.

PUENTE. Don Juan José Elegio de la Puente, a *floridiano* and *contador* of Cuba. Juan Elegio de la Puente was an adviser to the captain general on matters relating to British East Florida.

PUENTE. Joseph María Elegio de la Puente, an observer for the captain general of Cuba, 1777–1778. Joseph Elegio de la Puente was the *contador*'s brother.

RENDON. Francisco Rendon, a career government worker for Spain. Rendon was the Spanish observer in Philadelphia from 1780 to 1785.

TORRE. Don Felipe de Fonsdeviela y Ondeano, Marqués de la Torre (b. 1725, d. 1784), captain general of Cuba, 1771–1777.

ULLOA. Don Antonio de Ulloa y de la Torre Guiral (b. 1716, d. 1795), governor of Louisiana, 1765–1766.

UNZAGA. Don Luis de Unzaga y Amezaga, governor of Louisiana, 1770–1777, and captain general of Cuba, 1782–1785.

Sources

UNPUBLISHED PRIMARY SOURCES

This study is largely based on manuscripts found in the government archives of Spain. Although long the setting of research by students of Hispanic-American history, the archives have been little used by historians of the American Revolution. A word is therefore in order for readers unfamiliar with their structure and organization. The majority of public archives in Spain that hold government records from the eighteenth century are under the administration of the Dirección General de Archivos y Bibliotecas, an agency roughly analogous to the National Archives and Records Service in the United States of America. There is, however, no centralized repository. Instead, there are three major national archival facilities containing information relevant to eighteenth-century colonial history: the Archivo General de Indias, in Seville; the Archivo General de Simancas, in Simancas; and the Archivo Histórico Nacional, in Madrid. Although these three archives contain the bulk of the records bearing on the topic of this volume, numerous smaller, regional archival repositories in Spain also have relevant materials. For a general introduction to those repositories, see Gilbert C. Din, "Sources for Spanish Louisiana," in *A Guide to the History of Louisiana,* edited by Light Townsend Cummins and Glen Jeansonne (Westport, Conn., 1982), 127–37. For an overview of the records dealing with Spanish Louisiana and the Gulf Coast, see Paul Hoffman, "La documentación colonial en La Luisiana," *Archivo hispalense,* Nos. 207–208 (1985), 333–52; and Henry Putney Beers, *French and Spanish Records of Louisiana: A Bibliographical Guide to Archives and Manuscript Sources* (Baton Rouge, 1989).

The three major archives employ similar cataloging systems, which permit the retrieval of documents by researchers relatively efficiently once their organization is understood. Each facility organizes records generally according to the government agency or activity that created them—for example, the ministry of state, the audiencia de Santo Domingo, the captaincy general of Cuba. A researcher must consequently have some understanding of the lines of command within both the Spanish Indies and the home government during the historical era of concern. Within each agency grouping, there are usually subdivisions as well, depending upon the particular archive.

In all three of the major archives, the individual documents are stored in bundles, usually tied with string, known as *legajos*. Most *legajos* contain from five hundred to a thousand documents. Each facility maintains in its reading room a general catalog—known as the *inventario*—that lists every *legajo* in its collection by the subject of its contents and records the chronological period covered. Beyond the *inventario*, the archives maintain no finding aids except in rare, selected cases. Experience has shown that many of the *inventario* listings are too broad to be of utility to the researcher. In addition, since many of the *legajos* were bundled by government clerks at a time when the documents constituted operational records of government, some packets may never have been opened by modern archivists or researchers. The placement of particular documents within various *legajos* by subject is therefore often arbitrary by present-day standards and sometimes may suggest a preference for eclecticism to the researcher concerned with a particular topic. As a result, the researcher must examine folio by folio each *legajo* suspected of containing relevant documentation. Since most bundles have no internal organization, research in the major Spanish archives is time-consuming but often rewarding. In the course of the present study, over three hundred unindexed and uncalendared *legajos* (containing over 200,000 folios) were examined in their entirety. Of these, fifty-nine *legajos* yielded documents pertinent to the topic under consideration. Fortunately, in some cases researchers, historians, and microfilming projects have over the years prepared finding aids for particular sections of the archives; these will be noted below for each of the major archives.

In commemoration of the bicentennial of the United States in 1976, the government of Spain began a calendaring project to locate documents in its archives relating to the American Revolution. Although publication of the calendars that are the result came too late to assist in the basic research for this study, they are a considerable asset to any researcher who wishes to examine archival documents having a bearing on early relations with the United States. This calendar set, with volumes still appearing, is published as *Documentos relativos a la independencia de Norteamérica existentes en archivos españoles* (11 vols. to date; Madrid, 1976–86). Volumes dealing with specific archives are noted below.

The Archivo General de Indias, in Seville, is the most significant Spanish archive for the study of the English colonial experience in the New World, since it contains the majority of records from Spain's colonial office, the Consejo y Ministerio de Indias. The *legajos* are organized by the geographic locations in the Americas that produced the records, and there is a complete listing of the bundles in the reading-room *inventario*, of which only one manuscript copy exists. The Servicio Nacional de Microfilm of Spain is currently filming this *inventario* and plans to make it available to scholars throughout the world. The best guide to the AGI, although dated, is José María de la Peña y Cámara's *Archivo General de Indias de Sevilla: Guía del visitante* (Madrid, 1958). The AGI contains many, if not most, of the government records of the provinces of Louisiana and Cuba during the American Revolution. Some of those from the Papeles de Cuba and the audiencia de Santo Domingo have been microfilmed, and copies are in a number of repositories in the United States. During the 1970s, Aileen Moore Topping culled some of the letters written by Miralles and Rendon from various *legajos* and translated them into English. Typescripts of Moore's translations are deposited in the Manuscript Division of the Library of Congress. The microfilm collections and Topping's translations, however, do not include all the documentation relevant to the present volume. Since extensive research in the AGI and other repositories was necessary to develop the topic adequately anyway, the microfilms and translations were not used for this study.

The AGI has almost all the operational records of the captain general's office in Havana for the late eighteenth century. This set of documents is the most recent accession to the AGI, having been incorporated after the Spanish-American War. For a general idea of the captain general's records, see Roscoe R. Hill, *Descriptive Catalogue of Documents Relating to the History of the United States in the "Papeles Procedentes de Cuba" Deposited in the Archivo General de Indias at Seville* (Washington, D.C., 1916). The Papeles de Cuba section is currently the object of a microfilming project sponsored by the Spanish government and a consortium of universities in the United States, a number of whose libraries have microform copies of certain *legajos*. Also useful on the AGI is Cristóbal Bermúdez Plata's *Catálogo de documentos de la sección novena, redactado por el facultativo de archivo bajo la dirección del director del mismo* (Seville, 1945). The bicentennial history project calendar for the AGI is *Archivo General de Indias*, edited by Purificación Medina Encina and Saturnino Reyes Siles (2 vols., 3 parts; Madrid, 1977–80), in *Documentos relativos*. These volumes cover the sections Santo Domingo, Indiferente General, and Papeles de Cuba.

The Archivo General de Simancas is important for a consideration of Spain's diplomatic policy regarding the American Revolution, because it contains many records of the ministry of state. The section Secretaría de Estado preserves the records of the Spanish embassy in London up to the end of diplomatic relations between Spain and Great Britain, during the summer of 1779. This section also contains much of the personal correspondence of the minister of state regarding the American revolt. In addition, the AGS holds service records for most of the Spanish military officers who served in the American Revolution. For a general guide to the AGS, see Angel de la Plaza, *Archivo General de Simancas: Guía del investigador* (Valladolid, 1962). For specialized guides to the diplomatic and military records, see Julián Paz and Richardo Magdaleno, *Archivo General de Simancas, Secretaría de Estado, documentos relativos a Inglaterra, 1254–1834* (Madrid, 1947), and Concepción Alvarez Teran, *Archivo General de Simancas, Secretaría de Guerra (siglo XVIII), hojas de servicios de América* (Valladolid, 1958). The bicentennial history project calendar for the AGS is *Archivo General de Simancas*, edited by María Francisca Represa

Sources

Fernández (2 vols.; Madrid, 1976), *Documentos relativos*. These volumes cover primarily the section Secretaría de Estado.

The Archivo Histórico Nacional, in Madrid, is the major repository for diplomatic correspondence between officials of the Spanish government and the Continental Congress. These records are particularly rich for the period after 1778. The best general guide to the AHN is Luis Sánchez Belda's *Guía del Archivo Histórico Nacional (Madrid)* (Madrid, 1958). The Estado section of the AHN contains the better part of the documentation relative to the American Revolution, some of which has been microfilmed and is available in libraries in the United States. For a description of this filmed collection, see *Archivo Histórico Nacional, Sección de Estado, publicación número 16* (Madrid, 1974). There is an excellent calendar of the Estado section of the AHN: Miguel Gómez del Campillo, *Relaciones diplomáticas entre España y los Estados Unidos, según documentos del Archivo Histórico Nacional* (2 vols.; Madrid, 1944). The bicentennial history project calendar for the AHN is *Archivo Histórico Nacional*, edited by Pilar León Tello (2 vols.; Madrid, 1976), in *Documentos relativos*. This volume, like the earlier calendar by Gómez de Campillo, deals with the section Consejo de Estado.

Numerous smaller repositories in Spain contain material regarding Spanish participation in the American Revolution. Because of their number there can be no attempt here to list all such facilities. Only those particularly useful for the study will be noted. But two guides provide general information on most regional and special-interest archives: *Guía de los archivos de Madrid* (Madrid, 1952), and *Guía histórica y descriptiva de los archivos, bibliotecas y museos arqueológicos de España* (Madrid, 1916–21). The División de Manuscritos of the Biblioteca Nacional, in Madrid, contains sources relative to Louisiana and Cuba. For a guide to that collection, see Julián Paz, *Catálogo de manuscritos de América existentes de la Biblioteca Nacional de Madrid* (Madrid, 1933). The Real Academia de la História, in Madrid, also has several groups of records that contain documents pertaining to the Revolution: the Colección Mata Linares and the Colección Muñoz contain letters of José de Gálvez and various royal orders to the captain general of Cuba.

Some documents from Spanish archives concerning the American Revolution are available in the United States in microfilm, photocopy, or transcription. For a listing of microfilming projects undertaken by the Spanish government, consult the Dirección General de Archivos y Bibliotecas' *Publicaciones en microfilm-microficha* (Madrid, 1974, with supplements) and *Inventario de códices y documentos microfilmados, 1962–1974* (Madrid, 1975). Among the major archival repositories and libraries in the United States with copies of documents relating to Spain and the Revolution are the Library of Congress; the P. K. Yonge Library, of the University of Florida; the Troy H. Middleton Library, of Louisiana State University; the Howard-Tilton Memorial Library, of Tulane University; Loyola University of New Orleans; the Bancroft Library, of the University of California; and the Ayers Collection of the Newberry Library, in Chicago. For a general guide to filmed records from Spanish repositories, see José María de la Peña y Camara *et al.*, *Catálogo de documentos del Archivo General de Indias, sección V, Govierno, Audiencia de Santo*

Sources

Domingo, sobre la época española de Luisiana (2 vols.; New Orleans, 1968). For a good general guide to documents from Spanish archives in the United States, see Lino Gómez Canedo, *Los archivos de la história de América: Periodo colonial español,* Volume II (Mexico City, 1961). For materials relating to Louisiana, see Glenn R. Conrad and Carl A. Brasseaux, *A Selected Bibliography of Scholarly Literature on Colonial Louisiana and New France* (Lafayette, La., 1982).

Spanish participation in the American Revolution is a subject that has attracted study by generations of historians, and although much of this scholarship is not based upon research in the archives of Spain, it is often of merit. In fact, anyone who wishes to survey the role Spain played in the genesis of the United States is confronted with a voluminous literature—touching upon military affairs, diplomacy, the West Indies and the Gulf of Mexico, European theaters of conflict, commerce, and the like—written over the decades by dozens of scholars on both sides of the Atlantic. A bibliographic guide to this literature is Light Townsend Cummins' "Spanish Louisiana," in *A Guide to the History of Louisiana* (Westport, Conn., 1982). But, without presumption, it can probably be assumed that readers who have found their way to this relatively specialized monograph on Spanish espionage possess the ability to put themselves in touch with the larger body of literature on foreign participation in the American Revolution. Thus in the present bibliography there is no attempt at comprehensiveness regarding Spanish participation in the Revolution. Only sources and studies cited in the footnotes receive mention.

Manuscripts Consulted

AGI   ARCHIVO GENERAL DE INDIAS, SEVILLE
      Audiencia de Guatemala: Legajo 881
      Audiencia de México: Legajo 3189
      Audiencia de Santo Domingo: Legajos 1121, 1151, 1159, 1160, 1176, 1193, 1211, 1214, 1217, 1223–25, 1227, 1520, 1521, 1522, 1526, 1527, 1598-A, 2543, 2547, 2596–98, 2652
      Indiferente General: Legajos 656, 1606
      Papeles de Cuba: Legajos 81, 82, 112, 174-A, 174-B, 186-B, 188-C, 189-B, 190, 191, 560, 569, 1143, 1146, 1147, 1151, 1214, 1227, 1232, 1281–83, 1290–92, 1301, 1330, 2370
AGS   ARCHIVO GENERAL DE SIMANCAS
      Estado: Legajos 6988, 6990, 6991, 6993, 7000, 7016
AHN   ARCHIVO HISTÓRICO NACIONAL, MADRID
      Estado: Legajos 3882 bis, 3884 bis, 3885
BIBLIOTECA NACIONAL, MADRID
      Ms. 17616
HISTORICAL SOCIETY OF PENNSYLVANIA, PHILADELPHIA
      General Edward Hand Papers, 1771–1807
      Gratz Collection, 1383–1921
      Society Collection

Sources

HOWARD-TILTON MEMORIAL LIBRARY, TULANE UNIVERSITY, NEW ORLEANS
Beauregard Family Papers
Correspondence of the Governors of Spanish Louisiana
MORRISTOWN NATIONAL HISTORICAL PARK LIBRARY, MORRISTOWN, NEW JERSEY
Chevalier de La Luzerne Files
Juan de Miralles Files
Park Collection
MUNICIPAL ARCHIVES, PHILADELPHIA
Chancery Records
Probate Records
NATIONAL ARCHIVES, WASHINGTON, D.C.
Papers of the Continental Congress
PUBLIC RECORD OFFICE, LONDON
Colonial Office Papers, Part Five, America and the West Indies
REAL ACADEMIA DE LA HISTORIA, MADRID
Colección Mata Linares
Collección Muñoz

PUBLISHED PRIMARY SOURCES

Adams, Charles Francis, ed. *The Works of John Adams: Second President of the United States.* 10 vols. Boston, 1850–56.

Balch, Thomas Willing, ed. *Willing Letters and Papers, Edited with a Biographical Essay of Thomas Willing of Philadelphia, 1731–1821.* Philadelphia, 1922.

Boyd, Julian P., *et al.*, eds. *The Papers of Thomas Jefferson.* 22 vols. to date. Princeton, 1950–.

Burnett, Edmund Cody, ed. *Letters of the Members of the Continental Congress.* 8 vols. Washington, D.C., 1921–36.

Carter, Clarence E., ed. *The Correspondence of General Thomas Gage with the Secretaries of State and with the War Office and the Treasury, 1763–1775.* 2 vols. New Haven, 1931–33.

Clark, William B., *et al.*, eds. *Naval Documents of the American Revolution.* 9 vols. to date. Washington, D.C., 1964–.

Ferguson, E. James, ed. *The Papers of Robert Morris, 1781–1784.* 7 vols. to date. Pittsburgh, 1973–.

Fitzpatrick, John C., ed. *The Writings of George Washington, from the Original Manuscript Sources, 1745–1799.* 39 vols. Washington, D.C., 1931–44.

Ford, Worthington C., ed. *Journals of the Continental Congress.* 34 vols. Washington, D.C., 1904–37.

Gillon, Alexander. "Letters from Commodore Alexander Gillon in 1778 and 1779." *South Carolina Historical and Genealogical Magazine*, X (1909), 3–9, 75–82, 131–35.

Hargreaves-Mawdsley, W. N., ed. *Spain Under the Bourbons, 1700–1813: A Collection of Documents.* London, 1973.

Sources

Kinnaird, Lawrence, ed. *Spain in the Mississippi Valley, 1765–1794.* 3 vols. Washington, D.C., 1949.

Llaverías, Joaquín, ed. "Documentos acerca del estado de defensa de la Habana con un plano ó cuadro relativo al particular, 1766 a 1776." *Boletín de Archivo Nacional de Cuba,* XLIII (1946), 121–31.

Meng, John J., ed. *Despatches and Instructions of Conrad Alexandre Gérard, 1778–1780.* Baltimore, 1939.

Morris, Richard B., ed. *The Papers of John Jay.* 2 vols. New York, 1975–80. Vol. 1, *John Jay: The Making of a Revolutionary: Unpublished Papers;* Vol. 2, *John Jay: The Winning of the Peace: Unpublished Papers.*

Robertson, James A., trans. and ed. "Spanish Correspondence Concerning the American Revolution, 1779–1783." *Hispanic American Historical Review,* I (1918), 299–316.

Rodríguez, Amalia A., ed. *Cinco diarios del sitio de la Havana.* Havana, 1963.

Smith, Paul, ed. *Letters of Delegates to Congress, 1774–1789.* 16 vols. to date. Washington, D.C., 1976–.

Stevens, B. F., ed. *B. F. Stevens' Facsimiles of Manuscripts in European Archives Relating to America, 1773–1783, with Descriptions, Editorial Notes, Collations, References, and Translations.* 24 vols. London, 1889–95.

Wilkinson, James. *Memoirs of My Own Times.* 3 vols. Philadelphia, 1816.

SECONDARY SOURCES

Books

Abernethy, Thomas Perkins. *Western Lands and the American Revolution.* New York, 1937.

Alcázar Molina, Cayetano. *El Conde de Floridablanca: Notas para su estudio.* Madrid, 1929.

———. *Conde de Floridablanca: Su vida y su obra.* Múrcia, 1934.

Andregg, Charles H. *Management of Defense Intelligence.* Washington, D.C., 1968.

Anes Alvarez, Gonzalo. *El antiguo régimen: Los Borbones.* Madrid, 1975.

Augur, Helen. *The Secret War of Independence.* 1955; rpr. Westport, Conn., 1965.

Báez, Vicente. *La enciclopedia de Cuba, historia.* 4 vols. San Juan, 1971.

Ballesteros y Beretta, Antonio. *Historia de España y su influencia en la historia universal.* 2nd ed. 9 vols. 1929; rpr. Barcelona, 1964.

Bemis, Samuel Flagg. *The Diplomacy of the American Revolution.* New York, 1935.

———. *The Hussey-Cumberland Mission and American Independence: An Essay in the Diplomacy of the American Revolution.* 1931; rpr. Gloucester, Mass., 1968.

———. *Pinckney's Treaty: A Study of America's Advantage from Europe's Distress, 1783–1800.* Baltimore, 1926.

Billias, George A. *Elbridge Gerry: Founding Father and Republican Statesman.* New York, 1976.

Bobb, Bernard E. *The Viceregency of Antonio María Bacareli in New Spain, 1771–1779.* Austin, Tex., 1962.

Sources

Boeta, José Rodulfo. *Bernardo de Gálvez*. Madrid, 1976.

Brading, David. *Miners and Merchants in Bourbon Mexico, 1763–1810*. Cambridge, Eng., 1971.

Brasseaux, Carl A. *Denis-Nicolas Foucault and the New Orleans Rebellion of 1768*. Ruston, La., 1987.

Burson, Caroline. *The Stewardship of Don Esteban Miró*. New Orleans, 1940.

Casa Mena, Marqués de [José Montero de Pedro]. *Españoles en Nueva Orleans*. Madrid, 1979.

Caughey, John W. *Bernardo de Gálvez in Louisiana, 1776–1783*. Berkeley, Calif., 1934.

Clark, John G. *New Orleans, 1718–1812: An Economic History*. Baton Rouge, 1970.

Coe, Samuel G. *The Mission of William Carmichael to Spain*. Baltimore, 1928.

Coleman, Kenneth. *The American Revolution in Georgia, 1763–1789*. Athens, Ga., 1958.

Conrotte, Manuel. *La intervención de España en la independencia de la América del Norte*. Madrid, 1920.

Corwin, Edwin S. *French Policy and the American Alliance of 1778*. 1916; rpr. Gloucester, Mass., 1969.

Curry, Cecil B. *Code Number 72: Ben Franklin, Patriot or Spy?* Englewood Cliffs, N.J., 1972.

Du Fossat, Chevalier Guy Soniat. *Synopsis of the History of Louisiana from the Founding of the Colony to the End of the Year 1791*. Translated by Charles T. Soniat. New Orleans, 1903.

Dull, Jonathan R. *A Diplomatic History of the American Revolution*. New Haven, 1985.

——. *The French Navy and American Independence: A Study of Arms and Diplomacy, 1774–1787*. Princeton, 1975.

Floyd, Troy S., ed. *The Bourbon Reformers and Spanish Civilization: Builders or Destroyers?* Boston, 1966.

Freeman, Douglas Southall. *George Washington: A Biography*. 7 vols. New York, 1948–57.

García Melero, Luis Angel. *La independencia de los Estados Unidos de Norteamerica a través de la prensa española ("Gaceta de Madrid" y "Mercurio Histórico y Político")*. Madrid, 1977.

Gayarré, Charles. *The Spanish Domination*. 1866; rpr. Gretna, La., 1974. Vol. III of Gayarré, *A History of Louisiana*. 4 vols.

Gil Munilla, Octavo. *Malvinas: El conflicto anglo-español de 1770*. Seville, 1948.

——. *El Río de la Plata en la política internacional: Génesis del virreinato*. Seville, 1949.

Gold, Robert L. *Borderland Empires in Transition: The Triple-Nation Transfer of Florida*. Carbondale, Ill., 1969.

Gomez del Campillo, Miguel. *Relaciones diplomáticas entre España y los Estados Unidos, segun documentos del Archivo Histórico Nacional*. 2 vols. Madrid, 1944.

Guerra, Ramiro. *Manuel de historia de Cuba desde su descubrimiento hasta 1868*. 1938; rpr. Havana, 1971.

Harris, Wiliam R. *Intelligence and National Security: A Bibliography with Selected Annotations*. Cambridge, Mass., 1968.

Haynes, Robert V. *The Natchez District and the American Revolution.* Jackson, Miss., 1976.

Herr, Richard. *The Eighteenth Century Revolution in Spain.* Princeton, 1958.

———. *Spain.* Englewood Cliffs, N.J., 1971.

James, James A. *Oliver Pollock: The Life and Times of an Unknown Patriot.* 1937; rpr. Freeport, N.Y., 1970.

Johnson, Cecil. *British West Florida, 1763–1783.* New Haven, 1943.

Johnson, Willis Fletcher. *The History of Cuba.* 5 vols. New York, 1920.

Kendall, John S. *History of New Orleans.* 3 vols. Chicago, 1922.

Kite, Elizabeth S. *Beaumarchais and the War of American Independence.* 2 vols. Boston, 1918.

Konkle, Burton Alva. *Thomas Willing and the First American Financial System.* Philadelphia, 1937.

Kuethe, Allan J. *Cuba, 1753–1815: Crown, Military, and Society.* Knoxville, Tenn., 1986.

Liss, Peggy. *Atlantic Empires: The Network of Trade and Revolution, 1713–1826.* Baltimore, 1983.

Lyon, E. Wilson. *The Man Who Sold Louisiana: The Career of François Barbe-Marbois.* Norman, Okla., 1942.

McCowen, George Smith, Jr. *The British Occupation of Charleston, 1780–1782.* Columbia, S.C., 1972.

McCrady, Edward. *The History of South Carolina in the Revolution, 1775–1780.* New York, 1901.

McGovern, William M. *Strategic Intelligence and the Shape of Tomorrow.* Chicago, 1961.

Moore, John Preston. *Revolt in Louisiana: The Spanish Occupation, 1766–1770.* Baton Rouge, 1976.

Morales Padrón, Francisco. *Participación de España en la independencia política de los Estados Unidos.* 2nd ed. Madrid, 1963.

Morris, Richard B. *The Peacemakers: The Great Powers and American Independence.* New York, 1965.

Mowat, Charles L. *East Florida as a British Province, 1763–1784.* Berkeley, Calif., 1943.

Navarro García, Luis. *Hispanoamérica en el siglo XVIII.* Seville, 1975.

O'Donnell, William E. *The Chevalier de La Luzerne, French Minister to the United States, 1779–1784.* Bruges, 1938.

Olaechea, Rafael. *El Conde de Aranda y el "partido aragones."* Saragossa, 1967.

Panagopoulos, E. P. *New Smyrna: An Eighteenth Century Greek Odyssey.* Gainesville, Fla., 1966.

Pérez Herváas, José. *España y los Estados Unidos: Nuestra participación en la independencia de aquel país.* Barcelona, 1918.

Perkins, James B. *France in the American Revolution.* 1911; rpr. Williamstown, Mass., 1970.

Portell Vilá, Herminio. *Historia de Cuba en sus relaciones con los Estados Unidos y España.* 4 vols. Havana, 1938.

Sources

———. *Juan de Miralles, un habanero amigo de Jorge Washington.* Havana, 1947.
———. *Los "otros extranjeros" en la revolución norteamericana.* Miami, 1978.
Potts, Louis W. *Arthur Lee: A Virtuous Revolutionary.* Baton Rouge, 1981.
Priestley, Herbert I. *José de Gálvez: Visitor General of New Spain, 1765–1771.* Berkeley, Calif. 1916.
Quinn, Jane. *Minorcans in Florida: Their History and Heritage.* Saint Augustine, Fla., 1975.
Rodríguez Casado, Vicente. *La política marroquí de Carlos III.* Madrid, 1946.
———. *La política y los políticos en el reinado de Carlos III.* Madrid, 1962.
———. *Primeros años de dominación española en la Luisiana.* Madrid, 1942.
Rubio Argüelles, Angeles. *Un ministro de Carlos III, D. José de Gálvez y Gallardo . . . Marqués de Sonora.* Málaga, 1949.
Ruigómez de Hernández, María Pilar. *El gobierno español del despotismo illustrado ante la independencia de los Estados Unidos de América.* Madrid, 1978.
Rumeu de Armas, Antonio. *El testamento político del Conde de Floridablanca.* Madrid, 1962.
Sánchez-Fabrés Mirat, Elena. *Situación histórica de las Floridas en le segunda mitad del siglo XVIII, 1783–1819: Los problemas de una región de frontera.* Madrid, 1977.
Sarrailh, Jean. *La España ilustrada de la segunda mitad del siglo XVIII.* Madrid, 1957.
Senate Documents. 100th Cong., 2nd Sess., No. 34. *Biographical Directory of the United States Congress, 1774–1989.*
Sherman, Andrew M. *Historic Morristown: The Story of Its First Century.* Morristown, N.J., 1905.
Starr, J. Barton. *Tories, Dons, and Rebels: The American Revolution in British West Florida.* Gainesville, Fla., 1976.
Stinchcombe, William C. *The American Revolution and the French Alliance.* Syracuse, N.Y., 1969.
Stourzh, Gerald. *Benjamin Franklin and American Foreign Policy.* 2nd ed. Chicago, 1969.
Sucre Reyes, José. *La capitanía general de Venezuela.* Barcelona, 1969.
Tapia Ozcariz, Enrique de. *Carlos III y su época.* Madrid, 1966.
Thomas, Hugh. *Cuba; or, The Pursuit of Freedom.* London, 1971.
Torredemé Balado, Angel. *Iniciación a la historia del correo en Cuba.* Havana, 1945.
Torres Ramirez, Bibiano. *Alejandro O'Reilly en las Indias.* Seville, 1969.
U.S. Department of the Army. *Military Intelligence, Operational, ST30-6-2.* 1954.
Van Alstyne, Richard W. *Empire and Independence: The International History of the American Revolution.* New York, 1965.
Van Doren, Carl. *Secret History of the American Revolution.* New York, 1941.
Ver Steeg, Clarence L. *Robert Morris: Revolutionary Financier.* Philadelphia, 1954.
Whitaker, Arthur Preston. *The Spanish-American Frontier, 1783–1795: The Westward Movement and the Spanish Retreat in the Mississippi Valley.* 1927; rpr. Gloucester, Mass., 1962.
Wright, J. Leitch, Jr. *Anglo-Spanish Rivalry in North America.* Athens, Ga., 1971.

Sources

————. *Florida in the American Revolution.* Gainesville, Fla., 1975.
Wriston, Henry M. *Executive Agents in American Foreign Relations.* 1929; rpr. Gloucester, Mass., 1967.
Yela Utrilla, Juan Fernando. *España ante la independencia de los Estados Unidos.* 2nd ed. 2 vols. Lerida, 1925.

Articles

Abbey [Hanna], Kathryn. "Efforts of Spain to Maintain Sources of Information in the British Colonies Before 1779." *Mississippi Valley Historical Review,* XV (1928), 56–68.
————. "Spanish Projects for the Reoccupation of the Floridas During the American Revolution." *Hispanic American Historical Review,* IX (1929), 265–85.
Acosta Rodríguez, Antonio. "Problemas económicos y rebelión popular en Luisiana en 1768." In *Actos del congresso de historia de los Estados Unidos.* La Rábida, 1976.
Alcázar Molina, Cayetano. "Ideas políticas de Floridablanca: Del despotismo ilustrado a la revolución francesa y Napoleón, 1766–1801." *Revista de estudios políticos,* DXXIX (1955), 35–66.
Armillas Vicente, José Antonio. "Europa y la revolución americana: Un nuevo mito." In *Estudios del departamento de historia moderna, 1976.* Saragossa, 1976.
Bemis, Samuel Flagg. "British Secret Service and the French American Alliance." *American Historical Review,* XXIX (1924), 474–95.
Beerman, Eric. "Un bosquejo biográfico y genealógico del General Alejandro O'Reilly." *Hidalguía,* XXIV (1981), 225–44.
Bjork, David K. "Alexander O'Reilly and the Spanish Occupation of Louisiana, 1769–1770." In *New Spain and the Anglo-American West,* edited by George P. Hammond. Vol. I of 2 vols. Lancaster, Pa., 1932.
Born, John B., Jr. "Governor Johnstone and Trade in British West Florida, 1764–1767." *Bulletin of Wichita State University,* LXXV (1968), 3–22.
Boyd, Mark F., and José Navarro Latorre. "Spanish Interest in British Florida, and in the Progress of the American Revolution." *Florida Historical Quarterly,* XXXII (1953), 92–116.
Brown, Vera Lee. "Anglo-Spanish Relations in America in the Closing Years of the Colonial Era." *Hispanic American Historical Review,* V (1922), 325–483.
Caughey, John W. "Bernardo de Gálvez and the English Smugglers on the Mississippi, 1777." *Hispanic American Historical Review,* XII (1932), 46–58.
————. "The Panis Mission to Pensacola." *Hispanic American Historical Review,* X (1930), 480–89.
————. "Willing's Raid down the Mississippi, 1778." *Louisiana Historical Quarterly,* XV (1932), 5–36.
Covington, James W. "The Cuban Fishing *Ranchos:* A Spanish Enclave Within British Florida." In *Anglo-Spanish Confrontation on the Gulf Coast During the American Revolution,* edited by William Coker and Robert R. Rea. Pensacola, Fla., 1982.

Sources

Cummins, Light Townsend. "Luciano de Herrera and Spanish Espionage in British Saint Augustine." *El Escribano,* XVI (1979), 43–57.

――――. "Spanish Administration in the Southeastern Borderlands, 1763–1800." In *Latin American Frontiers: Proceedings of the P.C.C.L.A.S., 1977,* edited by Matt S. Meir. Berkeley, Calif., 1981.

――――. "Spanish Espionage in the South During the American Revolution." *Southern Studies,* XIX (1980), 39–49.

――――. "Spanish Historians and the Gulf Coast Campaigns." In *Anglo-Spanish Confrontation on the Gulf Coast During the American Revolution,* edited by William Coker and Robert R. Rea. Pensacola, Fla., 1982.

Downing, Margaret B. "Oliver Pollock, Patriot and Financier." *Illinois Catholic Historical Review,* II (1969), 196–207.

Faye, Stanley. "The Arkansas Post of Louisiana: Spanish Domination." *Louisiana Historical Quarterly,* XXVII (1944), 629–716.

Fletcher, Mildred S. "Louisiana as a Factor in French Diplomacy from 1763 to 1800." *Mississippi Valley Historical Review,* XVII (1930), 367–76.

Gold, Robert L. "Governor Bernardo de Gálvez and Spanish Espionage in Pensacola, 1777." In *The Spanish in the Mississippi Valley, 1762–1784,* edited by John F. McDermott. Urbana, Ill., 1974.

Griffin, Martin I. J. "Requiem for Don Juan Miralles." *American Catholic Historical Researches,* VI (1889), 60–72.

Haarman, Albert W. "The Spanish Conquest of British West Florida, 1779–1781." *Florida Historical Quarterly,* XXXIX (1960), 107–34.

Holmes, Jack D. L. "Juan de la Villebeuvre and Spanish Indian Policy in West Florida, 1784–1797." *Florida Historical Quarterly,* LVIII (1980), 387–99.

――――. "Some Economic Problems of Spanish Governors of Louisiana." *Hispanic American Historical Review,* XLII (1962), 521–43.

Hutson, James H. "The Partition Treaty and the Declaration of American Independence." *Journal of American History,* LVIII (1972), 877–96.

James, James A., "Oliver Pollock, Financier of the Revolution in the West." *Mississippi Valley Historical Review,* XVI (1929), 67–80.

――――. "Spanish Influence in the West During the Revolution." *Mississippi Valley Historical Review,* IV (1917), 193–208.

Kinnaird, Lawrence. "The Western Fringe of Revolution." *Western Historical Quarterly,* VII (1976), 253–70.

Lawson, Katherine S. "Luciano de Herrera, Spanish Spy in British Saint Augustine." *Florida Historical Quarterly,* XXIII (1945), 170–76.

Lewis, James A. "Anglo-American Entrepreneurs in Havana: The Background and Significance of the Expulsion, 1784–1785." In *The North American Role in the Spanish Imperial Economy, 1760–1819,* edited by Jacques A. Barbier and Allan J. Kuethe. Manchester, Eng., 1984.

McCadden, Helen M. "Juan de Miralles and the American Revolution." *The Americas,* XXIX (1973), 359–75.

Sources

Martinez Ortiz, José. "Un valenciano en la independencia de los Estados Unidos." *Revista de la historia de América,* L (1960), 488–95.

Moore, John Preston. "Antonio de Ulloa: A Profile of the First Spanish Governor of Louisiana." *Louisiana History,* VIII (1967), 189–218.

Morales Lezcano, Víctor. "Diplomática y política financiera de España durante la sublevación de las colonias ingleses en América, 1775–1783." *Anuario de estudios americanos,* XXVI (1969), 507–65.

Murphy, Orville T. "Charles Gravier de Vergennes: Profile of an Old Regime Diplomat." *Political Science Quarterly,* LXXXIII (1968), 400–418.

————. "The View from Versailles: Charles Gravier, Comte de Vergennes's Perceptions of the American Revolution." In *Diplomacy and Revolution: The Franco-American Alliance of 1778,* edited by Ronald Hoffman and Peter J. Albert. Charlottesville, Va., 1981.

Padgett, James A., ed. "Discussion in the Continental Congress Relative to Surrendering the Right to Navigate the Mississippi River." *Louisiana Historical Quarterly,* XXVI (1943), 12–36.

Rea, Robert R. "British West Florida, Stepchild of Diplomacy." In *Eighteenth-Century Florida and Its Borderlands,* edited by Samuel Proctor. Gainesville, Fla., 1975.

Rodríguez Casado, Vicente. "O'Reilly en la Luisiana." *Revista de Indias,* II (1941), 45–138.

Salvucci, Linda K. "Anglo-American Merchants and Stratagems for Success in Spanish Imperial Markets, 1783–1807." In *The North American Role in the Spanish Imperial Economy, 1760–1819,* edited by Jacques A. Barbier and Allan J. Kuethe. Manchester, Eng., 1984.

Stinchcombe, William C. "Americans Celebrate the Birth of the Dauphin." In *Diplomacy and Revolution: The Franco-American Alliance of 1778,* edited by Ronald Hoffman and Peter J. Albert. Charlottesville, Va., 1981.

Taylor, Garland. "Colonial Settlement and Early Revolutionary Activity in West Florida Up to 1779." *Mississippi Valley Historical Review,* XXII (1935), 351–60.

Topping, Aileen Moore. "'A Free Facetious Gentleman,' Jean Savy, Double Agent?" *Florida Historical Quarterly,* LVI (1978), 261–79.

Voltes Bou, Pedro. "Thomas Hussey y sus servicios a la política de Floridablanca." *Hispania,* XIX (1959), 92–141.

Walsh, James J. "The Chevalier de La Luzerne." *Records of the American Catholic Historical Society,* XVI (1905), 162–86.

Whitaker, Arthur Preston. "Antonio de Ulloa." *Hispanic American Historical Review,* XV (1935), 155–95.

Dissertations

Burke, Joseph H. "Spain's Attitude Toward the War for American Independence." Ph.D. dissertation, Catholic University of America, 1909.

Glascock, Melvin. "New Spain and the War for American Independence, 1779–1783." Ph.D. dissertation, Louisiana State University, 1969.

Lewis, James A. "New Spain and the American Revolution, 1779–1783: A Viceroyalty at War." Ph.D. dissertation, Duke University, 1975.

Otero, Michael A. "The American Mission of Diego de Gardoqui, 1785–1789." Ph.D. dissertation, University of California at Los Angeles, 1948.

Index

Index

Index

117*n*8, 120–22, 140–63, 203–204; friendships of, with prominent Americans, 118–20, 123–25, 130–32, 148, 154, 161, 203; and French ambassadors in Philadelphia, 120–21, 131, 143–45, 151–53; reception of, by Continental Congress, 122–23; interest of, in American-Spanish conquest of East Florida, 123, 138–39, 147, 150, 153–58; provision of information by, 125, 128–39, 163, 168, 203; desire of, for appointment as Spain's ambassador to United States, 140, 140n, 148; and Spanish prisoners of war, 142–46, 142*n*; and Catholic church, 146–47; personal goals of, 147–48, 150; problems of, owing to lack of formal status, 148–50; and Mississippi River navigation rights, 151, 152, 154, 155, 158–60; and Spanish land claims east of Mississippi River, 151, 152–53, 154–55, 158–59, 160; final illness and death of, 161–62, 168; estate of, 164, 164*nn*70, 71
Miró, Don Esteban, 169, 177
Mississippi River, navigation rights to, 151, 152, 154, 155, 158–60, 165–66, 169, 178, 179, 180, 192
Mobile, 12, 90, 113, 133, 161
Moñino, José. *See* Floridablanca, José Moñino, Conde de,
Morris, Robert: and Pollock, 51; and Willing, 85, 87; and Miralles, 105, 118, 118*n*12, 126–28, 131, 138; commercial activities of, 126–28, 173–75, 183; as executor of Miralles' estate, 164, 164*n*70; and Rendon, 173–75, 180–81, 181*n*, 188, 189, 190; appointment of, as superintendent of finance, 180–81, 181*n*, 189, 190
Mosquito Coast, 113–14
Murray, John. *See* Dunmore, John Murray, earl of

Natchez, 14, 86, 113, 160
Navarro y Valladares, Diego Joseph: as captain general of Cuba, 7, 61, 63, 64, 66, 72–79, 81, 94–96, 98–109; and Miralles, 122–23, 124, 129, 130, 148, 155, 162; and Rendon, 163, 165, 167, 171–72, 175
Navy. *See* British navy; Spanish navy
New Orleans, 47–53, 63, 78–89, 104–105. *See also* Louisiana
New Providence Island, 114
New Smyrna, 10–11, 19–20, 21, 25, 43, 101, 146–47, 200
Nicaragua, 114

Nitafatique, 97
North Africa, 198

Observers. *See* Spanish observers
O'Kelley, James, 15
Oller, José, 126, 126*n*33
Omoa, 114
O'Neil, Arturo, 177
O'Reilly, General Alejandro, 8, 13–14, 16–17, 18, 197–98
Otamendi, Miguel de, 194

Panis, Captain Jacinto, 90–91
Patronato real, 147
Peace of Paris, ix–x, 9, 11, 196
Peace of Utrecht, 4
Peale, Charles Willson, 118–19
Pensacola, 10, 11, 12, 23, 24, 48, 49, 55*n*4, 62–63, 82–83, 89–91, 97, 104, 113, 133, 155, 156, 161
Pensacola, Battle of, 176, 177
Pesos fuertes, 11, 40, 41, 45, 69, 79
Philip V (king of Spain), 7
Pittman, Captain Philip, 14
Pollock, Oliver, 48, 50–51, 63, 84–89, 128, 174, 201
Portugal, 28, 45, 55*n*4, 149
Prevost, General Augustine, 138
Pringle, John, 175
Prisoners of war, 142–46, 142*n*7, 175–76
Privateering, 42–43, 70, 78, 88, 101, 115, 128, 142, 144, 177
Providence Island, 48
Puente, Joseph María Elegio de la, 99–105
Puente, Juan José Elegio de la, 20–21, 37, 73–76, 73*n*67, 96, 99, 100, 104, 105, 129
Puente, María Elegio de la, 127, 129, 175
Puerto Rico, 31, 94, 138

Quakers, 76, 77
Queen Anne's War, ix

Raffelin, Antonio, 8, 69–72
Reed, Joseph, 119
Rendon, Francisco: appointment of, as Spanish observer, x, 167, 170–71; diplomatic and consular responsibilities of, 114, 171–81; appointment of, as Miralles' successor, 163–66; mission of, 167; and Luzerne, 170–73, 176–78, 183; provision of information by, 170–71, 182–92, 203; and American trade with Cuba, 171–75, 180, 204; and Spanish prisoners of war, 175–76; and Spanish ships seized by

227